RADICAL PHILOSOPHY

2.08
Series 2 / Autumn 2020

Editorial collective
Claudia Aradau
Brenna Bhandar
Victoria Browne
David Cunningham
Peter Hallward
Stewart Martin
Lucie Mercier
Daniel Nemenyi
Hannah Proctor
Rahul Rao
Martina Tazzioli
Chris Wilbert

Engineers
Daniel Nemenyi
Alex Sassmannshausen

Creative Commons BY-NC-ND
Radical Philosophy, Autumn 2020

ISSN 0300-211X
ISBN 978-1-9999793-7-9

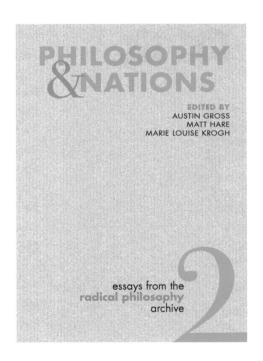

Beware: Medical Police

Brendan McQuade and Mark Neocleous

Cops forcibly removing someone from a bus for not wearing a face mask, arresting people for failure to socially distance on a crowded subway platform, moving people on if they look like they are socialising in excessive numbers, determining who can attend a public event. This is the new reality of policing the virus. The street-level enforcement of social distancing during the lockdown is just the start. Governments the world over have started rolling out new surveillance schemes and testing regimes in the name of public health. In the timid new world of the present and the brave new world of the future, policing meets health head-on. Medical policing is back. But did it ever stop?

For some, the gravity of the new conjuncture finally and decisively inaugurated by the Covid-19 pandemic suggests that revolution is now thinkable.[1] Yet it also means certain features of the class and racial dynamics of the modern capitalist system are set in stark relief. How many healthy people does it take to make an economy run? How many sick people can the health system handle? How many vulnerable migrant workers does it take to run a health system? How many dead friends, family members and lovers will the people tolerate? As pundits, quacks and hacks debate the number of corpses that would make an acceptable blood sacrifice to Capital – aka 'reopening of the economy' – the plague is exposing the strategic orientation of the state. In this orientation, the broader *police project* that has always been central to the fabrication of capitalist order – making and remaking the working class, policing the crises and keeping the great machinery of global accumulation churning – is now manifested most intensely in a series of measures around health and disease, infection and immunity, illness and well-being. For this reason, the term 'medical police' is once again a powerful critical resource.

The idea of medical police harkens back to the early modern period between the Renaissance and the Great Revolutions at the close the eighteenth and beginning of the nineteenth century. This was an extended historical epoch of systems transition when the modern order of things was still being consolidated and older ways of living were still being systemically destroyed. The plebs and the proles and the working class in the making were entangled in both the circuits of capital accumulation *and* the vestiges of pre-capitalist economies centred on the commons, which went beyond shared property (*the* commons) and entailed the shared knowledge and communal organisation of social life (practices of commoning). This systematic colonisation of the world was the process that Marx understood as 'primitive accumulation', the intervention of the state to transform commons into private property, dispossess and uproot the people from the land, and rebuild social order through the wage relation. During this period of dramatic and violent change, the nature of state power was stark, its oppressiveness plain and its function unambiguous. At the heart of this was the police power.[2]

At this time, 'police' meant everything that we would now call 'policy', including welfare, education, urban planning and, of course, law enforcement. Included in any list of police activities was a set of what we would now designate as matters of 'public health' but which went by the name 'medical police'. Reflecting this orientation, some of the first 'modern' police bodies comparable to contemporary law enforcement agencies possessed missions far broader than what we often think of as 'police' in the narrower sense. The Royal Irish Constabulary, for example, one of the first such bodies for managing the colonies and a model for the London Metropolitan Police, functioned as a war machine working as medical police.

After the failed rebellion of the United Irishmen in 1789, London deepened its control over Ireland with multi-faceted police projects executed by the Constabulary, which, in addition to enforcing the criminal law and repressing rebels, collected agricultural statistics and the decennial census, reported on evictions and loan frauds and inspected weights and measures. They were also quite explicitly designed to be medical police by legislators and administrators. This included identifying prostitutes and other people deemed immoral, loose or disorderly, not least because of the infectious diseases that they were said to spread. It also meant enforcing public health policy more generally: measures concerning the proper handling of dogs, the sale of livestock, the keeping of pigs and the removal of manure. Throughout the nineteenth century the Constabulary enforced the ban on wakes for those who had died from dangerous diseases, ensured that people disinfected their houses after inhabitants died of infectious disease and arrested people who did not vaccinate their children; the term 'conscientious objector' was first used to describe those among the working classes who resisted this medical police intervention in their lives. The Royal Irish Constabulary thus *policed* in the fullest sense of the term: it was the agent of law enforcement, the vessel for the exercise of multifarious police powers, and a prime force in the war of accumulation against the working class.

There is a tendency to misrecognise seemingly distinct and seemingly benign social policies as disconnected from each other and, more specifically, disconnected from police power. But as the example of the Royal Irish Constabulary attests, police power was in its origins a broad power concerned with the construction of a colonial social order and the promotion of commerce. It was police as *social policy* and hence *social policy as police*. It was, in other words, an art of government and an exercise in technologies of power through a network of institutions and animated by ways of knowing that produced modern social order. While policing was oppressive, its real *power* is manifest in the management of life and ways of living. Hence, medical police focused on the promotion of the collective health of the population which in turn involved the policing of the health of individuals. This health of individual bodies and the collective body politic was expected to underpin the economic productivity of the labour force.[3]

Such an art of government and such technologies of power are what Foucault later labelled as biopower and governmentality. In this sense, it is perhaps unsurprising that many intellectuals have recently turned to Foucault's neologisms to make sense of the current moment, especially to the notion of 'biopower';[4] even to the point of talking of a possible democratic biopolitics[5] or a 'dual biopower'.[6] It is significant that the same arguments ignore anything that Foucault had to say about the *policing* of the social field. It is also significant that they often seek to resist the language of warfare to describe the virus, even though Foucault insisted time and again that politics is a continuation of war by other means. In our view, the notion of 'medical police' as part of an expanded concept of police power focuses attention on important aspects of capitalist power that the Foucauldian invocation of 'biopower' tends to obscure. It focuses our attention on the fabrication of capitalist forms of order through both the relentless war of destruction against the commons and practices of commoning that still sustain the marginalised masses of humanity, and through the systematic colonisation of everyday practices of solidarity, life, love and care by the 'soft power' of social police. In this way, the lens of medical police offers greater clarity for the emergent conjuncture.

Responses

Such clarity also stems from a more enduring, less philosophical and much more direct demand, one that usefully kicks aside all the chatter about biopolitics: Fuck the Police! The words of NWA's great lumpen anthem, a slogan now being blasted in rowdy and disruptive anti-police actions across the United States, including the demand to defund and abolish police, plays on the commonly understood conception of police as hated agents of state violence, but it also points us to the expanded, original idea of police. In response to the current surge of medical police, can the crudity of 'Fuck the Police!' point to both a rejection of the violence of administration (the 'commonsense' idea of police) and a call for the abolition of the order of Capital that policing constitutes (the expanded idea of police)? Can 'Fuck the Police!' serve as a jarring reminder to kill the cop in your head and reject the police politics of bourgeois civilisation? To do so means avoiding the seduction of the prose of pacification and the temptation to get caught up in the pragmatic play of discourse that animates operations of

the state apparatus.[7] To say 'Fuck the Police!' is a reminder to resist becoming a cop, whether in the name of law and order, in the name of security or *even in the name of health security*. It is to confront, with sober senses, the strategic orientation of the state and the dynamics of contemporary police-wars of accumulation.

For a start, it is the *medical* policing of the crisis that has revealed the ubiquitous and amorphous nature of the police power in all its glory. The common refrain of those stopped by the police and questioned about their reason for being out of their homes has been that the reasons for the police stop have not been made fully clear and that such stops are not being enforced fairly or equally. What they have encountered is the mystical authority known as police discretion and what they have demanded is that the law should be clearer so that there is no room for such discretion. The critical theory of police power has long argued that discretion is the *sine qua non* of policing. As countless members of oppressed social groups and political movements all over the world will attest, the permissive nature of the law surrounding the police stop – walking too fast, walking too slowly or not walking at all can all be invoked as grounds for a stop – means that the stops have always been used unfairly and have always resulted in unequal treatment.

Now that members of the white bourgeoisie are experiencing those same powers (though to nowhere near the same extent) complaints against the powers are heard far and wide in the mainstream media. What has brought such powers into sharp focus is precisely the surge of medical policing to contain the pandemic. Where the police might once have stopped certain kinds of people from gathering on the street to talk, using discretionary powers to question them over whatever reason the police choose at that moment ('suspicion'), now the police stop other kinds of people on medical grounds and for reasons of health security. Nonetheless, flagrant racial and class disparities remain, most obviously in the ways that the discretionary nature of medical police replicates and intersects with the exercise of discretionary power in other 'policy' fields.

That the practices of medical police are being ratcheted up during the lockdown is a sign of what we might be facing when the lockdown eases, in what will become the new 'normality'. Much has been made, for example, of the projects to restart the machinery of accumulation the world over. China has rolled out a new Health Code which analyses usage data from mobile payment and social media apps to colour-code the relative risk/threat of each user. Hong Kong is enforcing quarantines with tracking bracelets synced to smart phones. South Korea fused data from CCTV cameras, mobile payment apps and smart phones to re-trace the steps of infected people, the very surveillance that has allowed South Korea to be held up as an exemplary case of 'curve-flattening'. Similar new measures for advanced physical surveillance include facial recognition cameras equipped with heat-sensors. Police in China, Italy and the UAE are already wearing 'smart helmets' capable of detecting body temperatures in addition to employing facial recognition capabilities, number plate recognition and QR code readers.

In the face of the virus and the proposals for testing, civil libertarians are struggling to respond. Surely it is irresponsible to condemn such benevolent surveillance in the name of public health? Surely selling our digital souls to the state is the price to pay for regaining our freedoms and maintaining our health? Even those known previously for their privacy campaign work have come out in favour of a massive surveillance program to fight the virus: how many times are we going to read the line 'I am a privacy advocate and have fought against surveillance but right now and in the name of health ...'?

It is no surprise that the civil libertarians are flummoxed. Their entire politics is premised on the foundational liberal belief that we can and should live atomised lives, that human societies are nothing more than the aggregation of private individuals. But 'privacy' is a particular claim articulated within a particular context. Privacy has no essential essence. It is a concession that the consolidating administrative state made to 'the public', a shifting boundary with demarcations set and reset by the state. Privacy is a tool of regulation, not resistance, and key to this regulation is information. But the virus has revealed something that has been inherent in medical police ever since life was redefined as information and the body as an information technology: the fact that the body is simultaneously the site of disease and information creates the opportunity for it to be policed through that very information. This enables any authority which can rightly claim access to that information – employers, credit card companies and insurance companies as well as the state – to keep constant watch over the body's biochemical processes and shape the behaviour of the subject. The issue here is not the fact of surveillance or the infringement of privacy but the *formation of the pacified subject*. The issue, in other words, is not surveillance, but ways in which the police power fabricates forms of subjectivity and submission.

The whole refrain of 'privacy' and surveillance' focuses our attention on the wrong thing: it focuses on the police of health *information* when it is the *police of health* that is the more pressing issue. In this regard, the proposal of many countries for Immunity Passports is telling.

Even though epidemiologists doubt their efficacy, the Immunity Passport may well turn out to be the new normal. Already, China's Health Code is functioning as a de-facto Immunity Passport, albeit one based on data analysis and not antibody testing. Chile launched an Immunity Card program in April. In May, Estonia started testing out digital Immunity Passports for businesses. Currently, the UK, Italy, Germany, Portugal, France, India, the US, Canada, Sweden, Spain, South Africa, Mexico, United Arab Emirates and the Netherlands are developing versions of Immunity Passports.

Everything about the Immunity Passport escapes the easy criticisms made by those who focus on privacy and surveillance. In contrast, the Immunity Passport does take us to the heart of medical police. Passports have always been an expression of power: the sovereign grant of travel that doubles-up as a document of bona fide citizenship. A passport can be denied, cancelled or seized by the police. The Immunity Passport (or 'CoviPass') will be a new document of state and corporate power, permitting the holder to go about their business in the market. As generations of racialised migrants in many countries will attest, only if you have the passport or certification can you participate fully in society.

The Immunity Passport will be a new form of pacification: it allows the state to declare not only who is (or is not) permitted to work and trade – as the CoviPass.com website makes clear, its main task is an 'end-to-end secure return to work protocol' – but also to decide who can drink with friends, go to a sports game, engage in sociability; first work, then live. The fact that no such immunity could ever be guaranteed by the Passport, since they have no idea whether people are genuinely 'immune', reveals the state's desperation to announce that capital is back in business and to keep it that way. An Immunity Passport would thus be a document of a bona fide ability to be a good citizen. It would constitute a 'health certificate' and 'work permit' in one document. It would be the ultimate document of medical police.

In 1788 the Director General of Public Health of Austrian Lombardy, Johann Peter Frank, introduced the fourth volume of his *System of Complete Medical Police* by announcing that medical police is concerned with 'the work, life, and health of the citizenry'. One finds a similar sentence in virtually every text in police science. It is life itself that is the object of police. Frank's comment is a reminder that, for police, life is where 'work' and 'health' come together. Just a few years later in his *Science of Rights*, the philosopher Johann Gottlieb Fichte suggested that the chief principle of a well-regulated police is that 'each citizen shall be at all times and places ... recognised as this or that person'. For police to be able to recognise a person, each should carry with them a 'certificate' or even something that might be called a 'pass'. This would contain their description and might even hold a portrait of them. The police would then have the power to ask any person for their 'pass'. Fichte's concern was with identification and thus identity. The police must be able to either know who you are or to demand that you reveal who you are: 'Let me see your ID!' Many baulked at Fichte's proposal for such a 'pass' to better police what he openly described as the 'police-state'; even Hegel thought the idea was a police measure too far. Yet his proposal is now the norm.

The Immunity Passport takes this one step further. In that sense, such a passport might well turn out to be the epitome of medical police: the power to demand a certificate of *health* as well as identity: 'Let me see your Health ID!' This would be an exercise of the police power to ensure that the world remains open, first and foremost,

only to those declared 'healthy' and thus *fit for work*. The Immunity Passport will be the epitome of health security.

The supreme concept of bourgeois society

Health security? As we have already commented, a large part of the left has baulked at the language of war being used in this pandemic. 'Our country is at war', 'the world is at war', 'invisible enemy', 'wartime government', 'wartime President', 'medical personnel are frontline workers', 'each and every one of us directly enlisted', 'a coronavirus war economy', a *health war*, to use President Macron's phrase. On and on it goes, and on and on goes the left's insistence that the language of war is inappropriate. Maybe it is. But the language of war and health has coincided since at least the launching of the 'germ warfare' theory of disease in the mid-nineteenth century. Surely there are more salutary arguments for the left to be making, nearly 200 years later? Now, the idea of the virus as a health war certainly sits comfortably with two trends of twenty-first century bellicosity: on the one hand, the idea that 'a new and deadly virus has emerged – the virus is terrorism' (as Tony Blair put it in a speech to the US Congress in July 2003, and he was far from alone in thinking so), and, on the other hand, the fact that scientists now commonly resort to describing viruses in the language of terrorism studies (for example, as 'bioterrorism'). As an indication of where this is going, note that the UK's Joint Biosecurity Centre (JBC) established to collect and analyse data about infection rates, identify local spikes and recommend appropriate responses is to be led by a senior counter-terrorism official, will be modelled on the Joint Terrorism Analysis Centre, and will use a model of 'levels of threat' that is adopted from the same techniques used to assess terror threats. Yet the real issue that emerges from this combined argument that terrorism is a virus and viruses are a kind of terrorism is that we should be thinking less about the rhetoric of war and more about the rhetoric of security. Descriptions of viruses read like they have been penned by security intellectuals and descriptions of terrorism read like they have been penned by virologists, and what gets imprinted on our minds is one idea: *health security*. This requires arguments from the left that are far more sophisticated than a pacifistic plea for less use of the language of war.

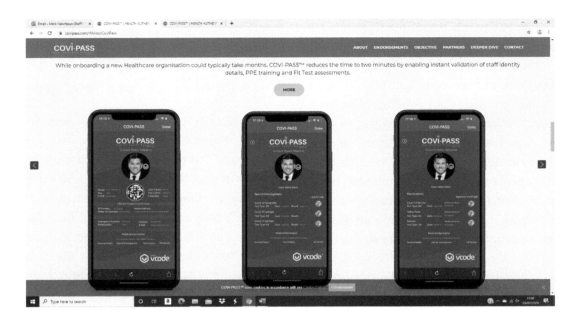

Marx long ago pointed out that 'security' is the supreme concept of bourgeois society and that this is why it coincides with the concept of police. It is clear that a left politics must involve a critique of security along the lines envisaged by Marx, and we ourselves have pursued this idea in other publications. One reason so many on the left find the idea of a critique of security so problematic is because they wish to hold on to something positive in the idea of security, some softer and person-centred notion of security. 'Health security' would appear to be one such notion. It is the centrality of 'health' to the new 'surveillance' measures that has flummoxed so many civil libertarians and radicals. We are confronted, then, with the war power and the police power coagulating around the notion of health security. Health and security coincide to reinforce the power of medical police. Yet this is precisely one of the ways in which 'security' and 'police' reinforce their power, through seemingly softer and apparently person-centred practices to do with things such as health. Pacification is the more successful the more it is done in the name of life itself. In our view, however, health security and medical police coincide.

Precisely how we might develop and configure our own collective notion of health without succumbing to 'health security' and the 'medical police' will turn out to be one of the pressing questions for the foreseeable future, not least because in a society racked with terrors, the terror of disease is among the highest. This is why 'health security' can so easily go unchallenged. But challenge it we must, and while we recognise that some form

of socialised medicine for the many is better than privatised insurance for the few, the problem is much deeper than the structure of the 'healthcare system'.

In this regard, we could do worse than revisit the critique of 'health' as a category that was made so trenchantly in earlier social struggles, from René Dubos's *Mirage of Health* (1959) through to Ivan Illich's *Medical Nemesis* (1979), Howard Waitzkin's *Second Sickness* (1983), and, of course, some of Foucault's work in the mid-1970s on the 'investment' in the healthy body demanded of us by capital. Much of this work on health was as powerful as the concomitant radical work on prisons and asylums, and involved an equally trenchant critique: 'health is a thoroughly bourgeois concept', the Socialist Patients Collective of the University of Heidelberg commented in *Turn Illness into a Weapon* (1972).[8] Under conditions of capitalist exploitation, to be declared healthy means nothing other than to be declared 'fit for work', which is the very thing the police power was instituted for in the first place. The reason 'disease' always has moral and political as well as medical implications (disease as dis-ease) is because 'health' likewise has moral and political implications. If health is a performance in a social script, as Illich put it in *Medical Nemesis*, that script is written for us by capital. Written out of the play are those who capital and the state are clearly willing to sacrifice to the virus: the elderly and those in nursing homes, prisons and asylums, and those, disproportionately racial and ethnic minorities, rendered 'vulnerable' due to 'underlying health issues'. This is the discretion of police power condensed into social relations, as Poulantzas would say, the materiality of the state and its strategic orientation toward the needs of capital expressed in the nursing-home-as-morgue.

We must therefore emphatically reject the police politics that accompanies the possessive individualism of bourgeois order. We must also emphatically reject the platitudes of the discourse around 'biopolitics' and 'privacy'. What we are up against is medical police conducted in the name of health security. Against this we need to assert an expansive solidarity that succumbs to neither medical police nor health security. This means learning and understanding how to care for each other – minds and bodies, fragilities and pleasures. And it means doing so without succumbing to the idea that our bodies are always already at war, without buying into bourgeois notions of illness, and without thinking that wellbeing is something that needs to be either policed or secured. All of which is a challenge that demands a positive politics rooted in a conception of human need, one that not only seeks to meet human needs as needs but builds momentum toward systems transition. This is precisely what has been articulated in the George Floyd Rebellion: an emphatic rejection – once again, Fuck the Police! – combined with an expansive solidarity oriented toward the construction of a new world: defund, abolition and commit instead to care and need.

The antithesis of police is the commons, a fact that is quite explicit in early modern writings on police. Perhaps as part of the new struggles against police powers we need also to articulate a new commons (of health) against the (medical) police? In a sense, the pandemic has already made some of this work a top priority, with ad-hoc efforts at mutual aid. Such efforts have been overtaken by the anti-police protests that have spiralled out of the George Floyd Rebellion, the terrifying spectre haunting the bourgeois imagination: the spectre of the commons, of the 'communism' of a non-policed order, of a world beyond police. Whether these struggles against policing in all its forms can grow into a sustained project of anti-capitalist world-making remains to be seen. It's not yet clear how we might move on from defensive efforts to mitigate the worst harms of police, whether medical or otherwise, and in that sense the challenge of abolition inspires both wonder and terror. Will popular responses to pandemic produce new solidarities and in-

stitutions capable of providing for 'public health' in such a way that the 'normal' plagues of our times – addiction, suicide, depression – get the same level of collective attention as the 'exceptional' pandemic? Will the revolt be mollified by divesting the armed uniform police only to be reinvested into the 'softer power' of social police? Or will the break be further reaching? The new conjuncture of pandemic and depression presents new possibilities. In the face of a moment both awesome and frightening, we must resist the seductions of security, including 'health security'. Beware: medical police. Recreate the commons.

Brendan McQuade teaches at the University of Southern Maine. His book Pacifying the Homeland: Intelligence Fusion and Mass Surveillance *was published by University of California Press in 2019. Mark Neocleous' books include* War Power, Police Power *(2014) and* A Critical Theory of Police Power, *which is forthcoming with Verso.*

Notes

1. Ben Tarnoff, 'These Are Conditions in Which Revolution Becomes Thinkable', *Commune*, 7 April 2020, https://commun-emag.com/these-are-conditions-in-which-revolution-becomes-thinkable/
2. Mark Neocleous, *War Power, Police Power* (Edinburgh: Edinburgh University Press, 2014), 53–74.
3. Mark Neocleous, *A Critical Theory of Police Power* (London: Verso, 2021).
4. See the collection 'Coronavirus and Philosophers', *European Journal of Psychoanalysis* online, no date, with a section from Foucault's *Discipline and Punish* followed by contributions from Agamben, Nancy, Esposito, and others, https://www.journal-psychoanalysis.eu/coronavirus-and-philosophers/. Likewise, Gerasimos Kakoliris, 'A Foucauldian Enquiry in the Origins of the COVID-19 Pandemic', *Critical Legal Thinking*, 11 May 2020, https://criticallegalthinking.com/2020/05/11/a-foucauldian-enquiry-in-the-origins-of-the-covid-19-pandemic-management-critique-in-times-of-coronavirus/
5. Panagiotis Sotiris, 'Against Agamben: Is a Democratic Biopolitics Possible?', *Viewpoint Magazine*, 20 March 2020, https://www.viewpointmag.com/2020/03/20/against-agamben-democratic-biopolitics/
6. Alberto Toscano, 'Beyond the Plague State', *The Bullet*, 14 May 2020, https://socialistproject.ca/2020/05/beyond-the-plague-state/
7. Brendan McQuade, *Pacifying the Homeland: Intelligence Fusion and Mass Supervision* (Oakland, CA: University of California Press, 2019).
8. SPK [Socialist Patients Collective of the University of Heidelberg], *Turn Illness into a Weapon* (1972), trans. Huber (SPK, 1993), 15.

Pandemic suspension

Alexei Penzin

The Lisbon earthquake of November 1755 was the most devastating natural disaster of the eighteenth century, and probably the first disaster on such a scale in modernity. It was an event that profoundly disturbed many Enlightenment philosophers.[1] Kant wrote three scientific studies that attempted to explain it from the standpoint of natural history, and some commentators have hypothesised that its reverberations can be detected in his famous elaboration of the aesthetic category of sublime.[2] Besides writing a poem about the earthquake, Voltaire employed it in his famous *Candide* as an example of a horrific and meaningless natural disaster that disproved Leibniz's optimistic theodicy of 'pre-established harmony', for the obvious reason that it would be impossible to incorporate into even the most sophisticated plot of divine providence.[3] Rousseau wrote a letter to Voltaire objecting to the latter's pessimism, and arguing, from the perspective of his general critique of civilisation, that the huge number of casualties in Lisbon was due to the density of populations in such big cities.[4]

These philosophical and theological controversies had immediate political consequences. The Portuguese Prime Minister sided with the naturalistic explanation of the event, so his policies included rebuilding Lisbon and the implementation of near 'war communism' measures, such as commandeering grain stocks and distributing them among the population to prevent a mass famine. Religious circles, predictably more concerned with the salvation of souls, opposed these policies, claiming the best measures were incessant prayers and fasting, and prophesying a second earthquake that would reveal, finally, God's convoluted providence and punish the sinners who doubted his will.[5]

Radical thinkers of the twentieth century retained a philosophical memory of the earthquake. Adorno briefly mentions the earthquake in a section on Auschwitz in *Negative Dialectics* (1966), presenting it as a 'visible disaster of the first nature' that 'sufficed to cure Voltaire of the theodicy of Leibniz'.[6] Although Adorno purports to echo Voltaire, his argument that the disaster was 'insignificant in comparison with the second, social one [Auschwitz], which defies human imagination as it distils a real hell from human evil', rather intensifies and modernises Rousseau's argument that 'the sufferings nature imposes on us are less cruel than those we add on ourselves'.[7]

These examples demonstrate how the philosophers of the Enlightenment applied their 'signature' ideas and concepts to the Lisbon earthquake. They also indicate how philosophers 'capitalise' on events with this order of notoriety in their drive to symbolic 'primitive accumulation'. The same drive can be discerned amongst the philosophers who have responded to the COVID-19 pandemic – including Agamben, Nancy, Žižek, et al. However, this is more a case of 'first as tragedy, then as farce', to use Marx's famous dictum from the *Eighteenth Brumaire*. Due to the quick deflation of intellectual and critical commentary in the 24/7 flows of texts, images and data, it is difficult to recognise what specific philosophical assumptions have been shaken by the pandemic, and how successful the philosophers have been in their attempts to 'capitalise' (or perhaps, waste) their concepts, or to exert any influence on current politics. Is there a new pessimism about the viral dangers of globalisation, which now appears more than ever as an extension of Enlightenment progressivism and cosmopolitanism? Has the pandemic revealed the persistence of Promethean illusions of human dominance of the earth, recently promulgated through the notion of the Anthropocene?[8] Given the urgency of providing society-scale protective measures and the impossibility of doing so through egotistic interests of profit-making, should the role of the state become greater, perhaps ascending to a new socialism, if not to say communism?[9] Or, *vice versa*, is this a new escalation of the 'biosecurity paradigm' enforced by the state, which threatens to destroy the last remnants of human dignity and decent life?[10]

Many controversies have arisen already in response to these hypotheses, and it is unlikely that they will be resolved until the whole situation has crystallised. However, if we cannot yet fully assess the 'objective' aspects of the pandemic, we can still criticise the subjective attitudes of the philosophers themselves. The sudden proliferation of philosophers' statements around the pandemic, claiming that the internal logic of their pre-existing concepts suddenly began to merge with the external logic of the new situation, lays bare a 'pre-established harmony' of the narcissistic mechanism of coincidences. In addition to the real virus that kills people, tragically accelerated by late capitalism's merciless greed and austerity, there is a comic mental fever of resurging philosophical narcissism, or the 'omnipotence of thoughts' described and ridiculed by Freud.[11]

How does one avoid catching *this* virus? Definitely not through self-humiliation, formal condemnations of anthropocentric arrogance and philosophical narcissism, or worshiping various nonhuman agents including the virus itself.[12] Rather, one has to take precautionary measures, as towards the real epidemic: physical distancing from the contagious idealism of stuffy philosophical caves and social solidarity.

Ideal suspension

We do not know yet how capitalism will *end*, but we can already glimpse what its 'pause' or, better still, its temporary and partial *suspension* looks like. This knowledge has been generated after the global coronavirus outbreak and the lockdown that followed in different time zones and in many countries. Images of empty, melancholic streets and wild animals wandering around cities flooded social media. For a moment, they exposed not just an exaggerated and frightening collapse of the distinction between nature and culture, but presented us with the immaterial ruins of social life, now replaced with bizarre animal caricatures. These images epitomised the break in social life by exposing the silent and eerie space of streets and squares, designed especially to contain, facil-

itate and manage human traffic.[13] This break, pause and decrease in social life is particularly illuminating, since it was made more visible – and more problematic – by the incessant, continuous character of capitalism: the so-called '24/7'.[14]

At the everyday level, a short or longer break during a public session, meeting, class or process of manual work means a relief, which offers an opportunity to refresh and recover. Such a break is a microscopic parcel of overall social reproduction. It allows individuals to recover physical and mental energies, and re-enter the irreversible flow of everyday life and work engagements. Yet the pandemic lockdown has been very far from a 'comfort break'. On the contrary, it has been filled with enormous anxiety, panic and disorientation – at least over the first weeks and months of the outbreak, until the emergency became more routinised. Of course, the global pause in many social activities did not include 'key workers' who suffered drastic increases in their work, now associated with the dangers brought about by the virus.

From the specific theoretical angle developed in this article, I suggest that one should add the adjective 'ideal' to the experience of 'suspension' caused by the pandemic. This ideal suspension has neutralised, if only for a moment, the very sense of the normality and naturalness of capitalism, which has in fact proved to be a very *artificial* formation, whose many aspects can be temporarily 'cancelled' or at least put on pause. In mainstream ideological discourse, the critical attributes of artificiality and unnaturalness used to be applied only to the opposite of capitalism. We were told for decades that socialism, not to mention communism, 'did not work' and collapsed because it was artificial and unnatural for humans, who are driven by egotistic interests that can be 'harmonised' only through the market. This strange reversal of capitalism and communism continued at the level of policies for handling emergencies. In order to sustain the political-economic continuity of capitalism, neoliberal or neoconservative governments have been forced to undertake or at least promise the kinds of temporary measures that have always been associated with left politics: nationalisation of railways, suspensions of rent and mortgage payments and, in some cases, a form of basic income. In the momentary suspension of the smooth functioning of the ideological apparatuses of the media and culture industry, a previously suppressed sense of the profound normality of production and consumption 'according to basic needs', free from the *jouissances* of consumerism and mass entertainment, has flashed into view.[15]

Masochism and insurrection

The effects of de-familiarisation caused by the event of suspension are well known in twentieth-century critical and philosophical thought. The Russian Formalist School discussed *ostranenie,* or de-familiarisation, as a key literary device that de-automatises (or suspends) our routinised perception of things and situations.[16] For Bertolt Brecht, who received and developed this idea in the 1930s, the *Verfremdungseffekt* (estrangement-effect) serves not only as a powerful artistic device, but also as a consciousness-raising technique that, instead of emphatic immersion into the entertaining spectacle, activates the critical attitude of the reader or spectator.[17] Taking these concepts as a starting point, one can argue that the pandemic suspension has produced a massive effect of de-familiarisation and, for a moment, exposed the artificial and contingent character of the capitalist rationality that is obsessively imposed on all aspects of society and individual life. As Elettra Stimili asks: 'Without

the virus, how much longer would many unquestionable things – things suddenly suspended and, in the suspension, laid bare – have continued to be taken as necessary?' Stimili produces an eloquent list of such 'things': 'The globalised economy of invasive tourism, television contests, air traffic, budgetary limits, the spectacle of sports competitions, shopping malls, fitness rooms, mass gatherings, the comfort of office jobs, all the drunken sociability we knew; and, on the other side of the coin, the anguished metropolitan solitudes, the education not equal for all, the class, gender and race injustices, the exploitation, and the job insecurity.'[18]

In his *Coldness and Cruelty* (1967), Deleuze presents the figure of suspension as an operation that creates a realm of the *ideal* that sustains the unfolding of masochist practices. Deleuze writes that these practices 'climb toward the Ideal', also suggesting that they historically originate in some 'idealistic initiation rites'. This produces an 'idealistic neutralisation' of real objects, by which they remain 'suspended or neutralised in the ideal'.[19] Deleuze means here not only literal, physical suspensions, which shape various self-torture rituals, but also an arresting of the whole temporality and spatiality of these practices, noting: 'Waiting and suspense are essential characteristics of the masochistic experience'.[20] Deleuze suggests that masochism can be conceived outside of the confines of psychoanalytic interpretation, although a theory of social suspension would need to develop these elements further, seeing them as modalities that can emerge not only on the basis of sexuality and desire, but also on the basis of diverse material infrastructures and events of individual or social existence.[21]

Bracketing, for a moment, the justified medical rationality of protective measures, one can argue that the temporary capitalism of pandemic cancellations and lockdowns acquires some traits of masochistic practices: an endless suspense, applied in this case not only to the individual, but also social bodies. The new rules and rituals, such as social distancing, resemble a masochistic 'coldness'. Even wearing masks mimics the props of masochist ritual. The national 're-openings' create a thrilling suspense in the anticipation of the new waves of pandemic. This reflects well the masochistic dynamics of pain and pleasure. While Deleuze criticised the simple complementarity of sadism and masochism, there is a complementarity in the oscillation between the sadistic pole of the unrestrained social and economic activity, and the reactive masochistic clinging to protective suspensions. This signals, perhaps, a post-pandemic tendency towards masochistic capitalism: oscillating between the neoliberal economic rationality that constantly issues decrees about the necessity to re-open and to go on, and the consequent self-punishments of lockdowns and the coldness of distancing.[22]

In his monumental recent study of Sergei Eisenstein's life and work, the post-Soviet philosopher Valery Podoroga focuses on the figure of 'being-in-suspense' as a crucial modality of Eisenstein's autobiographical self-reflections, which drew heavily on his studies in psychoanalysis. Podoroga elaborates this figure through a theoretical framework of masochism, which draws on Deleuze among others (such as Theodor Reik).[23] Podoroga tends to downplay the political engagement of Eisenstein's works and emphasise instead a dynamic of often-violent suspensions. Indeed, the figure of suspension is vividly present in Eisenstein's cinema. Examples include the horse suspended by its bridles after falling from a bridge in *October* (1928), or the dead sailor hung on the ship ropes in *Battleship Potemkin* (1925). In *Strike* (1925), one of the key scenes shows the legs of the worker who had taken his life by hanging himself in the factory hall after a manager humiliated him.

Instead of emphasising only the 'masochistic' suspensions in Eisenstein's oeuvre, at the cost of his political engagement, I suggest it is possible to negotiate an encounter between 'objective' capitalist violence, workers' struggles (captured in the scenes at the factory and the strike rallies) and Eisenstein's political engagement.[24] Indeed, the cinematic representation of the strike itself is also predicated on suspension, this time as a form of insurrectional political struggle that consists in the collective workers' decision to *suspend* the assembly line or any other work process. This indicates a form of suspension that is insurrectional, rather than merely masochistic.

Such a form of suspension is further elaborated in the recently discovered work of the Italian thinker Furio Jesi, *Spartakus*, dedicated to the Spartacist uprising in Germany in 1919. Jesi conceives of this uprising in terms of a 'suspension [*la sospensione*] of historical time and space'.[25] A sequence of insurrectional events suspend the flow of 'normal' or 'bourgeois' historical time and its pre-established territoriality, endowing the events with

a self-sufficiency and autonomy. Jesi considers various other kinds of events that generate such a suspension, including war, although it is not difficult to extend this to include general strikes or the current pandemic.

Watching Eisenstein's *Strike* against the current background of the pandemic rewards the viewer with intriguing parallels, such as the scenes in which, after the beginning of the strike, the animals (cats, ravens, foxes, etc.) start to invade and explore the abandoned factory spaces. These scenes are exemplary of Eisenstein's 'montage of attractions' aimed at rhetorical emphasis on the standstill of production that allows nature to reoccupy former spaces of incessant labour activity. Although such scenes present a rhetorical figure, they are also similar to those 'nature returns' images that flooded social media after the beginning of the national lockdowns. The obsessive and violent continuity of capitalist production encounters the pandemic suspension.

Intermezzo

Some important elements for a theory of a social suspension under conditions of capitalism can be found in the work of Alfred Sohn-Rethel, one of the outstanding fellow-travellers of the Frankfurt School. These help to elucidate another register of suspension, related rather to the everyday, which in turn leads to the theoretical elaborations of Sohn-Rethel's later work. In his lesser known but remarkable collection, *Das Ideal des Kaputten* [The Ideal of the Broken-Down], published posthumously in 1991, Sohn-Rethel discusses various forms of everyday disruptions in the free, essayistic form of travel recollections, stories and anecdotes. The collection opens with a skilfully written essay about an enormous traffic jam in Naples in the 1920s, provoked by a stereotypically stubborn donkey that suddenly stood still, blocking all traffic through Via Chiaia. This suspension allows Sohn-Rethel to create a panoramic view of the social life of the city and its economics as a background for this minuscule episode from everyday life. In another essay he discusses 'Neapolitan technology', that is, the refunctioning of broken devices and machines: 'In this city mechanisms cannot function as civilisation's continuum [*Kontinuum*], the role for which they are predestined: Naples turns everything on its head.'[26] As we will see, the problem of the continuum maintained by machines and mechanisms as the means of production within capitalist civilisation (or better, this specific form of barbarity) resonates with the late Sohn-Rethel's theory of 'advanced capitalism', formulated in his *Intellectual and Manual Labour*.

Sohn-Rethel's essays and stories in *Das Ideal des Kaputten* cover not only technological aspects of various interruptions and breaks, but also describe purely contingent and sometimes absurd or comic incidents of a very rare kind, based on an almost ideal or perfect combination of contingent factors. Although Sohn-Rethel never comments on the enigmatic title of his collection, 'Das Ideal' hints at this specific and significant modality of suspension. Still, these stories are also predicated on the intertwinement of technology and modern social life, such as in his essay about Dudley Zoo in Britain.[27] This story is dear to me as it mentions Wolverhampton and the Black Country, which I know intimately, passing them by on the train in my pre-pandemic then-regular commuting from London to the university where I teach. In the German original, Sohn-Rethel mentions the 'melancholischen' character of the Black Country – a claim that I completely endorse.[28]

In stark contrast to the Black Country's melancholic character, the story is short but explosive in its dynamics and humour. The family of Sohn-Rethel's friend, with three children, finally decides to make a trip to Dudley Zoo in their 'new red car'. After spending several hours in the zoo, they return to the gates where they parked and discover that their car has disappeared. Soon, zookeepers run up to them to explain what happened: around noon, a group of several elephants, guided by their keepers, came through the gates and one of them, probably with a circus past, noticed the shiny red car, and 'with full dignity' ('mit voller Würde'), as Sohn-Rethel adds, sat on the car's hood, seriously damaging it. The damaged but still functional car was then removed from the parking lot to escape the attention of curious crowds of visitors. The adventure continued on the way home in the crippled car. The family got stuck in a traffic jam and were approached by a policeman who asked why the car was damaged. 'The elephant sat on our hood', the father explained. Taken then to a police station for investigation after such an answer, he was suspected of being mad until the police called the Zoo to find out that his story was true.

Sohn-Rethel does not provide much commentary for this and several other short stories included in the collection, but their subversive humour speaks for itself. The automatic flow of the everyday is suspended though a sudden intervention made, characteristically, by animals, creating a surreal chain of episodes. (Besides the donkey and the elephant, rats feature in another story.) While in Eisenstein's *Strike* the animals emerge on the stage after the moment of suspension, in Sohn-Rethel's 'elephant story' the animal generates the disruption.

One can interpret this story in the spirit of the Frankfurt School as emphasising the resistance of colonised and exploited nature, the animals, which remain the only lively element in the cold, administrated world of late capitalism. While *Strike*, born in the epicentre of a victorious socialist revolution, represents a human-made political disruption of the production line, Sohn-Rethel's rebellious animals present a weak and displaced version of the same. The disruption of continuity shifts from production processes to forms of leisure and the everyday, human beings are replaced by the animals, and all this against the background of the creeping fascism that forced the German thinker to escape to Britain.

Interrupting the capitalist continuum

For further insights into the current pandemic suspensions and their significance, one needs to establish a connection between the insurgent 'elephant in the room' and Sohn-Rethel's better-known late theoretical work. Some important observations on the questions of continuity and suspension of capitalist production can be discovered in his opus magnum, *Intellectual and Manual*

Labour, originally published in 1970. This book is commonly known for its first part, which delivers a provocative critique of Kant's epistemology as the scientific consciousness of a 'real abstraction' derived from the exchange of commodities. But the book is also remarkable for its theory of an advanced stage of capitalism formulated in its third part, entitled 'The Dual Economics of Advanced Capitalism'. According to Sohn-Rethel, at the stage of 'advanced capitalism', production takes the form of a continuous 'flow'.[29] Sohn-Rethel's discussion refers to several passages from Marx's *Grundrisse* that stress the continuity of capitalist production and the necessity of constant value-metamorphosis.[30] With this background, the stakes of *Das Ideal des Kaputten* and its dramatisations of sudden breaks and suspensions in social life can be seen in a different light. They are not just peculiar and elegant exercises in essayistic writing, with the exciting narratives of various suspensions of the everyday. They present a utopian or an 'ideal' counterpoint to one of the key theoretical issues of *Intellectual and Manual Labour*, that is, the monotonous continuity of capitalist production and its effects upon society.

The passages from Marx's *Grundrisse* quoted by Sohn-Rethel explain the necessity of continuity [*Kontinuität*] for capital. They deserve perhaps even more attention than they receive by Sohn-Rethel, and can be related to Marx's other mature works to make evident their theoretical systematicity. For instance, in the second volume of *Capital*, Marx briefly notes that 'continuity is the characteristic feature of capitalist production and is required by its technical basis even if it is not always completely attainable'.[31] By 'technical basis' Marx means the factory's machinery, which, ideally, should function without interruption in order not to ruin the value contained in the machines.

The notion of continuity is examined in several other passages from the *Grundrisse*.[32] Marx points out the importance of 'the continuity of production processes' in its capitalist mode and identifies its three aspects. The first two concern the production process and circulation of capital. Marx claims that the continuity of production belongs to the very 'concept of capital' and can be an 'externally compelling condition' in which the expansion of fixed capital (or machinery) plays a key role. For circulating capital, an interruption is only a loss of surplus value, whereas for fixed capital (machinery) an interruption des-

troys the 'original value itself'.[33] Therefore, continuity is specific to capitalist production, critically distinguishing it from the prior organisations of economic life. Marx's third aspect of continuity deals with the credit system. Its main function is to maintain the continuity of production against various contingencies by making funds available to production processes: 'suspension of this chance element by capital itself is *credit*'.[34]

This continuity became an essential aspect of contemporary capitalism in its 24/7 mode of operation: automated production lines, online shopping, communications, banking, media, the Internet, call centres, surveillance, and so on. An incessant and restless activity is the dominant paradigm, which functions as an empty form that is forcefully imposed on all possible human activities and interactions. It would not be an exaggeration to say that, for a brief moment, the COVID-19 pandemic has posed a threat to the very metamorphosis of value. While society has had to practice social distancing, as a suspension of the contagious social continuum, the capitalist state has been desperately introducing more and more new 'emergency measures' that have aimed at maintaining economic continuity at any price. The pandemic suspension – amplified by erratic neoliberal policies – has created an enormous panic not only because it poses a real and ongoing threat to millions of human lives, but also because it threatens the continuum of capitalism, which its guardians are desperately trying to maintain through massive restructuring, deployment of digital technologies and new modes of online work.

In this way, the global breaks in social life have created, at the levels noted here, an ideal but nonetheless significant suspension, which has de-familiarised the received naturalness of capitalism and exposed its obsessive artificiality. This has activated an entire social and political symptomology. It is this that my essay has attempted to interpret in terms of the 'masochistic' and insurrectional tendencies within the pandemic crisis. Nonetheless, the crucial question remains: how can we use the lessons of this crisis to turn the 'ideal suspension' into a real social transformation?

Alexei Penzin is Reader in Art at the University of Wolverhampton and an Associate Research Fellow at the Institute of Philosophy, Moscow. He is the author of a forthcoming book on Sleep and Subjectivity in Capitalist Modernity.

Notes

1. As Susan Neiman claimed, 'The eighteenth century used the word *Lisbon* much as we use the word *Auschwitz* today'. See Susan Neiman, *Evil in Modern Thought: an Alternative History of Philosophy* (Princeton: Princeton University Press, 2015), 1.

2. Gene Ray, 'Reading the Lisbon Earthquake: Adorno, Lyotard, and the Contemporary Sublime', *The Yale Journal of Criticism* 17:1 (2004), 7–11. In the text of the Third Critique Kant mentions 'earthquakes' only once, together with 'storms' and 'tempests', as an example of the 'dynamic sublime' in nature, but he does not refer explicitly to the Lisbon earthquake.

3. See 'The Lisbon Earthquake: Rousseau versus Voltaire', in Voltaire, *Candide and Related Texts*, trans. and ed. David Wootton (Indianapolis: Hackett, 2000), 95–122.

4. See Voltaire, *Candide and Related Texts*, 110–111.

5. Neiman, *Evil in Modern Thought*, 248–249.

6. Theodor Adorno, *Negative Dialectics*, trans. E.B. Ashton (New York: Continuum, 1995), 361.

7. Jean-Jacques Rousseau, 'Letter to Voltaire on Optimism' (1756), in Voltaire, *Candide and Related Texts*, 111.

8. As simply put in an article from the *Guardian*, 'The idea of the Anthropocene conjures notions of human omnipotence. But Covid-19 has revealed the astonishing fragility of our societies'. Richard Horton, 'Coronavirus is the greatest global science policy failure in a generation', *The Guardian*, 9 April 2020, https://www.theguardian.com/commentisfree/2020/apr/09/deadly-virus-britain-failed-prepare-mers-sars-ebola-coronavirus? .

9. See Slavoj Žižek's *Pandemic! Covid-19 Shakes the World* (New York and London: OR Books, 2020), for his thoughts about a 'reinvention of communism' after pandemics, as the only alternative to the new barbarity.

10. Giorgio Agamben, 'Biosecurity and Politics', *Medium*, 11 May 2020, https://medium.com/@ddean3000/biosecurity-and-politics-giorgio-agamben-396f9ab3b6f4. See also 'Coronavirus and Philosophers: M. Foucault, G. Agamben, J.L. Nancy, R. Esposito, S. Benvenuto, D. Dwivedi, S. Mohan, R. Ronchi, M. de Carolis', *The European Journal of Psychoanalysis*, March-April, 2020, https://www.journal-psychoanalysis.eu/coronavirus-and-philosophers/.

11. Freud took as the name for this principle an expression used by one of his patients. See Sigmund Freud, 'The Uncanny' (1919), in *Standard Edition*, trans. James Strachey, Vol. 17 (London: Hogarth Press, 1953-1974), 240–241.

12. See, for example, a kind of ironic worshipping in the publications by 'The Society of the Friends of the Virus', organised by 16 Beaver Group, at centreparrhesia.org.

13. A group of scientists recently registered a record-breaking 50% global reduction of anthropogenic seismic noise resulting from the pandemic. See Thomas Lecocq et al, 'Global quieting of high-frequency seismic noise due to COVID-19 pandemic lockdown measures', *Science*, 23 Jul 2020, doi: 10.1126/science.abd2438.

14. See Jonathan Crary, *24/7: Late Capitalism and the Ends of Sleep* (London: Verso, 2013).

15. As Mark Fisher wrote, even 'tiny' and ephemeral events 'can tear a hole in the grey curtain of reaction which has marked the horizons of possibility under capitalist realism'. See Mark Fisher, *Capitalist Realism: Is There No Alternative?* (Winchester: Zero Books, 2009), 81.

16. Viktor Shklovsky, 'Art as Technique' in *Viktor Shklovsky: A Reader*, ed. and trans. Alexandra Berlina (London: Bloomsbury, 2016), 73–96. 'Ostranenie' is not only a literary or artistic technique. As a detachment from the perceptive automatisms of the everyday, it retains connections to social and political experience and can, in its turn, be used for their characterisation. Against the presentation of *ostranenie* as an apolitical modernist concept, many commentators have noted the links between the invention of this concept and Shklovsky's biographical and political experience, such as the revolution and his short emigration to Berlin. See, for example, Svetlana Boym, 'Estrangement as a Lifestyle: Shklovsky and Brodsky', in *Exile and Creativity*, ed. Susan Suleiman (Durham, NC: Duke University Press, 1998), 241–63.

17. Bertolt Brecht, 'On Chinese Acting', trans. Eric Bentley, *The Tulane Drama Review* 6:1 (1961), 130–136.

18. See Elettra Stimili, 'Apocalyptic Time', *Political Theology* 21:5 (2020), 392.

19. See Gilles Deleuze, 'Coldness and Cruelty' in *Masochism* (NY: Zone Books, 1991), 21, 32.

20. Ibid., 70.

21. Theodor Reik discusses a 'non-sexual, social masochism' in his *Masochism in Modern Man*, one of the classical studies of masochism that first drew attention to the 'factor of suspense'. See Theodor Reik, *Masochism and Modern Man*, trans. Margaret H. Beigel and Gertrud M. Kurth (New York: Farrar, Straus, 1941), 71.

22. About the masochist as a 'perfect subject of capitalism' from the perspective of Lacaninan psychoanalysis, see also Samo Tomši, *The Capitalist Unconscious: Marx and Lacan* (London and New York: Verso, 2015), 229.

23. See Valery Podoroga, *Vtoroi Ekran. Sergei Eizenshtein i kinematograf nasiliia* [The Second Screen: Sergei Eisenstein and the Cinema of Violence], Vol. 1 (Moscow: Sh. P. Breus, 2016), 211.

24. Ibid., 128–174. Eisenstein's subjective obsession with images of violent suspensions originate, Podoroga suggests, in the events of his early psychobiography. Podoroga scrupulously analyses the autobiographic materials from Eisenstein's memoirs and also uses Eisenstein's own attempts at psychoanalytical interpretation of his childhood, presenting his analysis as a fulfillment of these endeavours. The details of Eisenstein's family dispositions included a heavily disciplinary atmosphere and the despotic omnipresence of his father. An analysis of the spatial arrangements of Eisenstein's family house and of many visual documents articulates some prototypes and devices that will populate the future 'second screen'. For example, Podoroga focuses on a method of photography, popular at the time of Eisenstein's childhood, that used invisible holders, which 'suspended' the figure of the child in an artificial pose, to create an 'ideal' image.

25. See Furio Jesi, *Spartakus: The Symbology of the Revolt*, ed. Andrea Cavalletti, trans. Alberto Toscano (London, New York

and Calcutta: Seagull Press, 2014), 58. I would like to thank an anonymous reviewer from the RP editorial collective who drew my attention to this inspiring work.

26. This English translation is from a fragment of the essay translated by John Garvey and posted on February 15, 2018, entitled 'The Ideal of the Broken Down: On the Neapolitan Approach to Things Technical', at hardcrackers.com/ideal-broken-neapolitan-approach-things-technical.

27. During the Second World War, Sohn-Rethel, unlike his colleagues from the Frankfurt School who moved to the US, preferred Britain. He spent 35 years there, from 1937 to 1972. According to an interview, 'he hardly ever came out of his room' (quoted in Jairus Banaji, 'Alfred Sohn-Rethel', at http://www.historicalmaterialism.org/node/1183). Two stories from *Das Ideal des Kaputten* reflect Sohn-Rethel's experience of this exile.

28. See Alfred Sohn-Rethel, *Das Ideal des Kaputten*, ed. Bettina Wassman (Frickingen: Verlag Ulrich Seutter, 2009), 41.

29. Sohn-Rethel describes 'flow production' as follows: 'The entirety of a workshop or factory is integrated into one continuous process in the service of the rule of speed. ... This continuity is now implemented by a machine, a conveyor belt or other transfer mechanism subjecting to the set speed the action of all the productive machinery and the human labour serving it'. Alfred Sohn-Rethel, *Intellectual and Manual Labour* (Atlantic Highlands, NJ: Humanities Press, 1978), 161.

30. Sohn-Rethel, *Intellectual and Manual Labour*, 142–143.

31. Karl Marx, *Capital: A Critique of Political Economy, Volume 2*, trans. David Fernbach (London: Penguin Classics, 1992), 182.

32. For a detailed discussion of the concept of continuity in Marx, see my chapter '"Il faut continuer": Always-On Capitalism and Subjectivity', in *Politics of the Many: Contemporary Radical Thought and the Crisis of Agency*, eds. Rebecca Carson, Benjamin Halligan, Stefano Pippa and Alexei Penzin (London: Bloomsbury Academic, forthcoming 2021).

33. Karl Marx, *Grundrisse: Foundations of the Critique of Political Economy*, trans. Martin Nicolaus (London: Penguin Classics, 1993), 719.

34. Marx, *Grundrisse*, 535.

The theatre of economic categories
Rediscovering *Capital* in the late 1960s
Kyle Baasch

Marx prefaces the first edition of the first volume of *Capital* with a laconic proviso. 'To avoid any possible misunderstandings', he writes, 'a word. I do not by any means depict the capitalist and the landowner in rosy colours. But individuals are dealt with here only insofar as they are the personifications of economic categories, bearers of particular class relations and interests.'[1] He could not have foreseen that a full century after it was first penned, this pithy codicil to a thousand-page work would be the source of *all* possible misunderstandings and the fulcrum around which so many unresolved questions in the interpretation of his critique of political economy would pivot, such as its relationship to the natural sciences, its conception of human freedom and its usefulness for the analysis of culture.

Most decisive in the annals of institutionalised misunderstandings of Marx in the latter half of the twentieth century is simply 'a word'. What does it mean to be the 'bearer' [*Träger*] of a class relation? In much of the French and English Marxist literature written in the wake of the publication of *Reading Capital*, the joint intellectual project that emerged out of Louis Althusser's seminar at the École normale supérieure in the spring of 1965, *Träger* often figures as the only German word in an otherwise monolingual text and serves as incontrovertible proof of the anti-humanistic point of departure in Marx's economic writings. This Teutonic stain is often called upon to lend an air of philological rigour to Marxist scholarship, but in *Reading Capital* it evidences indolence: an appeal to the authenticity of the German excuses the critic from the task of investigating the various valences that the word contains in the original language and from locating the contexts in which the word actually appears in Marx's writings. Accordingly, the legion of recent publications recommending a return to *Reading Capital*, this 'watershed in Marxist philosophy and critical theory more generally' with its 'dazzling array of concepts that can still today be said to constitute the syntax of radical philosophy', should be approached with critical trepidation.[2] Perhaps one ought to return to *Reading Capital* precisely to discover that this tremendously influential text is not a serviceable explication of Marx's work, and to realise finally that the discourse of radical philosophy is compromised by its uncritical application of those so-called 'dazzling' concepts that Structural Marxism first imported into leftist sociological common sense.

This is the return to *Reading Capital* recommended here: to determine whether this text in fact deserves a place in the pantheon of 'key interventions in twentieth-century critical theory',[3] and to reflect on how a term that would have been associated during Althusser's time exclusively with the methodological approach of a group of Marxist social theorists based in Frankfurt could today self-evidently be used as a promiscuous umbrella term under which a highly antithetical Parisian intellectual movement takes refuge. In other words, the aim here is to critically examine the mechanisms through which the Structuralist interpretation of Marx became unproblematically synonymous with critical theory, in light of the fact that the self-proclaimed Critical Theory developed by Horkheimer and his colleagues at the Institute for Social Research in Frankfurt in the 1930s, which reaches its apotheosis in and around the sociological writings and advanced seminars of Theodor Adorno at Goethe University in the 1960s, is fundamentally incompatible with the research programme carried out contemporaneously in Paris.

In Frankfurt, it was recognised that the antinomy of agency and structure that took shape in the French confrontation of Existentialism and Structuralism in the 1960s was merely the re-emergence of a *fin de siècle* sociological problematic that pits structure against agency.[4] Ironically, the Critical Theorists of Frankfurt recognised that it was none other than Marx himself who had pre-emptively criticised this spurious sociological antinomy, and insisted that his approach shows how it is possible to criticise the deleterious nature of an unmastered economic totality that weighs upon impotent humans without regressing to an anthropological or ontological theory of the individual as *causa sui*.

Despite the number of references and allusions to Adorno and his milieu in the canon of contemporary critical theory, the reception of the Frankfurt School's most characteristically Marxist works occurred well after the institutionalisation of Structural Marxism by Anglophone journals and universities in the late 1960s and 1970s. French Structuralism and its predominantly English commentators alike offer a trans-historical model of the relation between individuals and social structures, inspired by rationalist metaphysics, which allows the reader to apply Marx's critique of social domination to spheres beyond the specifically economic. This has been highly attractive to a readership wishing to tap Marx without wishing to engage with his economics. The drawback of this approach, however, is its neglect of the salt of Marx's writings: the analyses of the historically specific mechanisms through which individuals are constituted as economic subjects, the dynamics through which capitalist society reproduces itself and the directional logic of the capitalist mode of production on which the possibility of its transcendence is grounded. Structural Marxism and its legacy, in other words, fail to appreciate the relation of freedom and necessity that is insisted upon by Marx's work, and which is inseparable from a German philosophical tradition oriented towards the reconciliation of spirit and flesh. By contrast, this discourse of reconciliation offers *sine qua non* origins for the original and persuasive interpretation of Marx that underpins Frankfurt School Critical Theory in the 1960s, which locates the desideratum of Marx's materialism in 'the generation of a state in which the blind pressure of material relations over humans is broken, and in which the question of freedom would first be truly meaningful'.[5]

Reading *Capital* in French

The interpretation of Marx that emerged in Paris in the 1960s in the work of Althusser and his students is shaped by the attempt to creatively reinterpret Marx's economic writings so as to conform with the Structuralist paradigm that dominated French intellectual thought at the time, namely, the linguistics-inspired work of figures such as Claude Lévi-Strauss and Jacques Lacan, as well as the anti-evolutionary theories of science established by Gaston Bachelard and Georges Canguilhem. This retrofitting of Marx's work to the fashion of the times is cunningly presented as a new orthodoxy that is able to appreciate the scientific revolution contained in *Capital* as if for the first time. This revolution is argued to have been overlooked by a century of the twin interpretive follies of economism and historicism, which are conveniently shown to be victims of an identical methodological error: the presupposition of a 'subject', an extraordinarily flexible term that is attributed by Althusser and his students to a panoply of conceptual entities ranging from methodological individualism's rational actor, to the proletariat qua Lukácsian 'subject of history', to the Hegelian *Begriff*, to the economy as such in the eyes of dogmatic Marxist economics. An adequate understanding of Marx's writings, according to Structural Marxism, presupposes that one reject the possibility of these seemingly self-determining agents.

In *Reading Capital*, first published in French in 1965, this assimilation of Marx is carried out by way of carefully chosen references to the original German text that represent contentious interpretations at best and philological irresponsibility at worst, perhaps best illustrated by the almost ideographic presence of the italicised German word *Träger* throughout the text.[6] This word is by no means unequivocal. In German, the verb *tragen* contains a raft of connotations, including to bear, to carry, to support or to wear. It shares many of these with the French verb *porter*, although in the case of bearing the weight of a physical structure, *supporter* is more appropriate. One might schematically differentiate two senses of the agent noun: one in which the *Träger* is an entity distinguishable from the content that it bears or carries, such as the bearer of a title or the wearer of an article of clothing, and another in which the *Träger* is a fun-

damental ingredient of that which it carries, such as a support beam. In any case, in the 1872 French edition of *Capital*, which served as the primary reference text in the 1960s, 'bearers of particular class relations and interests', from the 'Preface to the First Edition', is translated as 'les *supports* d'interêts et de rapports de classes determines'.[7]

Marx presided over the French translation of *Capital* and claimed to be proud of its even greater organisational clarity over the painstakingly revised second German edition of 1872 after which it was modelled. However, he admitted that he was often forced to 'aplatir', or flatten, the complex German presentation, and that future translations should diligently compare the German and French editions, especially in the first chapter.[8] The French edition is highly inconsistent in its translation of the more idiosyncratic terms that decorate the opening chapters, amongst which *Träger* is one. *Träger* appears some twenty times throughout the 1872 German edition, and in the French, after the preface, it is rendered as *support* in only one of these instances. 'Bearer of value' [*Wertträger* or *Träger von Wert*] is consistently translated as *porte-valeur*; twice the term appears as *soutien*. Often, especially in the opening chapters, the word is simply omitted in the corresponding French passage.

Althusser and his students were at least partially aware of the shortcomings of the French edition of *Capital* and followed Marx in emphasising the necessity of reading the 'German original, at least for the fundamental theoretical chapters and all the passages where Marx's key concepts come to the surface'.[9] This is one reason why *Reading Capital* is dotted with italicised German words and occasional comments on issues of translation. For example, in Étienne Balibar's contribution to *Reading Capital*, he claims that when Marx wrote about the individual, he 'systematically used the term *Träger* ... which is most often rendered in French as *support*'.[10] But this is not true. And even within *Reading Capital*, this term of such seeming importance is inconsistently translated. In Althusser's contribution to *Reading Capital*, *Träger* is rendered once as *support*, twice as *porteur*.[11] In order to establish which, if either, of these terms is most adequate, it is worth examining the opening paragraph of the second chapter of *Capital*, in which the term *Träger* appears in language that bears remarkable similarity to the 'Preface to the First Edition'. Marx writes:

As we proceed to develop our investigation, we shall find, in general, that the economic character masks of persons [*Charaktermasken der Personen*] are only the personifications of economic relations; it is as bearers [*Träger*] of the latter that they confront one another.[12]

Here, Marx compares the personification and *bearing* of economic relations with the *wearing* of masks. It is as wearers of masks that individuals confront one another on a market, which suggests that individuals are not identical with these masks.

Balibar may not have been familiar with this use of the term *Träger* in such close proximity to the concept of *Charaktermaske*, for the corresponding sentence is so warped in the French edition that any reference to a bearer of masks or economic relations is entirely omitted. However, Balibar does make reference to the original German text, locating an occurrence of *Charaktermaske* (originally translated as *le caractère économique*), and attempts to bring it into relation with the concept of *Träger* in order to make a general claim about Marx's theory of the individual. He states that, in the first volume of *Capital*

> we find all the images which Marx uses to help us grasp the mode of existence of the agents of the production process as the *supports (Träger)* of the structure. On the stage of reproduction ... the individuals quite literally *come forward masked ... they are nothing more than masks*.[13]

This passage warrants close scrutiny, for the terms that are borrowed from *Capital* are re-purposed in a manner that is at odds with Marx's consistent and systematic intentions. Marx uses the term 'mode of existence' [*Existenzweise*] in later chapters to refer to the existence of abstract categories such as value or capital in the concrete form of commodities or gold. This is entirely different from 'mode of expression' [*Ausdrucksweise*], a term prominently featured in the first chapter, which is used to emphasise the distinction between an object's socially mediated form and its concrete constitution. The commodity labour-power is thus one of capital's modes of existence insofar as it functions as a living body in the capitalistic production process, but one of the individual's modes of expression insofar as the individual appears on the labour market as the commodity labour-power. To describe a social determination as the individual's 'mode of existence' would be a category error: only social categories have modes of existence; concrete individuals

simply exist, and express themselves or appear in various ways. By collapsing this crucial distinction between existence and appearance, Balibar fails to appreciate the significance of the concept of the 'character mask', which in Marx's usage indicates a non-identity between the empirical and social individual. For Balibar, by contrast, individuals are 'nothing more than masks', or entirely reducible to the theatrical role that they are destined to perform in a mode of production-qua-performance. In the following chapter of *Capital*, Marx addresses this conflation of the character mask with its concrete bearer and associates it with the positivistic and necessarily apologetic methods of vulgar political economy:

> the practical agents of capitalist production and their ideological word-spinners are as incapable of thinking of the means of production separately from the antagonistic character masks that presently adhere [*ankleben*] to them as a slave-owner is incapable of thinking of the worker himself as distinct from his character as a slave.[14]

It is worth dwelling on these shifts in which Marx's presentation of the non-identity of the living and potentially free individual with the form in which the individual necessarily appears in capitalist society is obscured, for the Structuralist cliché of the absence of the individual qua subject in *Capital* has become so commonplace that most contemporary readers of Marx have little inclination to confront the complex socialisation process that is actually presented in the opening chapters of the book. When one reads the treacherously difficult opening chapters of *Capital*, it is immediately clear that Marx distinguishes between, on the one hand, objects of labour as sensuous objects, which he describes as the object's 'homely, natural form', and on the other hand, the object's 'value form', or the form in which objects of labour appear socially.[15] This distinction holds for individuals as well, insofar as they are concrete individuals in one instance and bearers of value in another. It is, furthermore, *only* within these opening chapters that the social process through which empirical individuals and concrete objects are constituted as bearers of economic categories, or wearers of masks, is even cursorily presented; the rest of the book unfolds under the presupposition that this socialisation process takes place successfully and vanishes without a trace.

Since Althusser's intervention into Marxist scholarship, it has become increasingly common to distinguish

between, on the one hand, humanistic interpretations of *Capital* that take the opening chapters of the book as their point of departure, and on the other, a more informed and anti-humanistic mode of interpretation that ironically insists upon the conceptual inadequacy of these most carefully revised chapters of the book. In his 1969 preface to a new French edition of the first volume of *Capital*, Althusser claims that the language that Marx uses in the first part of the book should be read as 'survivals' of a Hegelian philosophical heritage 'on the way to supersession', and even demands that the reader skip these opening chapters because of their 'flagrant and extremely harmful' Hegelian influence.[16] This assertion is perhaps less informed by a conclusively established 'epistemological break' between the young and mature Marx, and more the result of Althusser's own difficulty in comprehending these opening chapters. In the summer of 1967, two years after the composition of *Reading Capital*, Althusser remarks in a letter to his wife of his attempt to 'focus all of my efforts on *Capital* and on trying to see things clearly in the questions where I don't understand anything', namely 'the very beginning'. He adds:

> If you see Étienne [Balibar], tell him that I will ask him questions about the following concepts: 1.) What is the value-*form*? 2.) What is the difference between *value* and *exchange-value*, of which Marx says it's not value, but is a form of manifestation (*Erscheinungsform*)? 3.) Is there not, in spite of everything, a relationship between the value-form and exchange value, Marx playing on the word *form*? Étienne will surely understand what I am referring to.[17]

These are not easy questions, but they are nevertheless the kinds of questions to which an interpretation of *Capital* that insists upon a careful understanding of the text's most difficult and key concepts should be able to respond.

To be sure, Structural Marxism does have an account of the social process through which concrete individuals come to take on a social function, although it is an account that remains at odds with Marx. This is Althusser's concept of 'interpellation', perhaps his most well-known contribution to contemporary social theory, which he first introduced into his writings in 1966, just a few months after the publication of *Reading Capital*, and which is modelled on a form of socialisation that he thought he had found in Marx's *Capital*.[18] Althusser writes that 'in every social formation, the base requires *la function-support* (*Träger*) as a function to be assumed, as a place to be occupied in the technical and social division of labour'.[19] Althusser conceives of social formations on the order of an architectural blueprint, and the division of labour as a list of structural components, with all of the *Träger* – now conceived as support beams – laid out *in abstracto*, awaiting the right individual to occupy each specific structural position. 'The structure *requires Träger*', he writes, and 'ideological discourse *recruits* them for it by interpellating individuals *as subjects* to assume the function of *Träger*'.[20]

The looseness and imprecision of such formulations is foreign to the discourse of modern political economy. The latter, from Adam Smith to Marx, is concerned with the way in which individuals contribute, through seemingly self-interested economic decisions, to the reproduction of a social process that takes place behind their backs and beyond their comprehension, and the way in which this same social process consequently directs or diminishes the individual capacity to act. Althusser, convinced of the originality of Marx's inquiry, did not see these commonalities, and instead claimed to discover in *Capital* a conception of the relation between society and individual that is curiously modelled on early modern rationalist ethics – namely, Spinoza's relation between substance and mode – and a conception of the relation between consciousness and materiality that is likewise modelled on Spinozist metaphysics – namely, the parallelism of thought and extension.[21] What appears in the discourse of political economy as a tumultuous interaction between self-interested individuals is transformed in Althusser's social theory into a kind of bureaucratic police state that manipulates individuals with the assistance of 'ideology' into identifying with their own subjection, or rather, 'provid[es] them with reasons-of-a-subject ... for the functions defined by the structure as functions-of-a-*Träger*'.[22]

There is obviously great attraction to thinking of social coercion as a process in which individuals are compelled – in both the sense of forced and persuaded – to take on pre-established roles and functions in a process that ultimately harms them. The elasticity of the concept of interpellation allows one to conceive of forms of social subjection independent of the relationship between, for example, capitalist and wage-labourer. Furthermore,

the synonyms that Althusser employs to elaborate the interpellative process – such as 'recruitment' and 'requisition' – dramatically allegorise the imbalance of power between the interpellated and the interpellator. It is not surprising that much of the secondary literature on the concept of interpellation addresses its dramaturgical connotations.[23] Indeed, the most cited example of interpellation in Althusser's work is not a properly economic transaction at all, but that of a police officer who shouts 'Hey, you!' to the back of an unassuming individual and subsequently compels the respondent to assume the subject position of one who is being addressed. This kind of social interaction, in which individuals are called upon to identify with the aggressor by adopting the subject position that is imputed to them, is ubiquitous and quotidian, and one might convincingly conduct critical analyses of interpellative processes in carceral and educational institutions, as Foucault has done, or in sexual and kinship relations, all of which rely to varying degrees on the blueprint or script-like model that Althusser's concept of interpellation presupposes.

Marx's critique of political economy does not adopt a universally valid model of socialisation that fails to distinguish between the unique ways in which individuals are constituted as serfs here and proprietors of labour-power there, docile bodies in one instance and *homo economicus* in another. In fact, Althusser's theory of interpellation remains historically *anterior* to Marx's social theory, which demonstrates how capitalist society synthesises individuals into a social totality by way of private and apparently free transactions, thus rendering anachronistic the somewhat medieval conception of a social 'role' or 'function' that the individual is 'recruited' to assume. Moreover, by comprehending the bourgeois freedom enjoyed by the individual in a capitalist society as a 'specular' freedom offered by 'ideological discourse' – as though the concept of freedom were a sort of narcotic doled out to the masses, rather than a lived experience conditioned by legally non-coercive individual economic transactions – Structural Marxism forfeits any insight into the specific experiential process through which the individual comes to recognise that capitalism's promise and premise of freedom is constitutively withheld.

Reading Capital in English

One might imagine that the claims of Structural Marxism would not have survived the scrutiny of any intellectual culture with a deep familiarity with Marx's writings. But this is precisely what was lacking in England in the late 1960s. An adequate English translation of the first volume of *Capital* did not appear until 1976, almost 90 years after the first English translation of the book, and a good decade after serious interest in Marx's economic writings had taken shape in Western Europe. The available English edition of 1887 was a joint translation effort, undertaken by Samuel Moore, a long-time comrade of Marx, and Edward Aveling, Marx's son-in-law and best known for his writings on Charles Darwin. They worked independently of each other, with corrections made by Engels and Eleanor Marx herself. The resulting work is indicative of Engels' attempt to assimilate Marx's dialectics to a *Naturdialektik*, and thus the tension in the original German text between the concrete and its socially-mediated mode of expression is rendered almost systematically in language that obscures this tension. For example, in the 'Preface to the First Edition', individuals are now described neither as bearers nor supports, but as 'embodiments of particular class-relations and class-interests'. The commodity as a bearer of value [*Wertträger*], which was used by Marx to indicate the non-identity of the commodity's form of appearance with its so-called natural form, is now regularly rendered as a 'depository of value'.[24] The motif of the character mask is entirely omitted.

The *New Left Review* acted as a hub for the international exchange of Marx interpretations in the late 1960s, and the lack of a philologically sophisticated reading of Marx in England – or even the pretence thereof – left the country's extant Marxist traditions somewhat defenceless against foreign claims to Marxist orthodoxy. These English traditions, represented for example by E.P. Thompson's documentation of English working-class history and Raymond Williams' various extended commentaries on Marxist method from his early monographs on English literature and culture, were critical rehabilitations of a socially conservative and humanistic British romantic tradition that had fused with socialist currents in the twentieth century. They offered nuanced conceptions of the problem of the economic determination of the individual, but these were never formally systematised, and English Marxism generally lacked the obsession with methodology that characterised most continental engagements with Marx's writings at the time. It is therefore not surprising that when Nicos Poulantzas, a student of Althusser, waged a veritable sortie against the alleged conceptual impoverishment of the state of British Marxist discourse in the spring of 1967, his contribution was welcomed by the editors of the *New Left Review* as a 'searching criticism' of the work of Perry Anderson and Tom Nairn, representing 'an important advance over previous discussion', and was unequivocally lauded as 'a renewal of the internationalist traditions of the classic socialist movement', and thus a 'transcendence of national provincialism.'[25]

Poulantzas' impressive comprehension of an esoteric British Marxist discourse notwithstanding, his illumination of the latter's 'conceptual issues' takes the shape of a basic introduction to Structuralism's annihilation of the humanist subject: the admittedly simplistic reduction of history to the conscious action of individuals advocated by British Marxists is expeditiously replaced with an equally simplistic 'anti-historicist' conception of history as an entirely impersonal process. Poulantzas urged that one should understand individual consciousness as an effect of the structure of society, and introduced what would have appeared as a novel theoretical model that distinguishes between ideology, on the one hand, and 'social structures' or 'structures of production', on the other, without reducing the former to epiphenomena of the latter. 'Men' are defined as 'bearers of the social structure', and the dominant ideology is simply the '"cement" in the unity of the various levels of the social structure'.[26] Human ideas are a kind of carpenter's glue than cannot be conceived independently of the necessary link that they constitute within a complex structure.

Three years later, when an abridged version of Althusser's *Reading Capital* was translated into English for the first time, the term *Träger* was translated by Ben Brewster in all of its instances as 'support', including the passages where Althusser had rendered the term as *porteur*. What is more, Brewster translated Balibar's assertion that Marx's systematic use of the term *Träger* 'is most often rendered in French as *support*' by simply changing the word 'French' to 'English' and keeping the rest of the sentence intact.[27] *Träger* had never been rendered in English-language Marxist literature as 'support' before. Brewster, however, recognised the affinities between the sister concepts of *Träger* and *Charaktermaske* to a greater degree than can be found in Balibar's text, and writes in his glossary to *Reading Capital* under the entry 'Support' that 'biological men are only *supports* or bearers of the guises (*Charaktermasken*) assigned to them by the structure of relations in the social formation'.[28] This would have been the appropriate opportunity for Brewster to acknowledge that one cannot justifiably hold the conception of individuals as structural 'supports' as well as individuals as 'bearers of guises' as compatible interpretations of one and the same ambiguous German word, but he skirts this difficulty by repeating Balibar's claim that these masks are somehow 'assigned' to individuals by 'the structure of relations', eliding the socialisation process through which individuals don these character masks and the specific market relations in which these masks are perceived as valid. It is as though the capitalist mode of production were a sort of high school theatre production in which the drama teacher arbitrarily writes students' names and their designated characters on a cast list before the first rehearsal.

Given the prominence of the term *Träger* in the glossary of the English translation of *Reading Capital*, as well as its central position in *New Left Review* articles by Poulantzas amongst others, British Marxists were compelled to take up a position with respect to this tricky concept over the course of the following decade, now translated in almost equal measure as 'bearer' and 'support', occasionally 'carrier', and sometimes 'bearer or support'.[29] The term – both the German and its English variations – figures prominently in the writings of Perry Anderson, Stuart Hall and E.P. Thompson. It was perhaps Raymond Williams, otherwise sparing in his adoption of Structuralist vocabulary in his writings, who felt most pressured by the popularity of Structuralism to modify and expand his model of economic determination, and who emerged as one of the more vocal and consistent critics of Structural Marxism in a moment when Althusser exercised a certain popularity in English journals. This is in part because he had worked more diligently than the other British Marxists, and over the course of several decades, to produce a general Marxist theory of determination that was unproblematically compatible

with human freedom, but also perhaps because Williams' earliest efforts contained so many surprising similarities to those of Althusser, such as the rejection of the base-superstructure model of determination and the emphasis on the inextricable unity of being and consciousness. In both Williams and Althusser, the critique of dogmatic Marxist discourses is the point of departure. Most intriguing is that a widely anthologised letter by Engels from 1890, which Williams cites with vigour throughout his entire career to ground his theory of determination, is the same letter from which the Althusserian concept of 'determination-in-the-last-instance' is derived.[30]

These coincidences evidence an uncomfortable affinity. All of Williams' interventions into the problematic of determination are concerned with avoiding any model of causality that would isolate a particular *prima causa*, whether it be the economy or the transcendental subject, and he thus manages to reconcile the Structuralist rejection of 'expressive' and teleological causal models with a humanistic theory of social practice. In a sense, Williams opposes the Structuralist gravitation toward cold macrosociological analysis by foregrounding the complex web of economic, political and cultural determinants that work themselves out at ground level, through the intermediary of an individual consciousness confronted with decisions. But in Paris the existence of the conscious confrontation with decisions, motivations and norms is not rejected; it is simply relegated to the methodological ghetto of 'ideology'. In any case, the relationship between this humanistic model of determination and the ideas developed in the writings of Marx and Engels is not entirely obvious. In *Marxism and Literature*, Williams fixes on Engels' somewhat banal claim that 'we make our history ourselves, but, in the first place, under very definite assumptions and conditions', to suggest that the first part of this claim restores 'the idea of direct agency' to Marxism. He then uses this passage to construct a definition of determination as the 'setting of limits' to an otherwise free humanity.[31] It is, however, difficult to wrest a notion of agency from a letter that describes history as 'the product of a power which works as a whole *unconsciously* and without volition'.[32] As if correcting the enthusiasm for this letter that he demonstrated earlier in his career, Williams claims that if one were to follow Engels down the path indicated by some of the letter's darker sentences, one would 'fall back into a new passive and objectivist model' – this must be Structuralism's 'process without a subject' – in which 'society is the objectified (unconscious and unwilled) general process'.[33]

This irritation with the anti-humanistic attitude of Structuralism without a convincing systematic critique of its basic principles is characteristic of a certain strand of British Marxism in the wake of *Reading Capital*. By the early 1980s, the hegemony of Structural Marxism's mode of inquiry in Anglo-American cultural and social theory had successfully deprived the genuinely humanistic zeal of figures like Thompson and Williams of any shred of legitimacy. Stuart Hall, for example, argues that the French and the English approaches to social and cultural activity represent two useful Marxist methodological paradigms that one can toggle between without internal contradiction: a Structuralist paradigm, deriving from Althusser and his students, which conceives individuals as bearers or supports of structures, and a culturalist paradigm, exemplified by Williams' work, in which humans make their own history under given conditions.[34] Intent on marrying these seemingly incompatible approaches, Hall perceptively argues that they are merely

> different levels of abstraction. ... At the higher levels, Marx is working more with the notion of men and women as bearers of relations, but at the lower, more concrete levels, he works more with the notion of men and women as making their own history. But this second notion does not return us to the humanist subject, for in no sense does this second notion conceive of human beings as agents who can see through to the end of their practices.[35]

This rejection of the desideratum of a legitimately free and self-legislating human subject as some kind of embarrassing idealist philosophical trope is a concession to Structuralism's rhetorical finesse, and reveals that the apparently mutually exclusive paradigms of Structural and humanist Marxism that are often invoked in the discourse of contemporary critical theory are often two sides of the same franc; both reject *tout court* that Marxist 'kingdom of freedom' in which individuals would no longer be overdetermined by the mesh of social relations in which they find themselves, but would finally be 'ends in themselves'.[36] It is only in the German interpretation of Marx, where this unmistakably Christian eschatological discourse of reconciliation and salvation is part and parcel of the nation's philosophical history, that the incongruity of a properly Marxist conception of freedom with the French and English interpretations of Marx is finally thrown into relief.

Structuralism in Frankfurt

The post-war Marxist intellectual cultures of England and West Germany remained largely oblivious of each other's activities, but because of the monopoly that Anglophone journals exercised on the international dissemination of various Marxist intellectual currents in the 1960s and 70s, this mutual ignorance often appears as provincialism on the part of Germany in contrast to English internationalism. Perry Anderson buttresses this impression in *Considerations on Western Marxism* when he claims that 'within the entire corpus of Western Marxism there is not one single serious appraisal or sustained critique of the work of one major theorist by another, revealing close textual knowledge or minimal analytic care in its treatment'.[37] But this evidences a surprising ignorance of the work of Alfred Schmidt, the research assistant of Adorno and Horkheimer during the 1960s who ultimately occupied Horkheimer's chair at Goethe University for over 25 years. Schmidt had translated various major works of Henri Lefebvre, Jean-Paul Sartre and Maurice Merleau-Ponty into German throughout the 1960s, and published a monograph-length critique of Structural Marxism in 1971.[38] Schmidt was indeed a 'major theorist'. His 1960 dissertation on *The Concept of Nature in Marx*, which was translated by Ben Fowkes in 1971 for *New Left Books*, and which has since been translated into sixteen other languages, had a considerable influence on the West German student movements of the late 1960s and is the source of much of the sophisticated commentary on Marx that one finds in Adorno's *Negative Dialectics*.[39]

Anderson's limited familiarity with the intellectual culture of Frankfurt during the years in which he produced his influential tracts on Western Marxism and historical materialism compels his interpretation of Adorno's Marxism to limit itself to what is contained in the notoriously dense pages of *Negative Dialectics*. Several superficial similarities with Structuralism, such as Adorno's critique of nostalgic uses of the concept of reification and his preference for the later Marx over the younger, allow Anderson to hastily subsume Adorno under the Structuralist paradigm, and *Negative Dialectics* is said to 'reproduce' and 'echo' certain formulations found in the work that Althusser composed during same period.[40] Furthermore, Anderson claims that Adorno's Marxism, 'formed in another epoch', was strictly a university philosophy, and that by the 1960s Adorno's distance from political engagement had become 'well-nigh absolute' – a stereotype that lives on in the widespread yet poorly substantiated caricature of Adorno as the curmudgeonly enemy of the West German student movements of the late 1960s.[41] It is forgotten that in addition to his activities as the heterodox chair of the German Sociological Association, who had earnestly attempted to construct a mainstream empirical sociological research paradigm that takes the critique of political economy as its point of departure, Adorno was also one of the most prominent public intellectuals in post-war West Germany, with a gift for communicating sociologically complex ideas on television and radio in a remarkably lucid and accessible manner.[42]

There is at least some legitimacy to the comparison between Frankfurter and Structural Marxism, and Schmidt concedes that Structuralism's 'indisputable merit consists in the fact that after a period of spuriously subjective, naively anthropological interpretations of Marx, the critique of political economy returned to centre stage and was considered with conceptual rigour.'[43] Shortly after Adorno's death in 1969, Schmidt published a commemorative essay in which he even claimed, half-jokingly, that Adorno would perhaps have ironically described himself as an anti-humanist, in light of the barbarism of which the ideology of 'the human' is capable.[44] But these are distracting similarities, for the essence of Adorno's sociological theory in the 1960s lies in its unflagging methodological distinction between the concrete and the socially necessary semblance or forms of appearance through which the concrete is compelled to express itself.[45] One sees this most vividly in Adorno's deep antipathy toward the concept of 'role' that had become increasingly popular in American sociological discourse of the 1960s, particularly in the work of Talcott Parsons, which according to Adorno hypostatises the wrong state of affairs in which individuals 'act and dissimulate as something other than what they are', without comprehending the historically specific economic foundation that grounds this act of dissimulation.[46] Unsurprisingly, Adorno felt that Marx's concept of *Charaktermaske* effectively grounds this sociological dissimulation in a historically specific mode of production.[47] Adorno had no patience for sociological theories that attempted to 'derive the ontology of reality immediately from the theatre', and dedicated much of his late sociological writings to thinking the possibility of an unrestricted human freedom, which the transfiguration of everyday life into a stage performance invariably precludes.[48]

Adorno's advanced sociology seminar in the summer semester of 1969, titled 'Problems of Structuralism', only met once at its scheduled time and location. An hour before its second meeting, Adorno's lecture hall was occupied by upwards of 500 dissident students, and the seminar broke down into independent study-groups for the rest of the semester.[49] Virtually nothing of these meetings is known, but speculation need not travel very far, for many of Adorno's colleagues were deeply familiar with the work of Althusser, and by the time of Adorno's death, Althusser had already made a considerable impression in the intellectual culture of Goethe University.[50] The introduction of Althusser's ideas into Frankfurt occurred in much the same manner that his ideas found an

English readership: just a few months after his critique of British Marxism appeared in *New Left Review*, Poulantzas travelled to Goethe University in the spring of 1967 to present a paper at a conference organised by the Institute for Political Science in collaboration with the *Europäische Verlaganstalt*, which featured contributions by Alfred Schmidt, Oskar Negt, Ernest Mandel, Roman Rosdolsky *in absentia*, among many others.[51] Poulantzas had been invited as an ambassador of Althusserianism, and his paper offers a rudimentary lesson in the Structuralist interpretation of Marx's work, reaching its climax in the claim that

> the absence of a central subject in Marx indicates a break with economic anthropology, that is to say with the ideology of labour and needs, with such ideological concepts as alienation, reification, etc., with concepts that necessarily underwrite an essence, be it of the Hegelian or Feuerbachian type, and that have no scientific place in Marxism. ... 'Humans' are present in production only as *Träger* of structures, that is to say of relations of production, of structures that allocate to them their positions and functions, which are called social classes.[52]

Unlike in England, where such ideas were met with either the fascination of a young Marxist intelligentsia that thirsted for this level of methodological sophistication, or by the repulsion of an older generation that sensed the stoic and politically resigned implications of Structural Marxism, the mostly German audience agreed with the methodological prioritisation accorded to impersonal and self-regulating structures in the Althusserian position, but refused to accept this as a trans-historically valid state of affairs. Structural Marxism appeared to hypostatise – and thence affirm – that which is identified by Marx as the wrong life, and thus to sap *Capital* of its unmistakably critical tenor. 'That structures degrade humans to their mere *"Träger"* constitutes the scientific norm for you', Schmidt retorts to Poulantzas during the discussion of the latter's paper, 'whereas for Marx this was an object of criticism. I think that we are speaking of the same thing, only from two different sides.'[53]

The humanistic dimension of Schmidt's immediate response should not be seen as a recapitulation of a Marxist humanism akin to the French Existentialist Marxism of the 1950s – although Poulantzas, who bristled at every mention of individuals or humans, interpreted Schmidt's response in this way – but rather an interpretation of Marx that recognises the inextricability of the penetrating consciousness of the individual's unfreedom from the normative conception of the self-legislating individual as critique's desideratum. Furthermore, Schmidt emphasises that one can recognise *Capital*'s indebtedness to a Hegelian conception of world history without subscribing to Hegel's essentially affirmative conception of the overall historical process. Schmidt notes the unmistakably Hegelian character of Marx's conception of value as a 'self-moving' and 'automatic subject', derived immediately from the formula of M-C-M', or the law that value inexorably begets more value through its necessary metamorphoses; this lends capitalist society a certain autotelic, subject-like character.[54] Hegel's teleological philosophy is thus adequate to the analysis of capitalist society when its concepts are secularised, and it is shown to depict 'bourgeois society comprehended as ontology'; *Capital* represents a kind of parodic recapitulation of a Hegelian theodicy of world-spirit.[55]

This re-evaluation of Hegel had developed in Adorno's advanced seminars throughout the 1960s, and the significance accorded to Hegel's philosophy – particularly the *Logic* – in the analysis of Marx's work is a hallmark of the work of Adorno's students Helmut Reichelt and Hans-Georg Backhaus, the founding figures of what has come to be known as the *Neue Marx-Lektüre*.[56] In this interpretive tradition, it is methodologically appropriate to take the standpoint of conceptual realism, so long as the Hegelian *Begriff* is conceived as a 'conceptuality which holds sway in reality itself', or what is sometimes called an 'existing abstraction' [*daseinede Abstraktion*], grounded in the forms of commensurability carried out via the exchange of commodities.[57] But this 'second nature' of capitalist lawfulness does not constitute a normative totality or a kind of *Sittlichkeit* in which the individual finds himself at home in the social institutions that he has authorised, but is described by Adorno, in an ironic affirmation of Leibniz's *Monadology* – from which Althusser's conception of 'expressive totality' is ultimately derived – as a 'pre-established disharmony'.[58] If one is to read *Capital* as a teleological narrative, it is not as the predestined succession of various modes of production leading inevitably towards communism, but rather as a 'phenomenology of anti-spirit' [*Phänomenologie des Widergeistes*], in which reconciliation between the individual and the universal takes place at the expense of the individual.

The bad 'universal' is conceived by the Frankfurt School, in accordance with Marx, as the form of value in a capitalist society. Individuals buckle under the weight of the universal in their endeavour to make themselves economically attractive to others and to make their activity conform to society's economic demands. This is the experiential impetus of the Frankfurt School's critique of modern society. This universality of being-for-another and the blinding appearance of equivalence that it casts over all things is what Adorno describes as 'ideology' or 'socially necessary semblance'. Althusser, by contrast, comprehends ideology as a 'system of representations', in accordance with the linguistic conception of a symbolic order that mediates the field of individual experience, rather than an economically constituted (mis-)recognition of concrete reality as an expression of the universal category of value, and so it is assumed that 'ideology is as such an organic part of every social totality', and that the primacy of structures over individuals is a trans-historical constant.[59] This is quite far from Marx, however, who argues that after a 'long and tormented historical development', when the social production process is finally rationally organised, the social life process 'casts off its mystical veil of fog' [streift … ihren mystischen Nebelschleier ab].[60]

There is a tremendous difference between the conception of society as a kind of symbolic order and the conception of society as a self-moving totality of economic value, and Marx is clearly concerned with the latter. The progressive reconstitution of a social formation in value's image offers the semblance of something existing in-and-for-itself, in however parasitic and abstract a form, and grounds the generative materialist longing for the transubstantiation of this subject-*like* substance out of the abstract domain of value and into concrete human flesh. In other words, Marx's presentation of the social totality as an autotelic totality of value, as the self-reproduction of the abstract, is the enabling condition for Adorno's cherished and oft-repeated apothegm that 'life does not live', and allows him to speculatively anticipate the realisation of a world in which life *would* live, in which substance, or human flesh, would finally become subject, and not be subsumed under the heteronomous logic of the bad universal. Adorno's late work is thus marked by periodic references to the Christian doctrine of the resurrection of the flesh, in which he notices

ironic parallels with Marx's materialism, for in both he sees the longing for the realisation of the flesh as subject, or 'the emancipation of spirit from the primacy of material needs in the state of their fulfillment'.[61]

But until that flesh is risen, individuals in a capitalist society stand before one another as mutilated figures, conforming spontaneously under the pressure of a social mechanism that 'tames them to pure self-preservation while denying them the preservation of their selves'.[62] Critical Theory, as it developed in Germany as a reaction to positivistic and essentially affirmative tendencies in the social sciences, is animated by the refusal to allow this unbearable state of affairs have the last word. If this refusal is to substantiate itself, it cannot adopt a theoretical position that transfigures the radical stereotypicality of everyday life into yet another act in a trans-historical theatrical production, but must recognise the continued existence of the capitalist mode of production, 150 years after Marx's diagnosis, as a kind of grotesque second childishness. It must transform the grim sociological consciousness of what it means to bear a character mask in an economic drama into the implacable longing for the unrealised individuality that such economic categories both logically presuppose and materially refuse.

Kyle Baasch is a PhD student at the University of Minnesota in the Department of Cultural Studies and Comparative Literature.

Notes

1. Karl Marx, *Capital: A Critique of Political Economy, Volume 1*, trans. Ben Fowkes (New York: Penguin, 1976), 92. Translation amended.
2. Nick Nesbitt, 'Rereading *Reading Capital*', in *The Concept in Crisis: Reading Capital Today*, ed. Nick Nesbitt (Durham, NC: Duke University Press, 2017), 2. For other recent positive re-evaluations of *Reading Capital*, see Knox Peden, *Spinoza Contra Phenomenology* (Stanford: Stanford University Press, 2014); Warren Montag, *Althusser and his Contemporaries: Philosophy's Perpetual War* (Duke: Duke University Press, 2013); and the dossier of essays on Althusser published in *Viewpoint Magazine* in 2016, particularly Alex Demirović, 'Why Should We Read Althusser (Again?)', https://www.viewpoint-mag.com/2016/07/18/why-should-we-read-althusser-again/
3. Nesbitt, Rereading *Reading Capital*, 2.
4. Adorno compares Structuralism with Durkheimian sociology in passing in his only written comment on the movement published during his lifetime, although he probably had Lévi-Strauss in mind: see 'Einleitung zu Émile Durkheim, "Soziologie

und Philosophie'"(1967), in Theodor W. Adorno, *Gesammelte Schriften* [*GS*], ed. Rolf Tiedemann, 20 volumes (Frankfurt am Main: Suhrkamp, 1997), vol. 8, 245. Alfred Schmidt for his part compares Althusser with the structural-functionalism of Talcott Parsons. See Alfred Schmidt, 'Die Strukturalistische Angriff auf die Geschichte' [The Structuralist Attack on History] in *Beiträge zur marxistischen Erkenntnistheorie*, ed. Alfred Schmidt (Frankfurt am Main: Suhrkamp, 1969), 209.

5. Theodor W. Adorno, *Philosophische Terminologie: Band II* [Philosophical Terminology: Volume 2] (Frankfurt am Main: Suhrkamp, 1974), 197.

6. Commentary on *Reading Capital* in this article is limited to the contributions of Althusser and Balibar, owing to the fact that the contributions of Jacques Rancière, Roger Establet and Pierre Macherey were not included in the popular abridged edition of *Lire le capital* in 1969, nor in any English edition of *Reading Capital* until 2015, and therefore played a marginal role in the construction of Anglophone conceptions of a Marxist critical theory.

7. Karl Marx and Friedrich Engels, *Gesamtausgabe: Zweite Abteilung* (MEGA²) II.7: *Le Capital (1872-1875)* (Berlin: Dietz Verlag, 1979), 14. Italics added.

8. Karl Marx and Friedrich Engels, *Marx-Engels-Werke* (MEW) Vol. 34 (Berlin: Dietz Verlag, 2000), 358. The opening chapter of the second German edition is considerably different from that of the first edition. A list of changes included in the second edition can be found in Marx, *MEGA²* II.6, 1–54.

9. Louis Althusser and Etienne Balibar, *Reading Capital*, trans. Ben Brewser (London: New Left Books, 1970), 13–14.

10. Althusser and Balibar, *Reading Capital*, 283. Translation amended.

11. Louis Althusser and Étienne Balibar, *Lire le Capital: I* (Paris: Maspero, 1969), 45, 140; *Lire le Capital: II* (Paris: Maspero, 1969), 53.

12. Translation amended. The original reads: '*Wir werden überhaupt im Fortgang der Entwicklung finden, daß die ökonomischen Charaktermasken der Personen nur die Personifikationen der ökonomischen Verhältnisse sind, als deren Träger sie sich gegenübertreten.*' *MEW* Vol. 23, 100. The genitive *als deren Träger*, roughly 'as the bearers of which', referring ambiguously to both the character masks and the economic relations, is awkward to render outside of German, and it is probably for this reason that the final clause of the passage is usually either omitted or distorted in translation. The original French translation reads: '*Nous verrons d'ailleurs dans le cours du développement que les masques divers dont elles s'affublent suivant les circonstances, ne sont que les personnifications des rapports économiques qu'elles maintiennent les unes vis-à-vis des autres.*' *MEGA²* II.7, 64. The original English translation is closer to the French than to the German: 'The characters who appear on the economic stage are but the personifications of the economic relations that exist between them.' *MEGA²* II.9, 74. Ben Fowkes' 1976 edition reads: 'As we proceed to develop our investigation, we shall find, in general, that the characters who appear on the economic stage are merely the personifications of economic relations; it is as the bearers [*Träger*] of these economic relations that they come into contact with each other.' *Capital, Volume 1*, 179. Fowkes includes a

footnote explaining the concept of *Träger*, but it is unclear why he decided to replace 'character masks' with 'characters who appear on the economic stage', which obscures the dual significance of *Träger* as the bearer of a relation and the wearer of a mask. The four other instances of *Charaktermaske* in the original German text of volume 1 of *Capital* are translated by Fowkes as 'role', 'dramatis personae', 'economic character' and 'social mask' (170, 249, 711, 757), giving the impression that Marx played rather loosely with theatrical metaphors.

13. *Reading Capital*, 300. All italics in original.

14. Marx, *Capital, Volume 1*, 757. Translation amended. *Ankleben* is also the verb that Marx uses to illustrate the relationship between the commodity and the fetish-character that clings to it.

15. Marx, *Capital, Volume 1*, 138.

16. Louis Althusser, *Lenin and Philosophy and other Essays*, trans. Ben Brewster (London: Monthly Review Press, 1971), 94–95.

17. Louis Althusser, *Lettres à Hélène: 1947–1980*, ed. Olivier Corpet (Paris: Éditions Grasset & Fasquelle, 2011), 507. Italics in original. It is worth noting that *Erscheinungsform* was rendered as both *la forme phénoménale* and *la forme de manifestation* in the 1872 French translation.

18. Louis Althusser, 'Three Notes on the Theory of Discourses', in *The Humanist Controversy and other Writings*, ed. François Matheron, trans. G.M. Goshgarian (London: Verso, 2003), 33–84. Warren Montag notes that this is the first use of the term 'interpellation' in Althusser's writings, and offers an excellent account of how Althusser's development of this concept derives from his relationship with Lacanian psychoanalysis, but Montag does not address how Althusser's text is strongly characterised by obsessive and strange use of a German word that he had borrowed from Marx. See Montag, *Althusser and his Contemporaries*, 118–140.

19. Althusser, 'Three Notes', 51.

20. Ibid., 55.

21. The 'Three Notes' are the basis of a never-completed joint work that was intended to be, as Althusser describes it to Balibar, 'a true work of philosophy that can stand as our *Ethics*'. This interest in Spinoza inspires certain redundant and vague formulations in the text that mimic Spinoza's treatment of mind and body in the second book of his *Ethics*. An example is: 'Recruiting ideological subjects, ideological discourse establishes them as ideological subjects at the same time that it recruits them. Thus, in one and the same act, it produces the subjects that it recruits as subjects, establishing them as subjects'. See Althusser, 'Three Notes', 33; 54.

22. Ibid., 52.

23. One of the more important interpretations of this kind can be found in Judith Butler, *The Psychic Life of Power: Theories in Subjection* (Stanford: Stanford University Press, 1997), 106–131.

24. *MEGA²* II.9, 17, 30, 40, 44, 74.

25. New Left Review Editors, 'Introduction to Nicos Poulantzas', *New Left Review* I/43, (May/June 1967), 55–56. Italics in original.

26. Nicos Poulantzas, 'Marxist Political Theory in Britain' *New Left Review* I/43 (May/June 1967), 66. Two years later, Poulantzas introduced the German word *Träger* into the journal

in his 'The Problem of the Capitalist State', *New Left Review* I/58 (November/December 1969), 67–78.

27. Althusser and Balibar, *Reading Capital*, 283. This sentence has been redacted from the 2015 edition of *Reading Capital*, and all instances of 'support' have been changed to 'bearer'. Generally speaking, since the 1976 Fowkes translation of *Capital*, 'bearer' has been the standard translation of *Träger*.

28. Althusser and Balibar, *Reading Capital*, 358. Italics and parenthesis in original.

29. The most conspicuous appearance of the term *Träger* is E.P. Thompson's 1978 *The Poverty of Theory*, where it is the only German term to appear in the entire 200 page critique of Althusser, and appears in more instances than in all of *Capital* and *Reading Capital* combined, often mistakenly in lowercase, as though it were the German word for 'sluggish'. Significantly, Pierre Bourdieu frequently identifies the term *Träger*, as it appeared in Structuralist writing as *support*, as the foil against which he developed the concept of *habitus*. See Pierre Bourdieu, *The Logic of Practice* (Stanford: Stanford University Press, 1990), 41; *The Rules of Art* (Stanford: Stanford University Press, 1996), 179.

30. See Raymond Williams, *Culture and Society* (New York: Anchor Books, 1959), 285–6; *Marxism and Literature* (Oxford: Oxford University Press, 1977), 85–86; Louis Althusser, *For Marx* (London: Verso, 2006), 117–118.

31. Williams, *Marxism and Literature*, 85.

32. Friedrich Engels to Joseph Bloch, in *The Marx-Engels Reader*, ed. Robert Tucker (New York: Norton & Co., 1978), 761. Italics in original.

33. Williams, *Marxism and Literature*, 86.

34. Stuart Hall, 'Cultural Studies: Two Paradigms', in *Essential Essays*, vol. 1, ed. David Morley (Durham: Duke University Press, 1990), 47–70.

35. Stuart Hall, *Cultural Studies 1983* (Durham: Duke University Press, 2016), 103.

36. Karl Marx, *Capital, Volume 3*, trans. David Fernbach (London: Pelican Books, 1981), 959.

37. Perry Anderson, *Considerations on Western Marxism* (London: New Left Books, 1976), 69.

38. See Henri Lefebvre, *Probleme des Marxismus, heute* [Problems of Marxism Today], trans. Alfred Schmidt (Frankfurt am Main: Suhrkamp, 1965); Sartre et al., *Existentialismus und Marxismus: Eine Kontroverse zwischen Sartre, Garaudy, Hyppolite, Vigier und Orcel* [Existentialism and Marxism: A Controversy between Sartre, Garaudy, Hyppolite, Vigier and Orcel], trans. Alfred Schmidt (Frankfurt am Main: Suhrkamp, 1968); Maurice Merleau-Ponty, *Abenteuer der Dialektik* [Adventures of the Dialectic], trans. Alfred Schmidt (Frankfurt am Main: Suhrkamp, 1968); Alfred Schmidt, *History and Structure: An Essay on Hegelian-Marxist and Structuralist Theories of History* [1971], trans. Jeffrey Herf (Cambridge, MA: MIT Press, 1981). Although Jürgen Habermas is synonymous with the 'second generation' of Frankfurt School Critical Theory, this periodisation obscures the fact that, whereas Habermas made his rejection of the essence of Adorno's and Horkheimer's respective versions of critical theory readily apparent, Schmidt effectively carried the torch of Adorno and Horkheimer in Frankfurt throughout the final quarter of the twentieth century, and occupied himself in those years with the constellation of materialist concerns that occupy what he calls Adorno's '*Spätwerk*'.

39. Alfred Schmidt, *The Concept of Nature in Marx*, trans. Ben Fowkes (London: Verso, 2014), 12–13. Schmidt's monograph, for example, is the only secondary literature on Marx that is cited in *Negative Dialectics*, and with three citations, Schmidt is cited as frequently as all of Adorno's other living colleagues combined. Adorno references or recommends Schmidt's work to his students in many of his posthumously published lectures given in the 1960s.

40. Anderson, *Considerations*, 72–3.

41. Perry Anderson, *In the Tracks of Historical Materialism* (London: Verso, 1983), 58. Around the time of Adorno's death, it was rather Habermas who was widely recognised as the chief enemy of the student movement in Frankfurt.

42. It is estimated that Adorno spoke on the radio for a general audience on nearly 300 occasions throughout the 50s and 60s. See Michael Schwarz, 'Er redet leicht, schreibt schwer: Theodor W. Adorno am Mikrophon' [He speaks straightforwardly, writes heavily: Theodor W. Adorno at the microphone], *Studies in Contemporary History* 8 (2011), 454–465.

43. Alfred Schmidt, 'Statt eines Vorworts: Geschichte als verändernde Praxis' [In lieu of a foreword: History as transformative praxis], in Alfred Schmidt and Herbert Marcuse, *Existenzialistische Marx-Interpretation* [The Existentialist Interpretation of Marx] (Frankfurt am Main: Europäische Verlaganstalt, 1973), 9.

44. It should be noted that Schmidt's essay is titled 'Adorno – A Philosopher of Real Humanism', and that the contradiction between the essay's title and the affirmation of anti-humanism is intended to demonstrate the possibility of a Marxist humanism that does not take any extant humanisms as its point of departure. Alfred Schmidt, 'Adorno – ein Philosoph des realen Humanismus', in *Kritische Theorie, Humanismus, Aufklärung* (Stuttgart: Reclam, 1981), 27.

45. Adorno's writings are shot through with a nomenclature filled with references to veils and the nexus of blindness [*Verblendungszusammenhang*], which emphasises the illusory and mystificatory character of everyday life. The most recurrent of these terms is Adorno's standard definition of ideology as 'socially necessary semblance', which he derives from Marx's description of commodity fetishism as the 'objective semblance of the social determination of labour' in the first chapter of *Capital*.

46. Adorno, *Philosophische Elemente einer Theorie der Gesellschaft* [Philosophical Elements of a Theory of Society], eds. Tobias ten Brick and Marc Philip Nogueira (Frankfurt am Main: Suhrkamp 2008), 150. For a longer reflection on Talcott Parsons in which Adorno claims that he finds 'the normative use of the concept of role revolting', see Theodor Adorno and Helmut Becker, 'Education for Maturity and Responsibility', trans. Robert French et al., *History of the Human Sciences* 12:3 (1999), 27. References to the concept of 'character mask' can be found in most of Adorno's published lectures from the 1960s.

47. Adorno, 'Society', trans. Fredric Jameson, in *Can One Live After Auschwitz? A Philosophical Reader*, ed. Rolf Tiedemann (Stanford: Stanford University Press, 2003), 148. Translation amended.

48. Adorno, *Philosophische Elemente einer Theorie der Gesellschaft*,

151.

49. This is the famous 'Busenattentat', or breast attack, which was part of a wave of occupations and interruptions of Adorno's seminars towards the end of his life that led to a severe depression that likely contributed to his untimely death.

50. It is also worth noting that Adorno's student and mastermind of the Frankfurt SDS, Hans-Jürgen Krahl, favourably cites Rancière's contribution to the original edition of *Lire le capital* in a paper presented in Adorno's philosophy seminar already in the winter semester of 1966/7. See Hans-Jürgen Krahl, *Konstitution und Klassenkampf* (Frankfurt am Main: Verlag neuer Kritik, 1971), 31–83. None of the recent scholarship on Althusser acknowledges the Frankfurt engagement with Structuralism. Knox Peden, for example, claims that 'Adorno had nary an interest in Althusser's project'. See *Spinoza Contra Phenomenology*, 142. The opposite allegation is more convincingly proven.

51. Althusser had originally been scheduled to present a paper, and was replaced by Poulantzas at the last minute. This replacement in conjunction with Poulantzas' self-avowed limited facility with German is responsible for a weak defence of Structuralism that lags far behind the level of argumentative sophistication demonstrated by Poulantzas in his other writings published in the late 1960s. For a description of the Frankfurt Colloquium by its organiser, see Kevin Anderson, 'On Marx, Hegel, and Critical Theory in Postwar Germany: A Conversation with Iring Fetscher', *Studies in East European Thought* 50 (1998), 1–27. A rather biased presentation of the event that emphasises the anti-Althusserianism in the air is present in Ernest Mandel's correspondence with Roman Rosdolsky, cited at length in Jan Stutje, *Ernest Mandel: A Rebel's Dream Deferred*, trans. Christopher Beck and Peter Drucker (London: Verso, 2009), 129–131.

52. Nicos Poulantzas, 'Theorie und Geschichte: Kurze Bemerkungen über den Gegenstand des "Kapitals"' [Theory and History: Brief Remarks on the Object of *Capital*], in *Kritik der politischen Ökonomie heute. 100 Jahre 'Kapital'* [The Critique of Political Economy Today: 100 Years of *Capital*], eds. Walter Euchner and Alfred Schmidt (Frankfurt am Main: Europäische Verlaganstalt), 67. Poulantzas' essay was originally written in French, and translated into German by Schmidt for the conference. *Träger* is the only word originally written in German.

53. Discussion of Nicos Poulantzas' paper, in *100 Jahre 'Kapital'*, 73.

54. Marx, *Capital, Volume 1*, 255. It should be noted that the metamorphoses of M-C-M' take place only within the capitalist mode of production, and insofar as Schmidt sees a meaningful recapitulation of Hegelian themes in Marx, it is in the essentially conceptual nature of *capitalist* society, its reconfiguration of all human activity as an expression of social labour, and the self-moving character of its reproduction on an expanded scale. This should be differentiated from Marx's notion of the inevitability of crisis brought about by the law of the tendency of the profit rate to fall, which does not occupy a significant place in the Frankfurt interpretation of Marx.

55. Discussion of Alfred Schmidt's paper in *Kritik der politischen Ökonomie heute*, 27. The reconfiguration of Hegel's *Phenomenology* as a kind of self-development of hell was already a hallmark of Adorno's interpretation of Hegel in the 1950s. Adorno writes, 'Satanically, the world as grasped by the Hegelian system has only now, a hundred and fifty years later, proved itself to be a system in the literal sense, namely that of a radically societalized [*vergesellschaftete*] society'. Theodor Adorno, 'Aspects of Hegel's Philosophy', in *Hegel: Three Studies*, trans. Shierry Weber Nicholson (Cambridge: MIT Press, 1993), 27.

56. The *Neue Marx-Lektüre* would be unthinkable without the influence that Adorno's idiosyncratic understanding of Hegel exercised on his students, and recent texts emerging from this interpretative tradition, such as the work of Riccardo Bellofiore, Frank Engster and Werner Bonefeld, have showed a renewed interest in Adorno's philosophical and sociological writings from the 1960s. However, the *NML* is chiefly interested in Adorno's methodological holism, his conception of impersonal forms of economic domination, and the way in which he grounds semblance in social relations, subjectivity in objectivity. Adorno's complex treatment of the longing for freedom that is grounded in the consciousness of unfreedom – which distinguishes him most strongly from Althusser – is of less interest to the *NML*, and Adorno's reflections on culture and on intellectual and aesthetic experience are not accorded any significance by this tradition. For a careful treatment of Adorno's relation to the emergence of the *NML*, as well the most comprehensive account of the effect of French structuralism on the Frankfurt interpretation of Marx, see Ingo Elbe, *Marx im Westen* (Berlin: Akademie Verlag, 2010), 47–73.

57. Adorno, 'Sociology and Empirical Research', in Adorno et al., *The Positivist Dispute in German Sociology*, trans. G. Adey and D. Frisby (London: Deinmann, 1976), 35. The term *daseinde Abstraktion* is most closely associated with Hans-Jürgen Krahl, but can also be found in Schmidt's work. It bears many similarities with Alfred Sohn-Rethel's concept of 'real abstraction', and it is worth noting that when Sohn-Rethel was attempting to finally introduce his ideas to an advanced Marxist readership in 1969, he first and foremost wanted Schmidt's critical feedback. See Theodor W. Adorno and Alfred Sohn-Rethel, *Briefwechsel 1936-1969*, ed. Christoph Gödde (Munich: edition text+kritik, 1991), 155, 160ff.

58. Theodor W. Adorno, *Negative Dialectics*, trans. E.B. Ashton (New York: Seabury Press, 1973), 14.

59. Althusser, *For Marx*, 232.

60. Marx, *Capital, Volume 1*, 173. Translation amended.

61. Adorno, *Negative Dialectics*, 207. Translation amended.

62. Adorno, 'Society', 147–148. Translation amended.

Bodies in space

On the ends of vulnerability

Marina Vishmidt

> Weaker now, we mistakenly identify ourselves as our bodies.
>
> Ilona Sagar, 'Correspondence O', digital video, 2017

> I have had twenty-five or thirty souls, with their bodies, at once under my roof, and yet we often parted without being aware that we had come very near to one another.
>
> Henry David Thoreau, *Walden*, 1854

The last quarter of the twentieth century marked the emergence of 'the body' as a key heuristic in much post-structuralist and post-foundationalist cultural theory and philosophy. More recently, the terminology of 'bodies' has moved to the foreground in academic debates, but also gained traction in activist discourses and everyday forms of cultural speech. This is a terminology, primarily Anglophone, that speaks of bodies as subjects ('we are/there are bodies') rather than as objects ('we/they have bodies'). 'Bodies' as the basic unit that enumerates humans in (a) space assumes the status of a convention by means of a prior or ongoing shift to a consensus that invoking 'bodies' as such is to name them as the locus of socio-political agency in preference to or in distinction from terms such as 'person/s', 'people', 'individuals' or 'subjects'. The rationale for such a move is ostensibly its potential to take us beyond the humanist confines of such taxonomies, with their entrenched legacies of subject/object dualism, at best, and their openings to colonial, racist and patriarchal epistemologies, at worst. A 'posthumanist' turn in contemporary theory also constitutes, in this sense, part of the backdrop informing a discourse of 'bodies', suggesting a jettisoning of human privilege in allocations of value and significance across scales in a relational, intra-active universe, as well as a wider shift toward the 'object', the 'thing' and other non-personal forces such as 'affect' in many variants of post-phenomenological 'new materialism'.

Any survey of the terminological shift over the past decade would point to roughly this order of emancipatory motivation, stemming initially from radical campus politics but soon becoming a commonplace in grassroots political circles (with which academia has become increasingly porous) as well as art institutional spaces such as 2017's documenta, with its iterative talks programme called 'Parliament of Bodies'. This is a phenomenon traceable to the nexus between the nebulous category of 'identity politics' and progressive politics tout court as it has taken shape in the last decade of movements against capitalist crisis. These have often articulated themselves in biopolitical terms, that is to say, with the condition of bodies serving as the baselines for liveable life, whether politicised in revolt or its frequently lethal management of the state. Movements to protect lives and resist state and structural violence (Movement for Black Lives, NiUnaMenos); movements for social reproduction and against the destruction of the social and geophysical commons (Standing Rock); alongside movements for the defense of migrants and against the brutality of securitised borders everywhere. Needless to say, the defense of 'bodies' as such is hardly an apt description of these movements' wide agendas, with corporeal vulnerability and exposure to death looming larger for the groups organising against racialised and gendered state and social violence, while movements concerned with ecosystems and border management contend against vulnerability on a number of scales. Nonetheless, it can be noted that defense of living conditions and physical integrity is an element that more tangibly cuts across the agendas of a number of contemporary social movements than do any ideological precepts more conventionally understood.

The language of 'bodies' thus symptomatically appears to flag the vulnerability of growing numbers of the population abandoned without means of social and economic support *as* physical beings, as well as how those same conditions work to effect their reduction to the fragile, isolated quanta of consumption and discipline modelled by financialised structures of social reproduction and the platform capitalism that is currently their most efficient mode of delivery. Articulating the predicament in terms of 'bodies', rather than another term from the archive of political or psychological subjectivation, underlines the prioritisation of vulnerability, or, more generally, life, materiality and affect which constitutes the parameters of basic political analysis today. Vulnerability, or, more concretely, exposure and exclusion, seems so much a facet of daily experience for so much of the global population (even in the 'West') that, for many theorists, they suggest the parameters of any critical analysis that would prove adequate to both diagnosing this state and imagining forms of collective life otherwise. Depending on respective commitments in political theory, vulnerability as general condition – a general condition pertaining to isolated bodies - is geared to a demand for recognition and representation, where narratives of resistance should align with this basic understanding. Hence, as writers such as Asad Haider have observed in the related context of 'identity', a politics construed in such terms remains both sufficiently flexible, and sufficiently idealist, to unite positions across the spectrum from liberal to far-left. It also, decisively, points further right, as noted by the many commentators who have framed far-right positions as constituting a white identity politics.[1] Such a capacious spectrum, in the current climate, is quickly found to harbour ambiguous implications. If political actors are held to be acting politically insofar as they organise on the basis of their vulnerability, then no common horizon beyond pain management can be envisioned. And if pain management is the horizon, the opioid abuse of politics – blaming the outsiders, blaming the different – hovers close at hand.

If such a tendency is to read as symptomatic, what symptoms does the politics of vulnerability centring on 'bodies' express? This will form the main strand of the following essay. I will suggest that, at base, the discourse of 'bodies' presents us with the possibility of a pseudo-concreteness that often accompanies theoretical projects intolerant of the (real) abstraction that organises contemporary social life. It thus accepts the bio-, if not necro-, political, premises of the current dispensation – one that capitalises on the fragile, isolated and suffering body. The question of how and why such bodies are *produced* and mediated is necessarily elided, and this fragility, isolation and suffering is converted into ethical plenitude. Such a plenitude can be seen as both concrete and compensatory, whereas the brutal effects of social antagonism in the endurance of intensive social warfare from above, as it is invariably classed, gendered and racialised, seem impossible to remedy.[2] This then tends to confirm rather than challenge a status quo in which 'the reproduction of capitalism and the reproduction of organisms become indistinguishable'.[3] Though concentrating on 'bodies' as the main category of interest, 'the body' as an older, and certainly more capacious, category of analysis and description in philosophy and social theory cannot be entirely occluded, particularly as many of the theoretical debates that work with the discourse of 'bodies' draw upon earlier phenomenological, psychoanalytic or affect theory-derived notions of the body as the substance of their link to materialism, which is to say, the 'new materialism' where the body functions not as an abstraction, in Marx's terms, but rather as one of the many incarnations of an ever more pervasive vital matter.

What kinds of social relation make such a thing as 'the body' or 'bodies' not just legible but the basis for any form of political subjectivation that resonates with historical life in the present? Anxieties about division – philosophically into body and mind, politically by different ideologies or group affiliations – seem to be central to the embrace of contemporary 'bodies'-centric discourse. It is an anxiety that would thus seem to evoke, in its obverse, the old-fashioned idiom of 'souls' to refer to numerical aggregates or individuals, as the Thoreau passage in my epigraph illustrates, in its droll articulation of each with the other. As such, it carries with it, despite very divergent critical touchstones, an element of what could be called a 'jargon of authenticity' – the positing of something basic and fundamental as a substratum to all further thought; something which produces but is itself not produced, which conditions but is itself unconditioned. This resonates with Adorno's suggestion that at a specific historical point second nature becomes prior to first nature.[4] The body becomes a site where all politics has to begin but which itself manages to avoid scrutiny as a political problem or a contradictory enunciation. Eclipsed as well in this usage, interestingly, is the older usage of 'body' to refer to a corporate entity such as a group or organisation, no less than to 'bodies' as deceased. Contemporary 'bodies' are insistently material, physical, vital and animated, in an insistently empiricist register.

The following essay thus represents an attempt to undertake something of a genealogical survey of the transition to and establishment of the idiom of 'bodies', departing from its contemporary political and cultural currency, before developing its principal focus on those writers in political philosophy who have mobilised this idiom most explicitly in recent years, most obviously Judith Butler, and cataloguing the generative yet equivocal results of these projects. Particular prominence will be given in this regard to the elaboration of Hannah Arendt's concept of the public that Butler has been developing over the past nine years. Following this, another itinerary of 'bodies' will be drawn, seeking to demonstrate that 'bodies', like the individual in Gilbert Simondon's 'individuation', are not prior to but the outcome of capitalist processes of 'body-fication', the production of 'bodies' whose biopolitical character has to be taken as having a thoroughly historical and social character, thereby constituting a privileged instance of social abstraction rather than a social ontology of given-ness.

Assembling bodies

Judith Butler's 2011 essay 'Bodies in Alliance and the Politics of the Street' is concerned with understanding the occupation of urban public space as an emergent shape of resistance in the 'movements of the squares' in North Africa and in Spain, as well as emerging in the United States at that time, and shortly thereafter in the UK, with Occupy. In this article, which was revisited in other pieces and eventually became the book *Notes Toward a Theory of Performative Assembly*,[5] Butler drew together her interests in precarity and the ethics of vulnerability and exposure to develop an Arendtian argument about public space as the original scene of the political, but going beyond and in some ways counter to Arendt.

She does this mainly by noting that 'Arendt's view is confounded by its own gender politics, relying as it does on a distinction between the public and private domain that leaves the sphere of politics to men, and reproductive labour to women. If there is a body in the public sphere, it is masculine and unsupported, presumptively free to create, but not itself created.'[6] Thus, while Butler's concept of public space and political visibility is an Arendtian one, her concept of it as constituted by vulnerable and dependent bodies is not. That is, she agrees with Arendt that politics creates a public space and happens in public space, and that the political is a species of performative speech. However, the concept of the political as the space of public action is expanded to include the 'private' or the reproductive, which is jettisoned by Arendt in fidelity to the classical Greek conception of a de-socialised, eternal *oikos*. At the same time, bodily performativity is substituted for Arendt's prioritisation of speech, and a focus on need takes the place of her focus on action performed by independent agents for an audience. The political, for Butler, is generated in the space 'between' bodies, and relies on a recognition of mutual alterity, contingency and a dependency which can be understood as horizontal (dependency among the assembled) as well as vertical (on the infrastructures of reproduction of life provided, or not provided, by the state and the economy).

Yet, the simple expansion of the space designated as properly political in a formalist theory such as Arendt's proves less than capable of altering its intrinsically formalist character. If anything, the extension of political signification to the affective and the bodily are surer anchors for this ahistorical formalism, inasmuch as the vulnerable body makes an intuitive kind of sense as the ground of a political that is shared by everyone. This is so to the extent that their conditions of life are imbued with precarity, which functions both as a distinct feature of the historical present and an ontological premise of human existence – albeit, in some texts, it is relationality that is underlined rather than any anthropological constant, although it remains unclear whether the former is not confirmed after all as the latter.[7]

The emphasis on corporeality likewise resonates with the phenomenological and theological elements in her thinking that Butler has acknowledged in discussions of the influence of figures such as Maurice Merleau-Ponty, Emanuel Levinas and Martin Buber.[8] This is one aspect

that problematises Butler's move to re-introduce feminist dimensions such as collectivity, dependency, care, and in general, the social and material preconditions of appearance in public as a materialist challenge to Arendt's classicist (or antiquarian) concept of public space. The other is that the politics of vulnerability that is articulated through the needs and dependencies of living bodies is relatively lightly contextualised in socially and historically differentiated terms. The escalating inequities of crisis neoliberalism are sketched in, as well as specific episodes of contemporary protest and the gamut of state repression in which they can be located. In all these iterations, the visibility of living bodies to one another, to mediated witnesses and the state – a visibility which is a public articulation of the commonality of precarity, of exposure, of need – is the bedrock that connects ontological precarity to historical crises of social reproduction, here reformulated as a crisis of representation. The overriding theme of the politics of vulnerability generated thereby is that an acknowledgement of common need,

of common dependency, is *already* a 'common' in the sense of a common space of affect, of contestation, and of making a claim on commonly produced wealth and its institutions of governance. Affectability converts invariably into resistance; a resistance which is ethically valorised because it is about ontological precarity, and politically valorised because it is a *common* for all living, but especially human, beings.

The notion that the assembly of bodies is ontologically prior and in constitutive excess to the reasons for the assembly is not unique to Butler. It is a feature also of much thinking around the multitude and other principally but not exclusively post-anarchist approaches that downplay questions of ideology, power or organisation in favour of the dynamic of horizontality as its own end. A substantial degree of political ambiguity attends such a hypothesis, as already noted. Butler concedes this in later work, adding several caveats to the notion of assembly as the privileged site of contemporary politics.[9] These include that assembly can also be in digitally networked space or even in sites of incarceration, where the conditions do not permit large peaceful gatherings, and that vulnerability cannot be used as the criterion for making emancipatory political claims given the level of right-wing and neo-fascist backlash which couches its rhetoric precisely in the vocabulary of fear, invasion and defense from the barbaric other, be it marauding refugees or scholars of gender studies. This is not to mention the police officers who cease to feel safe when police impunity in deploying lethal force becomes a matter of popular objection. Finally, drawing on all these caveats, Butler hedges her bets against the optimism of the partisans of the 'multitude' as the political subject to reckon with.[10] Nonetheless, what is not at issue in any of these qualifications is the centrality of *bodies* as the minimal unit of 'the political', only the contingent purpose of their assembly.

In this light, the 'performative theory of assembly's choice to anchor its stakes in 'bodies' that generate rather than are contained by public space, which becomes a form of legibility that dramatises the material needs unmet in the society – needs which are both represented and compounded by these forms of collective manifestation – runs the risk of turning these bodies into an example of a 'simple' or 'chaotic abstraction', comparable to the basic notion of 'population' that Karl Marx cites in his discussion of dialectical method.[11] Bodies are depicted as implicated in webs of relationality, but bodies are also a given, insofar as they act precisely as a placeholder for the more complex notions of onto-theological precarity, and asymmetries of 'value' and 'grievability', that for Butler describe the social positioning of bodies in and beyond the site of assembly. 'Bodies' likewise act as placeholders for the often ahistorical notion of 'needs' – bodies have needs, we know what these needs are, and that they are invariant and non-negotiable. Because they are invariant and non-negotiable, their ethical status is equally invariant and non-negotiable; this is how they supply political possibility. So long as a category remains a simple abstraction, it remains a presupposition and not a category which can sustain a concrete process of inquiry capable of generating abstractions with greater analytical traction. As Kevin Floyd reconstructs Marx's method in the *Grundrisse*:

> In the two movements Marx describes here, movements leading to the establishment in thought of an internally

differentiated whole, theoretical abstractions are concretised: a chaotic conception of totality is concretised by way of ever simpler abstractions, and then these simple abstractions are themselves concretised in turn through an establishment of their determinate interconnections, through a more complex reconstruction of the totality with which the process began, now understood "as a rich totality of many determinations and relations."[12]

Simple abstractions are often encountered in formalist theories of 'the political', which Butler here, along with Arendt, shares with thinkers such as Chantal Mouffe, Ernesto Laclau, and, to a point, Jacques Rancière. The political has no content because it is a matter of contingency, not of any structural determinacy. While it is not unusual to encounter critiques from Marxist perspectives in response to this tendency, there are other projects, as we will see later, in political and critical theory that also look to the present-day echoes of histories of racialised and gendered commodification to articulate their critiques of the body as a category of self-ownership and a mode of recognition by the state that operates the more efficiently in its violent suspension.

My point is not to diagnose a 'deficit' of materialism at this juncture, since Butler has never located her work within the problematic of historical materialism. Rather it is intended to point to how theoretical engagements with 'bodies' denote a symptomatic anxiety about concreteness in their desire to bypass the materiality of social abstraction in favour of the predicament of the suffering body. An axiom central to liberal political theory can be seen at work here: the space of recognition by the state may be wholly transformed by means of its expansion, and inclusion thus becomes the horizon of transformation. This is the persistent liberalism which, in the language of Stefano Harney and Fred Moten, evacuates the conflictual 'plans' of movements and converts them into the 'policy' of managing the needs of 'abandoned populations', though only so long as any political capital may be yielded thereby.[13] As Butler notes, large groups of people assembling in public space can also provide legitimation to states, as a testimony to the freedom of assembly in ostensibly democratic polities.[14] Consequently, it is only the footage of police assault that can undermine the use-value of assembly in this register of legitimation. Naturally, it is the abused body which performs as the index of political legibility in this case, just as the speaking body performed in the other one.

The notion that emancipatory political thinking departs from bodies, or *the* body, is of course not altogether new. Indeed, a longer genealogy of this tendency would have to include all politicisations of the body, which encompasses pretty much any resistant or revolutionary movement, particularly those 'new social movements' which were motivated by their common address to people whose bodies were stigmatised through race, gender, sexuality or ability. The stronger meaning of 'the personal is political' always gestured to the somatic. Yet in the trajectory of Butler's own thought, and her relationship to feminist and queer theory, there is a curious development in this regard, which can only be very briefly recapitulated here.

Bodies That Matter was published in 1993, in part as a corrective to a certain reception of *Gender Trouble*.[15] If that text was deemed to be in danger of 'losing the body', in all its intractability and materiality, within a generalised notion of linguistic performance, with the second book Butler was concerned not with conjuring the tenuous self-evidence of 'the body' back onto the scene, but rather with developing a concept of the body as constructed, in alignment with the project of dismantling the established division between a socially constructed gender and a pre-discursive sex. The body as an inscribable surface which was not natural or prior to discourse, and, at least in this sense, incapable of serving as an ontological redoubt for a politics of resistance, was equally informed by the deconstructive framework of Derrida – and it is deconstruction that she mobilises against an unreflected or idealist concept of 'social construction'[16] – and by the power/knowledge framework of Foucault, with its examination of how the production of 'regulatory constraints' such as bodily and gender norms comes to be experienced as the most natural, unmediated and *material* thing in the world by the subject. These 'regulatory norms' evoke a materiality which is an effect of power; more succinctly, something like a corporeality or a materiality of the body (and its sex) cannot be conceived apart from the 'materialisation processes' activated by the meshwork of power. In a salient phrase, Butler calls power 'a constrained and iterative production', and it is in the margins of error and disruption *between* iterations that there is political agency for any individual or collective, which can capture those margins as significant

difference (as mattering), against the repetition of the same, timeless norm: 'an enabling disruption, the occasion for a radical rearticulation of the symbolic horizon in which bodies come to matter at all'.[17]

However, in this reading the distinction between construction and production does not come into focus, and there is a similar implicitness to the ontological gap between a re-articulation and a transformation of the 'horizon' in which a body registers as a body (as opposed to an abject or deformed 'thing' projected as deviant), and how it comes to discursively and socially 'matter'. In the two and a half decades since the publication of *Bodies That Matter*, Butler's preoccupations have shifted, to a degree, although much has also remained consistent, such as the founding deconstructive gesture that subsumes the political in the ethical.

This trajectory is complicated, though not diverted, by the broad proximity of the account in *Bodies That Matter*, as already noted, with Foucault's accounts of biopolitics in its moment of focusing on the disciplinary implementation of norms, rather than the later, more emphatically ethical tenor of the 'care of the self' writings. With that in mind, it is still important to inquire how it is that we go from the body as the construction of discursive power effects to a political theory, or a description of political performativity, in which 'bodies', whether taken as 'units in space' or as artefacts of a primary relationality, become *de facto* signifiers of agency and authenticity for any politics whatsoever. Surprisingly, the ultimate stakes of a critique of representation turn out to be the dismantling of the traces of representation carried by the idiom of 'people' or 'persons' in order to arrive, simply, at 'bodies' as such – presumed to be living (not dead) and human (not animal or machinic in an everyday sense) but otherwise free of any determinations or residual dualisms.

Weaker together

Foucault's discussions of the governance of populations as biological entities, in a way unprecedented enough as to be one of the distinctive marks of (European, national, colonial) modernity, is the source for most mobilisations of the concept of 'biopolitics' in recent theory. The concept of biopolitics makes the explicit linkage between economy and living capacity as the secret theology of the secular modern state, differentially applied to the de-valorised positions of women and enslaved or colonised subjects, although this is not a point explicitly developed by Foucault.[18] The recent terminology of 'bodies' seems like a working-out or an internalisation of these ideas as they have pervaded the academy and radical politics in the past few decades, alongside a number of feminist, queer and intersectional critiques of the control, management and production of bodies which in large part remain at the level of acknowledgement of a predicament rather than engaging in close historicisations; that is, which remain at the level of simple abstraction as outlined above. Yes, we are bodies, obviously, and no, 'we do not want to be governed like that', in Foucault's well-known phrase.

Notable in such a 'domestication' of Foucault's thesis of biopolitics is the bracketing of his own close historicisations, from the attention to capitalist requirements of labour discipline in *Discipline and Punish, Madness and Civilisation,*[19] or the emergence of 'the body' and 'bodies' as a terrain of class antagonism in nineteenth-century Europe in the first volume of *History of Sexuality*:

> There is little question that one of the primordial forms of class consciousness is the affirmation of the body, at least this was the case for the bourgeoisie during the 18th century. It converted the blue blood of the nobles into a sound organism and a healthy sexuality. One understands why it took such a long time and was so unwilling to acknowledge that other classes had a body and a sex - precisely those classes it was exploiting. ... Conflicts were necessary (in particular, conflicts over urban space: cohabitation, proximity, contamination, epidemics, such as the cholera outbreak of 1832, or again, prostitution and venereal diseases) in order for the proletariat to be granted a body and a sexuality.[20]

From an assertion of eugenic and social supremacy – the fitness to reproduce - the body nowadays seems to behave more legibly as a cipher for deprivation, and, in its declinations as 'surplus population' or 'wageless life',[21] it comes to stand in for the failure of reproduction as a survival strategy. Rather than the 'Body-without-Organs' of Deleuze and Guattari, as a vector of liberation de-linked from the natural teleologies of biological function and self-containment, there is something residual about the body figured thus. Bodies gathering in space, which exhibit their vulnerability as a kind of 'public secret' of crisis-capitalist ordinariness, seem, at the same time, to be exhibiting an acute loss of function; a sort of ultimate de-skilling, where neither labour nor political subjectivity can be found to avert the scandal of unsupported existence.

Butler's claim is that it is the melding of individualised, private and embodied troubles into public matters through the appearance of the many in the street which opens up a political space where it had long been foreclosed. The principal argument is that it is the dramatisation of collective vulnerability in this appearing – a set of structural vulnerabilities made literal by physically coming to and remaining in public spaces mediated by the violence of ownership, policing and damaged social relations, not to mention weather – that is the ground of the political. It is the sheer fact of 'bodies assembling' and making themselves visible, audible, impossible to ignore, prior to and constitutively in excess of any particular or general political demand. Thus, it is 'induced precarity' – a category which has latterly supplanted more prosaic terms such as 'capitalism' in Butler's vocabulary – that brings people together. In a sort of Heideggerian equality of 'being-towards-death', equally precarious, equally exposed, bodies themselves assemble, setting the scene for a new solidarity of precarity – an alliance of weakness, an equal and indivisible interest in improving their conditions of survival.

It is the very irreducibility of this ontological precarity of being a body among other bodies that, for Butler, prevents the conception from being re-routed into, as already noted, parts of the political spectrum less palatable to emancipatory, radically democratic desires. In her account, nationalist forms of togetherness need the minimal dualism of a 'people' who will affirm their collective strength against both a treacherous or absent sovereign and the invaders, as in her example of Pegida's slogan, recycled from East German anti-systemic movements of the 1980s, 'We are the people'.[22] An assembly of bodies, on the other hand, is impervious to such chauvinism, since it is predicated on weakness, although questions would still linger about whether the line between these identifications is quite so decisive as Butler implies, and whether 'bodies' can be said to constitute a type of identification at all.

Is anomie combined anomie overcome? Such a delineation of an unmediated vulnerability whose power stems from the sheer fact of coming together has a clarifying effect when considering the power of mass movements *as a mass*, in the way Marx describes the extra power and ability generated by the co-operation of many workers in a factory. But, as with Joshua Clover's periodisation of 'riots' as the ideal-typical form of revolutionary practice in the present,[23] this vision of a no-demands movement has a very circumscribed historical purchase, perhaps beginning in 2009, with the university occupations on the West Coast, and concluding with Occupy in 2011. The 'movements of the squares' fit it to a degree, though there the situation could be better described as a proliferation rather than absence of demands. It would be a stretch, however, to describe the itinerary of the past decade – ongoing insurrection in Hong Kong, Chile and Lebanon, the student strikes in Quebec, the movements of Palestinians against the separation wall, Black Lives Matter, or Extinction Rebellion, to cite just a few of the most-publicised recent instances of street politics – as primarily about the congregation of vulnerable and dependent bodies as a form of suasion to an uncaring capital and state. Moreover, bodily exposure, understood as a norm-breaking rather than norm-affirming practice, can be quite a truculent approach – just ask the rural women protesters in Nigeria's Igboland who halted the construction of an oil terminal in 2002 in part by means of this long-established tactic, a tactic that has been applied in multiple contexts where exposure is seen as an act of defiance rather than appeal.[24]

Vulner-*ability*?

The currency of bodies risks getting 'dis-embodied', or at least de-contextualised, if we stop at the borders of Butler's own recent trajectory and do not attend to its embedding in a larger sphere of reference and a 'common sense' on the liberal and progressive left, one which looks for both authenticity and popular political traction in the idiom of vulnerability. A new political realism announces itself here: a realism of the fragile, suffering body. As Robin D.G. Kelley has recently noted, the vulnerable body becomes a cipher of sorrow or, alternatively (in the white imagination), threat, which is made to 'increasingly stand in for actual people with names, experiences, dreams, and desires.'[25] Kelley suggests that the idiom of 'bodies' is not one that enhances concreteness and mutual understanding but that it is metaphysical, or fosters metaphysical explanations for everyday experience; one which Asad Haider has compared to 'afro-pessimist' theory's postulate of a universal, that is, ahistorical and planetary 'antiblackness'.

The lexicon of 'bodies' is now widespread enough to have become prevalent in cultural and art institutional spaces, particularly ones that wish to immunise themselves against a more reflexive and, presumably, discomfiting inquiry into their own elite conditions of possibility, and related issues of constitutive exclusion. Exemplary here, in an artworld context, is when documenta 14 curator Adam Szymczyk notes that the political salience of refugees registers as 'those who have nothing but their bodies', and who exert a call on representational strategies in the art field to once more turn to 'realism … as dealing with facts of biological and individual existence, with people who are suffering here and now from some kind of trauma or oppression.'[26] Szymczyk is interested in bodies as sites of inscription or bodies as signs, as emblems of a geopolitical crisis. If migratory movements are seen as composed of desperate masses travelling with 'nothing but their bodies', why not a 'Parliament of Bodies' as a suitable allegory for austerity-stricken times when politics has definitely 'failed', turning into a stand-off between a property-less 'rabble' and the police?[27]

A rhetorical nod to these and other outcasts from neoliberal security is the kind of gesture which is now habitual for the global institutions of contemporary art and which was reflected more controversially in the last documenta's double location in Kassel and in Athens. In turn, Kuo notes that Szymczyk's title is in pointed contrast to the 'thing-orientation' of other trends in recent theory, such as Bruno Latour's 2005 'Parliament of Things'. Here, the invocation of 'bodies' suggests that politics have been invited back into an arena of fetishism in a gesture partaking as much of constitution as of pathos, with the hope of sublating the polarisations of the situation of holding the documenta in Athens in an overall attention to the vulnerability that equally connects all bodies. Again, it is the projection of a political collectivity united by the sheer fact of exposure to harm (a strikingly uniform one, here), in other words, the undialectically biopolitical nature of this notion of bodies, which both takes power – Parliament - and evacuates power in the same moment, turning to appeal to a protective sovereign in the common fact of humiliating weakness – or to one another's empathy, undivided by antagonisms of property, race, gender or legal status. As the artist Jonas Staal, notes, in a paraphrase of Butler, 'This means that the collective gathering of bodies in the form of an assembly is an inherent act of resistance against the lack of care that a given regime provides to these bodies.'[28]

The terminology of 'bodies' seems almost unimaginable as a simple abstraction, given its address to immediacy and direct experience of the world *on one's skin*. Yet this is perhaps why it functions so adroitly as such an abstraction, in turn making the relation between experience and the pervasive social abstractions of contemporary capitalist life unimaginable, if all experience is direct and the somatic is immediately, indeterminately political. The only mediation whose presence is still desirable, it seems, is that of the art institution. But the disavowal of mediation in favour of the insistent, 'inherent resistance' of needs can be said to raise the question of realism in another key.

Political 'realism' has an unsavoury reputation in the history of the left, but it does come into the picture any time the exceptionally durable but reality-deficient supposition that equates the urgency of needs and the triggering of revolutionary social change is invoked. Such a 'functionalism' or 'economism' is the most characteristic guise of the rejection of political mediation in the history of the revolutionary left and its theoretical engagements in favour of a unilinear determinism that sustains neither historical nor conceptual scrutiny. At the same time, a history of reflection on the notion of 'need' as a social concept in critical thought, as already noted above, is long overdue.[29] The simple abstraction of 'need in general' can be paralleled to the self-evidence of 'bodies' (in general) as an elision of the specifically social (or, as Marx put it, 'historical and moral') determination of the 'most pressing, most undeniable', specifically in an era when algorithmic governance and untrammelled extraction across the social, cognitive and ecological spectrum means that the needs of capital to valorise, and that of humans and other life to survive, come to seem nearly inextricable in practice, if absolutely opposed in fact.

Returning to Butler, we can note that even if bodies are perceived as relational to infrastructures of care and reproduction, this relationality is politically valuable insofar as it is a source of dependency, not a source of power or of antagonism. These fundamentally biological units seem to have no political dimension besides this dependency, much less conflicting interests. Although significantly outside the parameters of the intentions of Butler and other advocates for a politics of vulnerability, there are relevant overlaps here with the field of 'humanitarian reason' which has been subject to various critiques over the past several decades. Accused of de-politicisation, or, at best a managerial, technocratic or solution-oriented politics, analysis of international human rights-driven approaches to crisis means engaging with the politics of management on the global scale, through its interfaces in the NGO complex and how it manages the 'bare lives' of those excluded from political subjectivity through their established status as permanently on the brink of death and needing to be rescued.

An inquiry into the origin of the lexicon of 'bodies' in the radical political and cultural imagination discloses multiple origins, and human rights discourses should not be left out of the picture. Didier Fassin observes on this point that 'Humanitarian reason pays more attention to the biological life of the destitute and unfortunate, the life in the name of which they are given aid, than to their biographical life, the life through which they could, independently, give a meaning to their own existence.'[30]

It is a short step from bracketing the political subjectivity of precarious bodies, inasmuch as they can present any demands that posit a form of collective subjectivity, whether propositional or antagonistic or both, which cannot be re-routed back through those bodies as their ultimate source of authority, to bracketing the political subjectivity and social relations of populations displaced by conflict the better to 'save' their precarious lives. How this biopolitical suspension of any life but that of administered bareness works in the context of truth and reconciliation processes is engaged by the legal scholar Josh Bowsher, who suggests that the neoliberal imperative of risk management forms the common thread between the 'passive victim' and the 'entrepreneurial subject'.[31]

How do you recognise a productive body?

So far, I have been concerned to pursue a dual-track inquiry into how 'bodies' are produced as a critical and discursive category, as well as what produces 'bodies' as a kind of non-universal universality that can be made to resonate across difference, precisely to the detriment of all political or ontological universalisms. In this final section, I will emphasise the latter – what produces bodies, and how bodies are made to produce.

The body, in the singular as in the plural, as a talisman of political performativity in a political and existential context characterised by individualisation, by individualised risk, and hence appearing as a 'simple aggregate' of precarity, is not simply a problem for thought, and its translations into ethical and aesthetic registers with equivocal implications. As already discussed, narratives which prioritise abstractions such as bodies and their needs are impelled by an *anti-abstracting* desire in the hope of arriving at something properly urgent and undeniable, without having to take the detour through subjectivity or antagonism. In this they rehearse, from the anti-authoritarian left, Foucault's account of the emergence of biopolitics as population management by the state, and all management as ineradicably biopolitical. But their focus on the demands of individuals before the state for the conditions which would allow them to have 'liveable lives' contains an important kernel of truth.

Capitalism is of course composed of isolated bodies, in production, in consumption, in reproduction. The body as a unit of labour power, that peculiar commodity which one both has and is, and one which, like any commodity, is in competition with all other commodities, comes in for consideration here. Biopolitics is an important reference for another reason; though Foucault has intermittently appeared in this analysis, it is in the mostly unheralded early 1970s work of Francois Guéry and Didier Deleule, *The Productive Body*, that the modern idiom of the body emerges as a naturalising, symptomatic one – one that is mediated by capitalist social relations such as the division of labour and the competition of capitals.[32] Guéry and Deleule's ideas are elaborated as a singular fusion of Marx and Foucault,[33] and set out from the start in polemical dialogue with Althusser, specifically with his division between ideology and science, and his concept of interpellation. Rather than focusing on how a cop's interception creates the subject, Guéry is more interested in how private property creates a cop with the right to intercept.

Guéry and Deleule's text, published initially as two separate essays, and translated in 2014 as one volume, extends commodity fetishism to all of society, and specifically to its concept of the body. 'Mind' and 'body' are both seen as reifications of capitalist social and productive relations, separated to create space for management as an agency of subsumption in industrial production. 'The body' is an artefact of individualising social relations produced by capitalist competition, which splits the social body into individualised productive bodies, and by real subsumption, which amplifies the division between mental and manual labour:

> As workers become easier to hire and fire, they are increasingly compelled to compete against one another and to consent to work for less money than others. This competition makes it seem to workers that they do not belong to a class or "social body," but must rely on their individual self or "biological body." Hence the "productive body" that has been created initially in the factory makes the biological body seem more important than the social body. As the work process becomes segmented, structural forces lead workers to begin to see themselves in terms of individual rather than group interests and demands.[34]

This evocation of a social dismemberment functional to domination and exploitation could be read alongside Marx's accounts of the structural as well as literal dismemberment of the worker's body by industrial machines: the body for the capitalist as an aggregation of muscles and nerves, as well as, today, an aggregation at a more molecular level: the quantified self.[35] In light of this thought of consumption as a latter-day extractive scene for the productive body, Butler's 'precarious assembly' can also be revisited: deprived of their individual purpose as productive (exploited) bodies, without a social body to fall back on, they are exposed to the harm attendant on being barred from access to the means of consumption, that is, to the means of physical reproduction.

Of course, the 'productiveness' of indebted populations, institutions and states for the international financial system, through all the scales of petty extraction that a terminally stagnant capitalism deploys,[36] could be useful as a corollary in updating the optic of Guéry and Deleule. This would note how exploitation of surplus labour is re-configured when systemic doldrums are such that extraction – in which industrial and financial processes of stripping already accumulated value prevail - is the main engine of accumulation rather than production.[37] Here we can clearly see, as Neilson and Mezzadra show, the intensification of work alongside the expansion of precarity and unemployment, the slashing of wages and social welfare, the privatisation of state and community commons, the militarisation of social life, and financialised primitive accumulation through debt personal and sovereign, as points in the same process. Concomitantly, the era of surplus population and 'wageless life' is one where there is a post-labour reification of the body, as vulnerable or threatening in itself – to be deflected, or accumulated out of sight – rather than a bearer of skills or potentials which can only be realised in connection with a social ensemble, be it a capitalist production unit or another collective form of life.

This move to project a unity, on the one hand, and an absolute irreducibility, on the other, this contemporary body without qualities, so to speak, needs to be examined further. Feminist labour scholar Melissa Wright, for example, is interested in how the bodies of women workers, especially those employed in electronics assembly in Mexico and China, come to represent, at the same time, tremendous value – employed in great numbers, admired for their docility, patience, nimble fingers, etc. – and the acme of waste and disposability for the transnational proprietors and managers of the companies in

question. (The social expression of the latter runs from reluctance to train or promote transient pools of 'girls' to the endemic murders of factory worker women and girls in Ciudad Juárez and elsewhere in Northern Mexico in the 1990s and early 2000s.)[38] Clearly there is no body in this equation without a certain kind of subjectivity – deficient, passive, adaptable – being associated with it, and Wright wants to emphasise that just as we are used to the critical vocabulary of the production of subjectivity as a feminist and materialist line of inquiry, we should also be asking how these bodies are produced, or, perhaps more aptly, 'manufactured' on the global factory floor of the gendered and racialised capitalist division of labour. Just as there is an abstraction of 'labour' as use value for capital, or the seller of the special commodity of labour power which Marx called variable capital and which contemporary apologists call human capital, the body that is the bearer of this labour power is also an abstraction insofar as it is produced in a specific social relationship characterised by the homogenising and unifying form of value. As Wright puts it:

> The disposable third world woman's body is not the same as the one that women workers bring into the workplace. Rather, it is a body manufactured during the labour process via discourses that combine bits and pieces of workers' bodies with industrial processes and managerial expectations. [...] this discursive production of the materially disposable third world woman's body does not, however, focus exclusively on the manufacturing of solely female bodies. It is a discursive process in which material entities cohere around an array of differences, such as first world/third world, female/male, valuable/disposable, and other traits often paired as binary opposites.[39]

Here we see that the common unit of analysis does not begin with a body or with bodies but *arrives* there. It is rather the crude empiricism of the boss, the owner and the manager – not to mention some academics – which begins and usually ends with bodies, bodies which come complete with subjectivities appropriate to and determined by the status of the disposable yet ultra-profitable exploited body, bound by gender and something called culture to occupy its allotted place. By contrast, the (gendered) bodies determined to be capable of advancing in the workplace hierarchy become individuated, bearers of skills and destinies *in principle* incalculable, hence not to be used up and discarded. This opens up a certain class relation of 'the body' comfortably anchored in the modern dualism that Guéry and Deleule specified as an artefact of a specific mode of production.

The Marxist and autonomist feminist impulse to attribute value production to bodies who are not recognised as engaging in 'official' channels of it, such as wage labour, is meant as a political gesture to centre reproductive labour. Yet, as Kevin Floyd notes, in his important analysis of the conjunction between an autonomist notion of the ubiquity of value production and extractive financialisation, this can lead to some tricky areas, such as biological materiality – tissues, cells, surrogate wombs - being seen as both a subject of labour and immanently value-productive, as soon as it appears under the commercial conditions of the biotech industry. For Floyd, the drive to read entities as bodies, these bodies as labouring, and their labour as value-productive, is to mis-identify 'the mediated capacities of capital' as 'the immediate capacities of labour'.[40] After all, for whom is labour the centre of the universe, source of all value, be it through work or debt? For capital. Who more than anything desires labour to be more and more productive, leading Marx to say that 'the notion of a productive labourer implies not merely a relation between work and useful effect, between labourer and product of labour, but also a specific, social relation of production, a relation that has sprung up historically and stamps the labourer as the direct means of creating surplus-value. To be a productive labourer is, therefore, not a piece of luck, but a misfortune'?[41] Beyond the ideological dimensions of productivity as an attribute of bodies here, there is the issue that it is not value-producing labour which is expanding but, rather, value-extracting capital in relation to labour and life seen increasingly as surplus to its requirements and as waste to be managed and maintained in docility, if not exported and killed.

A final question as regards the claims to the universality of the notion of a living body and the politics of its defence can be found in the work of Ann Anagnost, who discusses the 'corporeal politics of quality' or *suzhi*, in the emergent Chinese middle classes.[42] *Suzhi* is an intangible quality of breeding, education, an elixir of both social and human capital, as it were, from which surplus populations are debarred, and which must be carefully cultivated and hoarded by the urban bourgeoisie. Anagnost writes incisively about value as something which *travels* between different classes of bodies, with *suzhi* as an index of the changing relationship between value and bodies once rapid marketisation poses human life as the frontier for capital accumulation. In a strange disintermediation between labour and capital, she suggests that the extraction of value from one set of bodies is accumulated in another. This is a description that is uncanny, because it could be re-purposed to describe any type of direct domination (domestic service relations, chattel slavery...) but is actually being used to describe the transference of human capital – 'quality' – from those who have none to those who need it to maintain their class position. It is the double vision of this attempt to think the transfer of surplus labour from devalued body to the value-added body that contributes to the uncanniness, grounded in Marx's framing of value as 'differential' rather than substantial.

Coda

Does the diagnosis of 'bodies' as a disavowed form of abstraction that is both hegemonic within, yet inadequate to, the kinds of political subjectivity demanded by the present require us to invest in a counter-concept of subjectivity closer to universalism? Or will any resort to universalism signal a lapse into the presumptive common access to 'the human' practically denied by the existence of so many today, and for a long time, as capitalism's surplus and modernity's waste?

What this essay's itinerary through the ontologisation of vulnerability in the contemporary political idiom of 'bodies' has sought to demonstrate is that the concept has both a specific valence in the current moment and the recent past, and that it points to an abiding tendency in critical theory to blend 'first' and 'second' nature, and to mimetically adopt current forms of domination as the only conceivable forms in which emancipation can be imagined. In a very real sense, this expresses the overdetermination of emancipatory politics by such forms of domination, and the mimetic response to them that emerges for reasons of pragmatism as well as reasons of conviction. However, a close attention to *how* such forms get overdetermined, which is to say, how bodies are produced by means that further the ends of capitalist accumulation and population management, opens up an area which not only promises to undermine the 'abstraction-phobia' and thus the genres of liberalism that liberation politics today remain open to, but to get a handle on what other bodies are possible if these are seen as the consequence, rather than the precondition, of a socially and historically mediated mode of production. This, in turn, may be capable of redefining the political salience of experience as something collective, intractable and principally indeterminate rather than self-asserting, self-owning and claim-making.

While only being able to gesture to the field in which the question should be located, it has been this article's aim to show that the discourse of 'bodies', with its burden of naturalisation and proprietorial integrity, can be seen to form a hindrance to discovering what the political implications of that negation might be. An ontologised politics of vulnerable bodies can offer no resources apart from the connections of dependence between them and the extractive forces to which they appeal – which are either their own forces, alienated, or an external repressive agency. Thus recognition becomes the sole claim to amelioration possible to articulate here, since no other collective power, no form of social invention is conceivable, only relentless exposure (to harm, to one another) and the inescapability of this kind of life, lived in these same circumstances. This is a surplus population whose only subjectivity is its 'surplus-ness'; an actualised internalisation of the capital relation that demands recognition, and asks for counter-praxis.

Marina Vishmidt is a lecturer at Goldsmiths, University of London. She is the author of Speculation as a Mode of Production: Forms of Value Subjectivity in Art and Capital *(2018) and, with Kerstin Stakemeier,* Reproducing Autonomy: Work, Money, Crisis and Contemporary Art *(2016).*

Notes

1. Asad Haider, *Mistaken Identity: Class and Race in the Age of Trump* (London and New York: Verso, 2018).
2. Haider, *Mistaken Identity*, 101.
3. Elizabeth R. Johnson, 'Reconsidering Mimesis: Freedom and Acquiescence in the Anthropocene', *South Atlantic Quarterly* 115:2 (2016), 283.
4. '[T]he subject's powerlessness in a society petrified into a second nature becomes the motor of a flight into a purportedly first nature'. Theodor W. Adorno, *Aesthetic Theory*, trans. Robert Hullot-Kentor (London: Bloomsbury, 2013), 90.
5. Judith Butler, *Notes Toward a Theory of Performative Assembly* (Cambridge, MA: Harvard University Press, 2015).
6. Judith Butler, 'Bodies in Alliance and the Politics of the Street', first published in EIPCP *transversal* web journal September 2011; now available at https://scalar.usc.edu/works/bodies/Judith Butler: Bodies in Alliance and the Politics of the Street | eipcp.net.pdf
7. While this aspect cannot be explored in detail here, in this work Butler is drawing a line under the Western legacy of modern political theory that takes its cue from the realism of Hobbes, where existential fragility is the condition of the human isolated in the 'state of nature', who seeks refuge in society, which in turn hands over sovereignty to a monarch in return for safety. For Butler, existential fragility is the defining characteristic of *social* rather than *pre-social* life, though Hobbes would agree with her that it also only attains political significance there.
8. *The Other Journal* interview with Judith Butler, 'We Are Wordless Without One Another', *The Seattle School of Theology & Psychology* (December 2, 2017) https://theseattleschool.edu/blog/worldless-without-one-another-interview-judith-butler/
9. Judith Butler, 'Bodily Vulnerability, Coalitions and Street Politics', in Marta Kuzma and Peter Osborne (eds), *The State of Things* (Oslo: Office for Contemporary Art, 2012), 161-97; Judith Butler, 'Rethinking Vulnerability and Resistance', in Butler, Zeynep Gambetti and Leticia Sabsay (eds), *Vulnerability in Resistance* (Durham, NC and London: Duke University Press, 2016), 12-27.
10. Butler, 'Bodily Vulnerability', 166.
11. Karl Marx, *Grundrisse: Foundations of the Critique of Political Economy* (1939), trans. Martin Nicolaus (Harmondsworth: Penguin, 1973), 100-8.
12. Kevin Floyd, *The Reification of Desire: Toward a Queer Marxism* (Minneapolis and London: University of Minnesota Press, 2009), 28.
13. Stefano Harney and Fred Moten, *The Undercommons: Fugitive Planning & Black Study* (Wivehoe, New York and Port Watson: Minor Compositions, 2013), 70-82.
14. Butler, *Notes Toward a Theory of Performative Assembly*, 19.
15. Judith Butler, *Bodies That Matter: On the discursive limits of "sex"* (London and New York: Routledge, 1993). In the preface to the book, Butler genially sums up the type of critique she frequently encountered from other feminist theorists sceptical about the performative theory of gender elaborated in *Gender Trouble* as the remark 'But what about the materiality of the body, *Judy*?' Here, the de-formalisation of 'Judith' to 'Judy' is reckoned by Butler to function as a call to a kind of feminist 'common sense' she was seen to be at risk of flouting (Butler, *Bodies That Matter*, viii). The title of this essay is taken from another of Butler's references in the same text to the presumptive status of the body that she was accused of disregarding with an overly semiotic reading of gender.
16. Butler, *Bodies That Matter*, xiv-xvi.
17. Butler, *Bodies That Matter*, xxx.
18. Max Haiven and Scott Stoneman, 'Wal-Mart: The Panopticon of Time', *Globalization Working Papers* 09/1 (2009), 24.
19. Michel Foucault, *Discipline and Punish: The Birth of the Prison*, trans. Alan Sheridan (New York: Vintage, 1995); Michel Foucault, *Madness and Civilisation: A History of Insanity in the Age of*

Reason, trans. Richard Howard (New York: Vintage, 1988). Revealing on this theme are also the more recently translated and published lectures on 'the punitive society', which predate *Discipline and Punish* by three years but prefigure much of its research programme. See Michel Foucault, *The Punitive Society: Lectures at the Collège de France, 1972-1973*, trans. Graham Burchell (Basingstoke and New York: Palgrave Macmillan, 2015).

20. Michel Foucault, *The History of Sexuality, Vol I: An Introduction*, trans. Robert Hurley (New York: Pantheon, 1978), 126.

21. Some reference points for debates using this terminology in recent years include Endnotes Collective, 'Misery and Debt', *Endnotes* 2 (2010), 21–51; Susanne Soederberg, *Debtfare States and the Poverty Industry: Money, Discipline and the Surplus Population* (London and New York: Routledge, 2014). For 'wageless life', see Michael Denning, 'Wageless Life', *New Left Review* 66 (2010), 70–97.

22. Butler, *Notes Toward a Theory of Performative Assembly*, 3.

23. Joshua Clover, *Riot Strike Riot: The New Era of Uprisings* (London and New York: Verso, 2016).

24. Kathleen M. Fallon and Julie Moreau, 'Revisiting Repertoire Transition: Women's Nakedness as Potent Protests in Nigeria and Kenya', *Mobilization: An International Quarterly* 21:3 (2016), 323-40; Toyin Falola, *Colonialism and Violence in Nigeria* (Bloomington: Indiana University Press, 2009). For a mapping of this tactic between Nigeria and migrant women held in the Yarl's Wood removal centre in the UK, see also Imogen Tyler, 'Naked Protest: The Maternal Politics of Citizenship and Revolt', *Citizenship Studies* 17:2 (2013), 211-26.

25. Robin D.G. Kelley, 'Black Study, Black Struggle', *Boston Review* (March 2016), cited in Haider, *Mistaken Identity*, 39. Haider continues 'But in fact, Kelley points out, "what sustained enslaved African people was a *memory of freedom*, dreams of seizing it, and conspiracies to enact it" – a heritage of resistance that is erased by the rhetoric of "black bodies"'.

26. Michelle Kuo interview with Adam Szymczik, 'Documenta 14', *Artforum* (April 2017).

27. Kuo and Szymczik, 'Documenta 14'.

28. Jonas Staal, 'Assemblism', *e-flux journal* 80 (March 2017), 5.

29. One starting point could be Theodor W Adorno's 1942's 'Theses on Need', which makes an argument for a dialectical theory of need in capitalist society that would overcome distinctions between levels and types of needs that human beings might have. The hierarchy of needs was then a notion in wide circulation from depth psychology and other disciplines, for example, the 'primary' and 'secondary' needs (think of Abraham Maslow's 'pyramid of needs') or 'natural' and 'social' needs. As with other uses of binary distinction in critical thought – 'base' and 'superstructure', or 'sex' and 'gender', are two of the obvious ones – the analytic utility of those distinctions for denaturalising the social is soon extinguished in their leaving one of the terms as 'non-constructed' and the congealment over time into forms of identity thinking, or, as Adorno puts it in the essay, 'denial and domination'. 'Thesen über Bedürfnis' is collected in *Gesammelte Schriften*, Vol. 8: *Soziologische Schriften I* (Frankfurt am Main: Suhrkamp, 1998), pp. 392-6. It has recently been translated into English. See Keston Sutherland, 'Theses on Need', *QUID* 16 (2006) and another translation by Martin Shuster and Iain Macdonald, *Adorno Studies*, 1:1 (2017), 100–4.

30. Didier Fassin, *Humanitarian Reason: A Moral History of the Present*, trans. Rachel Gomme (Berkeley, Los Angeles and London: University of California Press, 2012), 254.

31. Josh Bowsher, '"Omnis et Singulatim": Establishing the Relationship Between Transitional Justice and Neoliberalism', *Law Critique* 29 (2018), 102.

32. François Guéry and Didier Deleule, *The Productive Body*, trans. Philip Barnard and Stephen Shapiro (Alresford, Hants.: Zero Books, 2014).

33. Two examples of recently published and translated work in this trajectory includes Christopher Chitty, 'Reassessing Foucault: Modern Sexuality and the Transition to Capitalism', *Viewpoint Magazine* (20 April 2017), and Pierre Macherey, 'The Productive Subject', trans. Tijana Okić, Patrick King, and Cory Knudson, *Viewpoint Magazine* (31 October 2015).

34. François Guéry and Didier Deleule, *The Productive Body*, 21.

35. The disaggregation of an anatomical image of a singular body into productive parts as intrinsic to the capitalist experience of labour can be seen in its generality and granularity in some notions of 'quantification', along with the legacy of Taylorist motion study. On the former, see Keston Sutherland, 'Marx in Jargon', *World Picture Journal* 1 (2008). A later version, 'Poetics of Capital', can be found in Eric Alliez, Peter Osborne and Eric-John Russell (eds), *Capitalism: Concept, Idea, Image: Aspects of Marx's Capital Today* (Kingston: Centre for Research in Modern European Philosophy, 2019).

36. Aaron Benanav, 'Automation and the Future of Work – I', *New Left Review* 119 (2019), 5–38; 'Automation and the Future of Work – II', *New Left Review* 120 (2019), 117–46.

37. This is a point that can be referred to the recent work of Neilson and Mezzadra who develop a concept of extraction as an operating system for contemporary capital, where industrial and financial processes of stripping accumulated value without 'producing' new value, prevail. See Sandro Mezzadra and Brett Neilson, 'On the multiple frontiers of extraction: excavating contemporary capitalism', *Cultural Studies* 31:2-3 (2017), 185–204. See also Sandro Mezzadra and Veronica Gago, 'A Critique of the Extractive Operations of Capital: Toward an Expanded Concept of Extractivism', *Rethinking Marxism* 29:4 (2017), 574–91.

38. Melissa W. Wright, *Disposable Women and Other Myths of Global Capitalism* (Abingdon and New York: Routledge, 2006).

39. Wright, *Disposable Women*, 45.

40. Kevin Floyd, 'Automatic Subjects: Gendered Labour and Abstract Life', *Historical Materialism* 24:2 (2016), 65.

41. Karl Marx, *Capital: A Critique of Political Economy*, Volume One, trans. Ben Fowkes (London: Penguin, 1990), 644.

42. Ann Anagnost, 'The Corporeal Politics of Quality (*Suzhi*)', *Public Culture* 16:2 (2004), 189–208.

Dossier: Decolonising the University

The combination of entrenched racism, the structural legacies of slavery and colonialism, and neoliberal austerity, together with far-reaching changes in the way students and teachers are encouraged to understand the purpose, provision and 'consumption' of higher education, has exacerbated the crisis of the public university in the UK and beyond. Needless to say, its consequences are being magnified and intensified with unprecedented speed by the impact of Covid-19 and the government's responses to it. The short articles that follow, along with further articles that will be collected in a dossier in a forthcoming issue, aim to engage with some of the many aspects of this complex and highly charged situation.

Neoliberal antiracism and the British university

Rahul Rao

While debates over race and higher education in the UK have long focused on questions of access, in recent years a host of campaigns have drawn attention to the alienation of students and staff of colour who succeed in entering white-dominated institutions. Their claims, often articulated on social media with the pithiness that hashtags require, have shone a light on the content and pedagogical premises of syllabi (#whyismycurriculumwhite), the underrepresentation of students and staff of colour particularly in more prestigious institutions and in the upper echelons of the profession (#whyisntmyprofessorblack) and the hostile built environment of British universities that reflects their entanglement in the histories of slavery, colonialism and apartheid (#Rhodesmustfall). Progress has been slow. Rhodes may indeed fall, but a recent *Guardian* investigation revealed that only a fifth of British universities have committed to reforming their curriculum to acknowledge the harmful legacies of colonialism and fewer than 1% of professors are Black.[1]

Decolonisation movements in British universities have been shaped by broader struggles around race relations in the UK and US. But the influence of African thinkers and student movements has also been palpable. At SOAS, the student society that has pushed most concertedly for a decolonisation of the institution – Decolonising Our Minds – takes its name from Ngũgĩ wa Thiong'o's landmark text.[2] Rhodes Must Fall (RMF) Oxford was directly inspired by the movement of the same name that had erupted at the University of Cape Town in 2015 and counted among its leaders some of the South African students who had participated in that earlier mobilisation. Important as these genealogical antecedents are, it seems vital to think through the differences between the structural contexts from which movements for the 'decolonisation' of the academy have emanated.

Decolonisation versus antiprivatisation?

Provoked by a deep frustration with the failure of South African universities to dismantle the legacies of apartheid in the academy, RMF Cape Town had also pointed to the whiteness of the curriculum alongside the still skewed racial demographics of staff and student populations. Yet six months after it burst on the scene, the wider student movement that it ignited across South Africa was asking questions about higher education funding, student fees and financial aid. Kelly Gillespie and Leigh-Ann Naidoo point out that while the 'decolonisation' protests predominantly took shape at elite historically white universities, antiprivatisation protests tended to be more popular, sweeping all national public universities including Black and working-class institutions.[3] RMF quickly morphed into a nation-wide movement called Fees Must Fall whose central demands included the scrapping of fee increments, insourcing of workers and a progressive shift in student funding from loans to scholarships. These movements in turn grew out of disillusionment with the failures of the ruling African National Congress. They reflect larger tensions in South African politics between those still beholden to its postapartheid nonracialism and neoliberal rapprochement with the market, and those especially from the 'Born Free' generations of young South Africans who are more enamoured of the Black Consciousness advocated by Steve Biko and the economic populism of Julius Malema.[4] As FMF activists explained, 'when we say fees must fall we mean we want the land back.'[5]

In the UK, by contrast, the movement against university tuition fees reached its apogee in 2010 before being defeated that year. Led by the National Campaign Against Fees and Cuts, the movement was triggered by the then Conservative-Liberal Democrat coalition government's decision to triple undergraduate student fees to £9,000 per year. Student anger manifested itself in a wave of occupations at more than fifty universities as well as a series of demonstrations, at one of which protesters briefly occupied the Conservative Party headquarters at Millbank in London. More than 50,000 students occupied Parliament Square on the day of the vote to raise fees. Despite being the largest instance of student unrest in the UK for decades, and indeed constituting the vanguard of an emerging opposition to the programme of cuts and austerity that would ravage the country over the next decade, the protests failed to avert the fee increase. But the issue of tuition fees has arguably remained of totemic significance for younger voters, peeling them away from the Liberal Democrats and fuelling the rise of Corbynism within the Labour Party, whose 2017 manifesto commitment to abolish tuition fees proved to be extremely popular.[6]

Calls for the decolonisation of the academy have been articulated largely in the wake of the defeat of the movement against fees and somewhat separately from it. This is not to imply that they lack a materialist dimension. It is difficult to see how demands for greater access to the academy for Black students and staff are realisable without a significant redistribution of resources. And it is striking to see the prominence of redistributive demands on the agendas of decolonisation movements. In its latest iteration, the Rhodes Must Fall Oxford campaign has called for reparatory scholarships and fellowships targeted at students and scholars of Afro-Caribbean and African descent, the latter in direct reference to the colonial provenance of the endowment that supports the Rhodes scholarships.[7] Yet the decolonisation agenda has also become deeply imbricated with the increasing marketisation of higher education in the UK in ways that are troubling.

The pitfalls of neoliberal antiracism

This imbrication is starkly evident in Kehinde Andrews's account of the advent of Europe's first Black Studies programme at Birmingham City University (BCU) in 2017. Andrews argues that the university's receptiveness to the programme stemmed from its potential to enhance its attractiveness in the increasingly competitive student market and the distinctiveness of its submission to the Research Excellence Framework (REF), the periodic exercise whereby UK universities are awarded public funding in accordance with their performance on an audit purporting to measure the quality of their research. Andrews further points out that the rise in tuition fees was accompanied by a lifting of the caps that previously allocated universities quotas for the number of undergraduates they could admit. He surmises that BCU might have been reluctant to support Black Studies in the circumstances of the steadier recruitment guaranteed by caps, for fear that it might have taken students away from more established programmes. By contrast, in the more thoroughly marketised environment enabled by the lifting of caps, universities were anxious to expand offerings to reach untapped markets. His conclusion in respect of BCU is unambiguous: 'we have a Black Studies degree as a direct result of the massive increase in fees for students.'[8]

If the REF offers universities a financial and market incentive to showcase their research on race, the

Teaching Excellence Framework (TEF) does something analogous in respect of pedagogy. Purporting to measure teaching excellence in the areas of 'teaching quality', 'learning environment' and educational and professional outcomes achieved by students, the TEF awards participating institutions gold, silver, bronze and 'provisional' ratings that have become yet another rubric by which universities are judged in the higher education market. Teaching quality is estimated via a range of metrics including graduate employment and earnings and 'student satisfaction' scores in a National Student Survey administered by the Office for Students (OfS), a quango largely modelled along the lines of a consumer protection agency that purports to safeguard the interests of students. The quality of learning environment is judged through data measuring student progression and retention. The OfS has recently set an ambitious target to eliminate awarding gaps between white and minority racialised students, in light of evidence that the latter are less likely to graduate with a first or upper second class degree than their white peers.[9] While attention to the racial awarding gap is long overdue, measures to close it will rely on a regulatory logic premised on market-based rewards and punishments.

Andrews is clear eyed about the risks of piggybacking on a neoliberal agenda. He points to the gentrification of Black Studies in the US as it became more professionalised and disengaged from Black communities, as a warning about the likelihood of its deradicalisation in the academy. Indeed appearing to view the institution of the university as irredeemably racist, he insists that the aim of Black Studies is not to decolonise the university so much as to infiltrate it and use its resources in the service of Black communities. He defends his engagement with the university as realistic rather than cynical, suggesting that 'the interests of Black communities are advanced only when they converge with those of mainstream society'.[10] Yet Black advancement that is contingent on a coincidence of interest with market neoliberalism is likely to be shallow, fragile and easily reversed.

At no time has this been clearer than in the current moment in which the financial shock of the Covid pandemic has exacerbated prior structural weaknesses, bringing many universities to the brink of unviability.[11] This has placed significant elements of the decolonisation agenda in jeopardy. Ngũgĩ's ideas may have inspired decolonising work at SOAS, but his identification of language as a primary terrain for the decolonisation of the mind has not insulated the teaching of African and Asian languages from curricular cuts on grounds of their putative financial unsustainability. In the wake of the killing of George Floyd, British universities were eager to proclaim that 'Black Lives Matter' on social media even as they proceeded to fire significant proportions of their academic precariat, whose ranks are disproportionately populated by women and racialised minorities, in anticipation of Covid-induced shortfalls in revenue.[12] That such contradictions are possible is illustrative of the fact that institutional commitments to decolonisation waver the moment they begin to entail a serious redistribution of resources.

These illustrations call to mind Sara Ahmed's account of campaigning to persuade her institution to take sexual harassment and sexual misconduct seriously at the same time as it was applying for an Athena SWAN award to showcase its efforts at advancing gender equality. Ahmed uses the term 'white feminism' to describe a liberal feminism that seeks inclusion in existing structures while leaving intact the structures themselves, including whiteness as a structure.[13] Catherine Rottenberg mobilises the term 'neoliberal feminism' to describe forms of feminism that acknowledge the fact of gender inequality while purporting to address it through mechanisms that entrench neoliberal commitments to individual responsibility and entrepreneurialism.[14] Neoliberal antiracism shares aspects of white feminism and neoliberal feminism. As we have seen, neoliberal antiracist initiatives rely for their effectiveness on the very market structures that produce racial exclusion. Ironically, they may also end up leaving intact the structures of racism and whiteness that they purport to attack. Think of the increasingly ubiquitous practice of anonymised marking which, although intending to correct for the 'unconscious bias' that produces racial awarding gaps, simply screens out information that triggers bias rather than recognising and rooting it out, while also assuming that individuals grading academic work are white or have internalised whiteness.

Central to the advent of neoliberal antiracism has been the move away from collective and materialist demands towards individualised, self-help models of change in struggles around racial justice.[15] Beginning in the UK in the early 1990s, these shifts were consonant with broader ideological trends evident in the demise of the welfare state and the reframing of progressive politics as a 'Third Way' between capitalism and communism. The renaming of student welfare as 'wellbeing' services strikes me as a metonymic instance of this shift in the everyday life of the university. When I queried this semantic change at SOAS, I was told that students were more likely to access these services if they were divested of the stigma associated with welfare. But the rebranding obscures troubling tectonic shifts. Wellbeing services bear the increasingly heavy burden of supporting students suffering the consequences of poor housing, schooling, healthcare and debt. It is possible that the epidemic of anxiety, learning difficulties and mental health crises that university students currently report may be the result of better diagnostic criteria and institutional awareness. An alternative reading would be that the individualised and pathologising frames of these diagnoses are ideologically preferable because they redirect activist energies away from struggles against the failures and abdications of the state towards a cultivation of individual 'resilience' as a means of coping with those failures. The decolonisation agenda confronts a similar tension between structural and individualised models of change. For all the attention that has been devoted to transforming structures such as curricula and hiring practices, an equal amount of energy has gone into initiatives such as mentoring schemes and workshops driven by the well-meaning but self-defeating aim of enabling Black students and staff to more comfortably inhabit those structures.

To criticise neoliberal antiracism can be politically difficult given that it is itself a besieged formation under attack from an unrepentant or unreflective whiteness in the academy. Within such an institutional landscape, even neoliberal antiracist initiatives can appear to offer respite from the pervasive whiteness of the university. But we might learn something here from Black feminism, which is unsparing in its criticism of white feminism despite their shared experience of subjection to patriarchy by demonstrating how that patriarchy is not experienced in the same way by differently positioned subjects because of their location at different intersections of race, class, ability, sexuality and other markers of (dis)advantage. As such, the argument against neoliberal antiracism is not simply the doctrinaire (white) Marxist claim that class has slipped out of the analysis, but the intersectional one that racism is not experienced in the same way by differently classed subjects. Categories such as BME or BAME (Black, Asian and minority ethnic), popular in the UK as umbrella terms for people of colour, are of limited analytical utility in capturing differences in the kinds of racism that might be experienced by class- and caste-privileged students of colour from a transnational elite paying the higher rate international fees on which British universities have increasingly come to depend, and those graduating from poorly resourced state schools and hailing from backgrounds that may be historically underrepresented at university.

Political blackness versus Afropessimism?

There are at least two other reasons why the critique of neoliberal antiracism cannot simply insist on a re-insertion of class into discussions of race. First, differently racialised subjects experience racism differently in ways that are irreducible to class. Statistics disaggregating students of colour regularly report significant disparities between students racialised as Black Caribbean, Bangladeshi, Pakistani, Indian, Chinese, mixed-race and white on a range of performance indicators including secondary school results, admission to prestigious universities and final degree classifications.[16] Second, the reality of racism among people of colour also demands discussion of different experiences of racialisation. Both factors have fuelled an impatience with the very categories in terms of which earlier antiracist movements conceptualised race and racialisation.

Writing about Rhodes Must Fall Oxford, Athinangamso Nkopo and Roseanne Chantiluke describe how they found umbrella terms such as 'people of colour' and the language of political blackness to be unhelpful and damaging. By way of example they describe how critiques of patriarchy levelled by non-Black women of colour against Black men were instrumentalised in an attempt to wrest control of what had been a Black-led movement. They criticise RMF Oxford's failure to clarify its political boundaries in the way that its progenitor in Cape Town did with its explicit commitment to Black Consciousness, Black feminism and Pan-Africanism.[17] Yet elsewhere Nkopo notes that tensions between differently racialised groups also erupted in the South African movement particularly around questions of tactics and the use of violence. Writing about the multiracial Fees Must Fall movement at Wits University in Johannesburg she says:

> These were almost always racially distinct fights, with our non-Black allies holding the same contorted expressions of knitted brows and half smiling teeth: what Frank Wilderson calls the expression of 'solidarity and anxiety' … They wanted changes here and there, more staff of colour, working staff in-sourced and some Biko in the curriculum. We needed the University to shut down by any means necessary. We had no place else to go after the fee statements came in saying we would be barred from exams, after our student cards stopped working because fees had not been paid, nowhere to sleep but on toilet floors and in libraries once the residences kicked us out, no desire to continue brewing in the hate of whitewashed philosophy, or colonial political thought. We needed to bring the University to heel in order to finally take our fight to the state. They needed to manage us, the Blacks, and with each day we appeared more and more unmanageable.[18]

While much of this comes across as a materialist critique pointing to the ways in which class differences might have mapped onto racialised ones, the nature of the critique shifts later in the piece when Nkopo speaks of divergent conceptions of suffering that are 'symptomatic of irreconcilable differences in how and where Blacks are ontologically positioned in relation to non-Blacks.'[19] She elaborates:

> What has been overlooked is that we fight or struggle as chattel first (slaves, Blacks, denied being itself), and then we organise our struggles in borrowed forms: students, labourers, missing-middle, children-disabled-and-women … We, the Black, the denied beings, the anti-human are often told to struggle as the poor, the unemployed, unemployable, unskilled, social-grant recipient, the queer. All the while we are structurally adjusted for the morphing condition Saidiya Hartman terms 'the afterlife of slavery'. What is constant is that we emerge always without our own grammar of suffering … [20]

Ironically, other participants in the MustFall mobilisations were troubled by what they saw as the borrowed grammar of Afropessimism that Nkopo is evidently inspired by. Thuli and Asher Gamedze, while acknowledging that the language of Afropessimism may be useful in naming systems of power, view it as a departure

from the Black radical tradition that has typically seen African cultural practices as forming the basis of Black revolt across time and space. In contrast, Afropessimism, in their view, sees enslaved Black people 'not as cultural subjects who brought entire cosmological worlds and practices with them, but as hopeless, utterly dislocated beings only existing as the sum total of their position in white supremacy'. Questioning the value of this understanding even in the Black diaspora, they argue that its problems are more pronounced on the African continent where 'although many of us are alienated from African cultural practices and contexts, those traditions persist and are more or less proximate whether or not one is immersed in them.'[21]

I have dwelt at some length on Afropessimist interventions and critiques thereof in the South African decolonisation struggles because they illustrate an itinerary of influence between the US, South Africa and the UK.[22] If Afropessimism has become a way of insisting on the primacy of a certain conception of race in struggles for social justice, it is instructive to note how audible its presence was even in the context of a movement in which struggles around class, labour and free education were more central than they have been in the UK. While there have been a number of useful critiques of Afropessimism,[23] my interest here is in thinking through some of its possible contact points with neoliberal antiracism.

Central to Afropessimist discourse is the claim that Blackness is defined by the distinction between the Human and the Slave. As Frank Wilderson III sees it, in contrast to other subaltern subjects such as the worker, native, etc. whose subordination does not entail a denial of their humanity, 'the antagonist of the Black is the Human being'.[24] This has implications for both what is to be done and who it can be done with: among other things, Afropessimism is pessimistic about the prospects of solidarity with 'non-black people of colour' (NBPOC) whose relative privilege, in its view, positions them as 'junior partners' to whiteness in imperialist and racist projects. Critics have pointed out that the extrication of Blackness in Afropessimist discourse from other axes of identity such as class, gender, sexuality and nationality obscures the ways in which Blackness is crosshatched or intersected by them. This makes it impossible to conceive of the tension-ridden positionalities of, say, the formerly enslaved Black Americans who became settlers in nineteenth century Liberia;[25] or of contemporary Black US citizens who, even as they endure degrading conditions at home, live on land stolen by white settlers from indigenous peoples and benefit from the US state's extraction of resources abroad;[26] or, more generally, of the differences between Black capitalists and workers anywhere in the world.

Kevin Okoth argues that the resulting 'flatness of Blackness' in Afropessimist thought has made it amenable to corporate capture.[27] By way of example Okoth describes the 2018 Nike advertisement featuring Colin Kaepernick as co-opting the football star's famous kneeling protest against police brutality in the US and thereby rebranding itself as a vehicle for Black emancipatory politics. To achieve this rebranding, the advertisement must delink African American struggles from those of racialised workers in the global South, on whose exploitation Nike's profits are premised. This delinking mirrors Afropessimism's denial of the possibility of anti-imperialist solidarity between differently racialised peoples, in contrast to earlier exemplars of the Black radical tradition such as the Black Panthers.[28] In offering a theoretical framework with pretensions to a radicalism that apparently 'requires no political action from Black writers and activists other than simply being Black', Okoth views Afropessimism as the quintessential product of the neoliberal university.[29]

While I share these critiques, I think materialist critics of Afropessimism have yet to come to grips with why it has such a strong affective purchase on student antiracist politics today. Even if its foundational premises cannot be widely shared, rooted as they are in the very particular history of slavery and its afterlives in the US, student organising around race well beyond the US is saturated with an Afropessimist-influenced language that distinguishes between Black and NBPOC and that commits itself to rooting out all manifestations of 'antiblackness'. It does not seem enough in the face of these trends to deploy an earlier rhetoric of political blackness as corrective without an adequate reckoning with why it lost its purchase. While I cannot offer the account I am calling for here, I am intrigued by Jesse McCarthy's suggestion that the psychic appeal of Afropessimism is a function of both the failure and success of antiracist politics. On the one hand, its appeal indexes the failure of prior frames of antiracist organising, evident in the spectre of unending

Black death as a result of the enduring racism of institutions such as the police and healthcare. On the other hand, it might speak to the 'survivor's guilt' that accompanies Black success, particularly in the predominantly middle-class spaces of the neoliberal academy. As McCarthy surmises, 'It feels good to suture your identity back to the collective, to pronounce that you share in equal measure the plight of all Black people throughout history. But that doesn't make it so.'[30]

Inside or outside the teaching machine?[31]

One of the signal achievements of movements for the decolonisation of the academy is that they have opened up a set of questions that are too big to confront from within the confines of the university. They have forced open national and global conversations on the politics of race and national belonging and on the legacies of slavery, colonialism and apartheid. The very enormity of these questions poses dilemmas about the extent to which it might be possible or advisable to address them within specific institutions. The problem is not just one of size or scale. If institutionalisation invariably transforms and tames decolonisation into a defanged neoliberal antiracism, perhaps we are better off working outside institutions.

Frantz Fanon confronted this question in relation to the hospital. Taking the view that the task of psychiatry is to repair the alienation of people from their environment, Fanon concluded in 1956 that this was no longer possible in the social conditions of colonial Algeria in which the Arab subject was made 'permanently an alien' in their own country. He describes his state of mind in the famous letter resigning his post at the Psychiatric Hospital at Blida-Joinville: 'there comes a moment when tenacity becomes morbid perseverance. Hope is then no longer an open door to the future but the illogical maintenance of a subjective attitude in organized contradiction with reality.'[32] Something of this spirit of militant exit animates a long line of antiracist education initiatives in the UK from the Black supplementary schools movement beginning in the 1960s to the recent announcement of plans to set up a Free Black University. Born of a frustration that 'this idea of transforming the university from the inside and having a decolonised curriculum isn't going to happen with the way the structures of the university are', the project envisages sustaining itself through crowdfunding but also by persuading existing universities to contribute as a means of discharging their reparative obligation to undo their complicity in slavery, eugenics and other sites of racism and racist knowledge production.[33]

Yet the work of finding spaces of reprieve and respite from the whiteness of the neoliberal academy might also unfold within the university through those unspectacular acts of refusal that Fred Moten and Stefano Harney famously describe:

> it cannot be denied that the university is a place of refuge, and it cannot be accepted that the university is a place of enlightenment. In the face of these conditions one can only sneak into the university and steal what one can. To abuse its hospitality, to spite its mission, to join its refugee colony, its gypsy encampment, to be in but not of – this is the path of the subversive intellectual in the modern university.[34]

At their best, decolonisation movements are 'in but not of' the university, using and abusing it for purposes that are not reducible to its mission. At SOAS, the student-run Decolonising Our Minds society has been a thorn in the institution's side, shaming it for its collaborations with the British and Israeli states, its casualisation and exploitation of labour, its complicity in the deportation of migrant workers and its complacence on questions of racism and sexism among other things.[35] In refusing the distinction between decolonisation and antiprivatisation, the campaign refuses to permit its institution to fly the decolonisation flag in light of its complicities with imperialist and capitalist violence and its implication in the market structures of UK higher education.

If decolonisation is not to be reduced to a metaphor in struggles around race in the university, then it is salutary to recall the context of its original referents. The tragedy of decolonisation movements, as Fanon prophetically foresaw, is that they were too easily content with flag independence, deferring questions of economic redistribution and social change to later 'stages' of revolution that never seemed to arrive.[36] Transported into the academy, a similar truncation of decolonisation delivers the shallowness of neoliberal antiracism. If we wish to resist this, we will need to take our fight beyond the confines of our respective institutions back to the racial capitalist state that sets the terms within which they function and compete with one another to their collect-ive detriment. Dalia Gebrial captures well the paradox that this entails when she observes that 'contemporary struggles in and around the university have a central, unresolved contradiction ... between being compelled to defend what once was from the attacks of neoliberal austerity, while fully understanding that what once was, was never truly public.'[37] The struggle against the marketisation of higher education and for the restoration of free public education will not be a sufficient condition for the decolonisation of the academy (we have only to recall the whiteness of the status quo ante to know this). But it is a necessary one.

Rahul Rao is Senior Lecturer in Politics at SOAS University of London and author of Out of Time: The Queer Politics of Postcoloniality *(2020). He is a member of the* Radical Philosophy *editorial collective.*

Notes

1. David Batty, 'Only a fifth of UK universities say they are "decolonising" curriculum', *Guardian*, 11 June 2020, https://www.theguardian.com/us-news/2020/jun/11/only-fifth-of-uk-universities-have-said-they-will-decolonise-curriculum; Richard Adams, 'Fewer than 1% of UK university professors are black, figures show', *Guardian*, 27 February 2020, https://www.theguardian.com/education/2020/feb/27/fewer-than-1-of-uk-university-professors-are-black-figures-show.
2. Ngũgĩ wa Thiong'o, *Decolonising the Mind: The Politics of Language in African Literature* (Harare: Zimbabwe Publishing House, 1994).
3. Kelly Gillespie and Leigh-Ann Naidoo, '#MustFall: The South African Student Movement and the Politics of Time', *South Atlantic Quarterly* 118:1 (2019), 191.
4. Heribert Adam, 'I will make you pay', *London Review of Books* 42:5 (2020), https://www.lrb.co.uk/the-paper/v42/n05/heribert-adam/i-will-make-you-pay.
5. Ahmed Veriava, 'Leaving Solomon House: A(n Impressionistic) Portrait of the FMF Movement at Wits', *South Atlantic Quarterly* 118:1 (2019), 195–204.
6. John Morgan, 'Have the 2010 student protests (eventually) killed £9k fees?', *Times Higher Education*, 3 January 2019, https://www.timeshighereducation.com/news/have-2010-student-protests-eventually-killed-ps9k-fees.
7. Rhodes Must Fall Oxford, https://www.instagram.com/p/CBN-a-Kjvh5/.
8. Kehinde Andrews, 'The Challenge of Black Studies in the Neoliberal Academy', in *Decolonising the University*, eds. Gurminder K. Bhambra, Dalia Gebrial and Kerem Nişancıoğlu (London: Pluto Press, 2018), 134.
9. Office for Students, 'Official statistic: Key performance measure 4', https://www.officeforstudents.org.uk/about/measures-of-our-success/participation-performance-measures/gap-in-

degree-outcomes-1sts-or-21s-between-white-students-and-black-students/.

10. Andrews, 'Challenge of Black Studies', 139, 134.

11. Chris Cook, 'Off campus', 26 May 2020, https://members.tortoisemedia.com/2020/05/26/universities-in-crisis-main-piece-off-campus-cc/content.html.

12. Fractionals For Fair Play, 'The Impact of the Transformation and Change Project on Casualised Staff at SOAS', August 2020, https://drive.google.com/file/d/1Rm_dtlvbCHg1sh4TBIVhP58tZGfy-pme/view.

13. Sara Ahmed, 'Rocking the Boat: Women of Colour as Diversity Workers', in *Dismantling Race in Higher Education: Racism, Whiteness and Decolonising the Academy*, eds. Jason Arday and Heidi Safia Mirza (Basingstoke: Palgrave, 2018), 340–41.

14. Catherine Rottenberg, 'The Rise of Neoliberal Feminism', *Cultural Studies* 28:3 (2014), 418–37.

15. Dalia Gebrial, 'Rhodes Must Fall: Oxford and Movements for Change', in *Decolonising the University*, eds. Gurminder K. Bhambra, Dalia Gebrial and Kerem Nişancıoğlu (London: Pluto Press, 2018), 29–34.

16. Vikki Bolivar, 'Ethnic Inequalities in Admission to Highly Selective Universities' and John T. E. Richardson, 'Understanding the Under-Attainment of Ethnic Minority Students in UK Higher Education: The Known Knowns and the Known Unknowns', in *Dismantling Race in Higher Education: Racism, Whiteness and Decolonising the Academy*, eds. Jason Arday and Heidi Safia Mirza (Basingstoke: Palgrave, 2018); Universities UK and National Union of Students, 'Black, Asian and Minority Ethnic Student Attainment at UK Universities: #Closingthegap', https://www.universitiesuk.ac.uk/policy-and-analysis/reports/Documents/2019/bame-student-attainment-uk-universities-closing-the-gap.pdf, 12.

17. Athinangamso Nkopo and Roseanne Chantiluke, 'Anti-Blackness, Intersectionality and People of Colour Politics', in *Rhodes Must Fall: The Struggle to Decolonise the Racist Heart of Empire*, eds. Roseanne Chantiluke, Brian Kwoba and Athinangamso Nkopo (London: Zed Books, 2018), 140.

18. Athinangamso Nkopo, 'Of Air. Running. Out.', in *Rhodes Must Fall: The Struggle to Decolonise the Racist Heart of Empire*, eds. Roseanne Chantiluke, Brian Kwoba and Athinangamso Nkopo (London: Zed Books, 2018), 159.

19. Nkopo, 'Of Air', 162.

20. Nkopo, 'Of Air, 166–67.

21. gamEdze and gamedZe, 'Anxiety, Afropessimism, and the University Shutdown', *South Atlantic Quarterly* 118:1 (2019),

22. The direction of this influence is not straightforward. It is possible that the South African receptiveness to the work of Frank Wilderson III, typically identified alongside Jared Sexton as a founding figure of Afropessimism, has something to do with his sojourn in South Africa between 1989 and 1996. Some have suggested that Wilderson's membership of the ANC and subsequent disillusionment with both the compromised liberalism of Mandela and the Marxist-Leninist revolutionary alternative that disappeared with the murder of Chris Hani, were pivotal to his conceptualisation of Afropessimism (Jesse McCarthy, 'On Afropessimism', *Los Angeles Review of Books*, 20 July 2020, https://lareviewofbooks.org/article/on-afropessimism/).

23. See for example Angela Davis and Gayatri Chakravorty Spivak in conversation with Nikita Dhawan, 'Planetary Utopias', *Radical Philosophy* 2.05 (Autumn 2019), 73–74.

24. Frank B. Wilderson III, *Afropessimism* (New York: Liveright, 2020), 241.

25. McCarthy, 'On Afropessimism'.

26. Vinson Cunningham, 'Blacking Out', *The New Yorker*, 20 July 2020, 61.

27. Kevin Ochieng Okoth, 'The Flatness of Blackness: Afro-Pessimism and the Erasure of Anti-Colonial Thought', *Salvage*, 16 January 2020, https://salvage.zone/issue-seven/the-flatness-of-blackness-afro-pessimism-and-the-erasure-of-anti-colonial-thought/.

28. Annie Olaloku-Teriba, 'Afro-Pessimism and the (Un)Logic of Anti-Blackness', *Historical Materialism* 26:2 (2018), http://www.historicalmaterialism.org/articles/afro-pessimism-and-unlogic-anti-blackness.

29. Okoth, 'The Flatness of Blackness'.

30. McCarthy, 'On Afropessimism'.

31. Gayatri Chakravorty Spivak, *Outside in the Teaching Machine* (New York: Routledge, 1993).

32. Frantz Fanon, 'Letter to the Resident Minister (1956)', in *Toward the African Revolution: Political Essays*, trans. Haakon Chevalier (New York: Grove Press, 1967), 53.

33. Melz Owusu, cited in Harriet Swain, 'Payback time: academic's plan to launch Free Black University in UK', *Guardian*, 27 June 2020, https://www.theguardian.com/education/2020/jun/27/payback-time-academics-plan-to-launch-free-black-university-in-uk.

34. Fred Moten and Stefano Harney, 'The University and the Undercommons: Seven Theses', *Social Text* 22:2 (2004), 101.

35. Decolonising Our Minds Society, *SOAS Disorientation Guide 2019*, https://drive.google.com/file/d/1trElvrOzYY8OIJ0LtcrZGZNY37vWdltq/view?fbclid=IwAR0zLGIJm_zT8MHIDGQevYFwuaYsBdNbM0IjrieEpRatqJ_GhX7akdLr2SA.

36. Frantz Fanon, 'The pitfalls of national consciousness', in *The Wretched of the Earth*, trans. Constance Farrington (London: Penguin, 2001 [1961]).

37. Gurminder K. Bhambra, Kerem Nişancıoğlu and Dalia Gebrial, 'Decolonising the university in 2020', *Identities* 27:4 (2020), 513.

Destruction styles
Black aesthetics of rupture and capture
Thulile Gamedze

Diagram A: rhodes explodes, corrodes, and loses head

I think that I and many others involved with the RhodesMustFall (RMF) movement at the University of Cape Town -- and beyond – might have preferred, on the 9th of April 2015, to see:

A. cecil's head explode, blast-site of bronze shards glistening in the afternoon sun, on the sprawling, clambering, continually inaccessible grounds of the university's main campus, or to watch him

B. corrode; to see him melt into chemical soup, nauseating smugness fallen to dusty, pungent metallic liquid, or to gather as he was

C. beheaded, the ugly likeness becoming a circulating prize, moving ritualistically for display between comrades' res and digs rooms.

But the motherfucker just got *airlifted*.

Until this moment, the texture of RhodesMustFall had been altogether different, the movement's 'decolonisation' denoting improvised – if strategic – instances of chaotic disruption, directed by radically critical readings of the South African status quo. But the awkward, unfamiliar ceremonial tone of the removal seemed to have

the unwarranted effect of instigating a feeling of 'unified resolve' to the insurgent action that had preceded it. Cecil John Rhodes' gentle elevation in the fresh autumn air was a sinister aesthetic reminder that the power of coloniality – evident, in this case, in the South African neoliberal university's response to decolonial critique – is an immeasurable capacity to co-opt and reconstruct that which undermines it.

Compare this institutionally paid-for airlift, for a moment, to Edward Colston's recent drowning in Bristol, the labour of heavy-lifting protestors never more at home (never less alienated) in their bodies, as they pulled him down and released nightmare to the depths. A world away from the weightlessness of air, from secured and safe removal, Colston fell heavy, drowned low and downward into deep water.

This comparison serves not to detract from the necessity of Rhodes' removal, but rather to emphasise the fact that the insurgent act need not be defined purely by its outcome (that the statue is gone) but should be read also with regard to the extent to which it attends

Diagram B: rhodes is lifted, colston is drowned

aesthetically to the historical or political problem at hand (Colston has been drowned!). The physical destruction of, or intervention in, coloniality's life is always *enacted* with significantly varying modes of style, tone, embodiment and performance, all formal and political choices that together can be regarded as an overall 'aesthetic'. When read in terms of their aesthetics, modes of destruction of colonial images and objects, and symbolic choices relating to the manner in which resistance is expressed by decolonisation movements, may take on a variety of political meanings that are less evident in readings of protest that centralise tangible outcomes. The act of destruction or insurgency should be seen as an act, visibilising through its aesthetic choices the connection between contemporary experiences of oppression (as patriarchy, racism, classism) and inherited historical traumas of the colonial project, in slavery, land theft, genocide, and so on. Our collaborative efforts then, in annihilations of white supremacy, are inevitably as aesthetic practitioners, illustrating expressions of resistance (better guerilla-facing than seated at the table) that further enunciate or diminish the *meaning* around which our protests are based.[1]

In this article, I draw from an overlying analysis of RMF's 2015 employment of the word 'decolonisation' at the University of Cape Town. I imagine the term as a located aesthetic set, whose reconfigured meaning in this context made possible the temporary rupture of space-time at the university, but whose capacity to signify radical Black disruption has greatly declined, with the word continually instrumentalised by a global neo-liberal academic discourse. I propose that the depoliticisation of the term has its origins in the actual climactic moment of Rhodes' removal and, more generally, that this institutionally-assisted 'insurgent' action can be politically unpacked, through aesthetic reasoning.

However, despite the slowing effect of neoliberal appropriation and capture of radical vocabularies, this time of abolitionist politics, expressed in the physical destruction of colonial symbols, is evidence that there exists a shared aesthetic (and political) impulse that transcends the limited possibility of rhetoric. In an intentionally aesthetic reading of contemporary Black embodiments of colonial destruction in the West, through the political lens of RMF in Cape Town, I reflect on a cross-spatial and cross-temporal parallel in meaning; a shared desire, perhaps, for the end of this world.

Decolonisation with RhodesMustFall, Cape Town

> The statue was therefore the natural starting point of this movement. Its removal will not mark the end but the beginning of the long overdue process of decolonising this university. In our belief, the experiences seeking to be addressed by this movement are not unique to an elite institution such as UCT, but rather reflect broader dynamics of a racist and patriarchal society that has remained unchanged since the end of formal apartheid.[2]

In early 2015, a much sampled, and largely broken, 'decolonisation' entered the mix of a group of radical Black student organisers at the University of Cape Town, mobilising around the image or phrase 'RhodesMustFall'.

Broken, because we must attend to the fact that decolonisation's re-re-re-re-re-emergence at this time was (and is) heavily annotated, the results of its historical processes in Africa having yielded much revolutionary independence struggle the ultimate outcome of which has been nations still structured by underdevelopment and exploitation intended to profit former colonisers. Regardless of the immense systemic failures of post-independence that the notion of 'decolonisation' brings with it, RMF found its employment necessary in the landscape of contemporary Cape Town – a city often described as South Africa's last colonial outpost. This is easily observable in Cape Town's stark geographical apartheid, where racial categories emerging from British colonialism and strengthened through white nationalist Afrikaner administration ('black', 'coloured', 'european') continue to determine where and how people live. Cape Town's racial divide largely determines peoples' access to resources, basic services, security, and level of exposure to the threat of government eviction and destruction of homes – a staple of life in the new South Africa.[3] As is well documented, the introduction of formal democracy in 1994 was a cosmetic intervention which both obfuscated and deepened the material inequalities of South African life through the implementation of deeply damaging neoliberal policies that arrived with the election of the African National Congress.[4] South Africa remained South Africa, only now with a heavily indebted Black government whose entrapment in racist economic negotiation meant that socialist measures, such as the nationalisation of land and natural resources, free education and free access to decent public healthcare, were impossible to implement with resources securely tied up in the private (white) sector. In Cape Town in particular, the failure of Azania's coming is glaringly obvious, the contentious UCT statue of Cecil Rhodes being just one of many littering the city alongside numerous other figures that pay tribute to the violence of British imperial rule in the Cape.[5]

Whilst RhodesMustFall came into being following an individual intervention with UCT's Rhodes statue, the movement's preoccupation with 'decolonisation' had no association with partisan, nationalist or individualised agendas.[6] Decolonisation, re-sampled, operated here with an ethics of non-partisanship, focused on what historical decolonisation processes had failed to rupture: systemic reproductions of white supremacy. Based broadly in the recognition of South Africa as a product of coloniality, the movement directed its attention to the ways in which the university was a culpable agent in deepening the hold of white supremacist power structures.

Furthermore, decolonisation's 'arrival' in the movement was conditional, welcome inasmuch as it was accompanied by modes, practices and methodologies seeking to undo the rendition of revolution in terms that too closely mimic the colonial status quo. This break with 'revolutionary' business as usual, in other words, wanted nothing to do with the image of struggle as one of individuals, martyrs or heroes exemplified by able-bodied young Black men. Instead, I believe there was a desire to, perhaps prefiguratively, embody the actuality of revolutionary work which, by nature, is collective and in refusing to adhere to modes of identity regulated by institutional power, is Queer. In this regard, there was no formal leadership and, in media representation, press conferences and interviews, concerted effort was made to ensure that different comrades spoke on behalf of RMF. The movement treated meetings and negotiations with the university's management as open invitations, where any and all members who wished to, could attend and speak, often overwhelming the staff in numbers. RMF thus refused 'representation', choosing to remain in flux and resistant to the efforts of institutions like the university and the predominantly white-owned press to define and epistemologically *resolve* its identity and work. Led conceptually and politically largely by gender studies, politics and law students, RMF's 'decolonisation' project outlined its 'three-pronged' approach as a meeting point of Black Consciousness (hereafter BC), Black Radical Feminism (particularly Kimberlé Crenshaw's work on intersectionality), and Pan Africanism.[7]

In many ways, the simultaneous take-up of these theoretical and political voices made for a rather eccentric and, at times, non-cohesive mixture of scholarship and strategy. The sharing of texts and ideas was improvisational, building in real-time, but the curriculum we were engaging was rife with irresolvable contradictions. How, for instance, does a Fanonian reading of violence through *The Wretched of the Earth* – a text in which the violation of Black womens' bodies forms a backdrop to both white settler colonialism and Black revolutionary struggle – converse with intersectionality, a vocabulary designed to be legible in the context of American jurisprudence and demanding that all forms of an individual's (simultaneous) oppression should be recognised (simultaneously)? What emerges from this and from DuBois' question *'how does it feel to be a problem?'*, when asked in South Africa, a country whose vast majority is Black, over one hundred years later?[8] How do we reckon with a history of BC that is immediately associated with expressions of masculinity? What *is* Pan-African solidarity from South Africa, when African nationals who move to the country are subject to forms of xenophobic attack – physical, social and administrative? Where does our systemic complicity lie in this unfolding as Black South Africans?[9] How, in the context of widespread 'gender-based-violence', not sparing any corner of any campus of UCT, does a group of Black students – trans, queer and cis – hope to organise and read together, through this deep mistrust and fear?[10] What can a curriculum *be* under such impossible conditions?

In Paolo Freire's terms, dialogue is able to facilitate a pedagogy of freedom, through the coming together of ideas that critically name peoples' worlds and experiences in a continually unfolding process. The dialogic imperative is that the word, in such a pedagogy, must simultaneously *reflect on* and *enact* the transformation of collective reality. As Freire argues, 'When a word is deprived of its dimension of action, reflection automatically suffers as well; and the word is changed into idle chatter, into verbalism, into an alienated and alienating "blah" ... On the other hand, if action is emphasized exclusively, to the detriment of reflection, the word is converted into activism. The latter – action for action's sake – negates the true praxis and makes dialogue impossible.'[11] So, at best, by virtue of its offering a meeting place for Black students (and workers at key times) to respond to and act against the manifest nature of oppression at the university, RMF could be said to have operated dialogically. At worst, aspects of the movement's internal failure, or coloniality (perhaps Freirian 'verbalism' or 'activism'), reproduced the oppression against which it purported to stand.[12] What I believe can be claimed here is that the sharing of theoretical work, rooted in personal experience and towards the creation of a collective Black study (and fugitivity), birthed a newly energised Black critique of the South African university that has had rippling ef-

fect.[13] This critique, by no means smooth, resolved or perfect, recognised the university as both a microcosm of, and a reproducing force in, the contemporary colonial landscape of South Africa and beyond.

RMF as a Black connective technology

> Means of communication were not constructed in the colonial period so that Africans could visit their friends.[14]
>
> We are oppressed because we are black. We must use that very concept to unite ourselves and to respond as a cohesive group. We must cling to each other with a tenacity that will shock the perpetrators of evil.[15]

Walter Rodney's *How Europe Underdeveloped Africa* offers a robust critique of the still-popular notion that Europe's colonialism 'benefited' Africa by providing services and infrastructure that the continent would not otherwise have had. Drawing on examples from across the continent, Rodney argues that colonial 'infrastructure' was built *only* to profit the coloniser, in the process deepening the oppression, enslavement and slow killing of indigenous peoples who were seen only as a cheap labour force. Of particular significance are the railways and transport routes which, far from enabling the coming together of Black people, resources and services, are oriented towards the sea for 'Black *export*' or Black repression (military deployment) thus instead producing fracture and alienation in the colony.[16] Rhodes himself was prone to citing the speculative plan for a railway from the 'Cape to Cairo', a notion exemplifying the scale of unchecked colonial exploitation in Africa and its desire to accumulate profit and alienate Black labour. Diagnosing colonial communicative devices as mechanisms precluding Black friendship, Rodney calls for a radical suspicion in our analysis of colonial infrastructural *purpose*.

The colonial university does not and cannot, by its very nature, provide connectivity between Black people for the benefit of Black people. Its infrastructures are designed with the opposite purpose – to appropriate and export Black knowledge (as we will see with 'decolonisation') – and to repress and gaslight Black expressions of opposition to oppressive conditions.

So in the sudden and impossible rupture caused by RMF, an initially haphazard but later more organised Black connective infrastructure was built, echoing historical appropriations in the colony in service of Black to-

police

azania

Diagram C: forced entry into Azania (House)

getherness. The movement's singing of the Pan-African protest hymn *Azania* can be recognised in this regard, as the take-up of a Black connective intervention repurposing Rhodes' conception of 'Cape to Cairo' into a form of cross-border solidarity.[17] In occupying the administrative heart of UCT (the Bremner building, renamed 'Azania House') RMF undermined its operative function, capturing the very architecture of business as usual and holding the institution to ransom. Occupation, of course, is always a refusal of the 'proper'/colonial channels of negotiation and prioritises work that facilitates connection and friendship, even as this priority is destined for trouble.

Additionally, RMF's pedagogy aligned itself with Black Consciousness, a movement whose revolutionary intent also outlined the importance of Black connective technology. BC's project, as articulated by Steve Biko, was and is to 'broaden the base of our operation', to centralise the 'totality of involvement', and to move always towards a unified Blackness.[18] The movement took up the BC refusal of apartheid identificatory ethnography, the notion that to be *black* is to claim a political identity of solidarity against white supremacy (referred to in this text as *Black*). In stark opposition to terms like 'PoC' or 'Brown' and 'Beige', BC refuses to sustain the structure of white supremacy in its language of self-identification. These terms, granting whiteness full political opacity, render the racialised body hypervisible, as the sum of shades by which it is negated from being white. This central critique of BC – a philosophy and politics frequently re-marginalised in South Africa and elsewhere – is a rad-

ical one in its insistence that resistance to white supremacy be premised on a systematic refusal of race as a valid mode of identification. In its choice of opacity of identity, BC is preoccupied with self-identification, which, I'd argue, finds political parallel in radical conceptions of Queerness.[19] Political Blackness allows a container of solidarity, where forms of oppression in classism, patriarchy, colourism, language hierarchy, and so on are simultaneously collectively validated as lived realities and recognised as violences sustained by race as an operative formation of a white supremacist world. Political Blackness asserts a basic precondition of humanity, that of recognition and love, inclusive and respectful of difference. In its use of BC, RMF was a Black-run movement, comprising members with diverse cultural and linguistic backgrounds, from historically racialised, segregated and oppressed groups that experienced different levels of oppression and exclusion under colonialism and apartheid.

'Decolonisation' under duress

During its first occupation in the lead-up to the statue's removal, the movement was highly visible and impossible to ignore. RMF action saw the disruption of university conferences and guest lectures, and the frequent vandalising of the university's surfaces and symbols. Keynotes of international professors were routinely redirected, in some way or other, to the contention at hand (decolonisation of the university), the role of chair in various talks, meetings and debates was decisively seized by fallists, and wheat pastes of Black revolutionaries appeared on campus overnight.

Something shifted through the university's decision to remove the Rhodes statue. Overnight, management seized power, claiming a kind of administrative role over the movement and differentiating between 'legitimate' and 'criminal' protest. Following the removal of the statue, the continued occupation of Azania House was interdicted and officially entered into the realm of criminal activity.[20] Students were arrested, and furthermore, on reading the interdict and its attached 'evidence', we became aware that the occupation had been spied on and documented by management from its inception. The institution's performance of 'transformation' through its strategic compliance (in Rhodes' removal) was exposed in all its disingenuity.

If we see things this way, the specificity of the *style* of Rhodes's removal, specifically in his mechanical airlift, created the kind of photo-op that readily boosted the image of this 'African university'. Let us consider that once loosened from its plinth, the statue could have been removed in a variety of ways – wrapped in a protective layer and rolled into the back of a truck, say; manually walked off the plinth, with the help of some heavy-lifters; taken care of unceremoniously, packed into a wooden crate and disappeared into the night.[21] But some undercover, perhaps even unintentional, aesthete of the university's administration created a spectacle of epic proportion, which I argue contributed to the securing of the university's image in the public eye, thereby marking it as an ethical agent in the manner it chose to characterise and punish the movement in the period afterwards.

RMF was now in a corner and, forced into a more explicitly hostile relation with the university and the law, had to re-think its aesthetic practices.

In a smaller occupation of a university administrative building – 'Avenue House' bordered on one side by Rhodes Avenue – work continued in the form of longer-term, less risky projects. For a short period, there was an RMF church of Black liberation theology on Sundays. Here, we produced a journal issue and, together with workers, made a documentary on outsourced labour at UCT.[22] Mysteriously, at some point during this period, the nose of a bronze Rhodes bust situated off-campus suddenly disappeared, violently ground off, never to return (the same statue has since been decapitated).[23] Work wound down in pace, and more radical interventions – like the

nose business – were carried out in secret (while the action resonates with those of RMF, it remains unclear who was responsible for it). It was only towards the end of the year, when RMF participated in the call for 'national shutdown' initiated by the FeesMustFall movement at the University of the Witwatersrand (Wits), that visible actions recommenced.[24] This energy would continue into 2016 through the protest intervention known as *Shackville*.

Shackville took place on 15 and 16 February 2016, with RMF/FMF members organising and protesting around housing for poor Black students, whom the university had rendered homeless. This homelessness, which occurs every year, is due to an administrative system that overbooks its facilities (to sustain profit margins) on the assumption that some students will not enrol. The effect of this is that poor Black students not local to Cape Town are left without safe accommodation in the vicinity of the university and forced to complete their studies whilst homeless in a very expensive city. *Shackville* blocked a main UCT driveway with an installation of a corrugated iron shack adorned with the words 'UCT HOUSING CRISIS'. After refusing to move the set up – which included a braai, or barbecue – private security and state police were called in on 16 February. After a student was beaten up and the installation destroyed by security and police, students retaliated, collecting some of the university's paintings from nearby student residences and burning them. 'The Shackville 5' included students who were expelled following the action and interdicted by the university. In ironic employment of the wretched history of the new South Africa, students later began pushing the university to hold a 'Shackville TRC' in which the five would be granted amnesty, and other protest actions that had taken place would be 'forgiven'.[25]

This final straw, in *Shackville*, saw what were once 'courageous university activists' rendered in honest colonial form: as barbarians under the rightful threat of the law. The shift was, of course, inevitable, and I believe greatly overdetermined by the power of the static image of Rhodes' removal by the university, which now shadowed all RMF work. Having visually arrested the movement's insurgency so close to its inception, the institution's aesthetic powerplay sidestepped the necessity for genuine and sincere engagement with the structural critique that fallist intervention continued to push.

Diagram D: Shackville, samples

The heavy-handed treatment of *Shackville* protestors was evidence of this.

'Decolonisation' at the conference

The spectacle of Rhodes' removal (as event, and as an aesthetic/political shift) may have contributed to the beginnings of opportunistic and regressive mobilisations of the word 'decolonisation' within neoliberal spacetime. We began to notice something we would continue to see for the next few years: the word unstuck from the meaning it had had in the RMF context and its surfacing in spaces where its presence would before have seemed implausible. As I've mentioned, the notion of decolonisation for us – beyond the shuffling of curricular content – had implications for the radical re-organisation of the structure of pedagogical space. The movement had sought to disturb institutional academic hierarchies that contrasted 'professional' knowledge with the perceived inadequacy of 'not knowing' (frequently mapped onto hierarchies of white versus Black, wealthy versus poor, heteronormative versus Queer, masculine versus non-masculine, and so on). In this regard, RMF founded its own sense of togetherness through the mutual sharing, validation and political theorisation of members' lived experiences of oppression at UCT, within the context of a disruption of the university's regular form, via occupation of its main administrative space.

In light of RMF's generalised suspicion and continued intervention in normatively organised academic spaces, 'decolonisation's' entry into paid-for conferences and panel discussions was jarring. The *form* of these academic spaces, in RMF's conception, was antithetical to decolonisation itself. What's more, as time went on, many of us involved in 'decolonisation' work were now faced with ethical conundrums. Suddenly recognised as 'specialists' on 'decolonisation', we were well-positioned to become agents in furthering the term's depoliticisation as invited panelists, conference presenters and recipients of international scholarships. Working through such invitations and attempting to decipher an event, publication or panel as either a site for the *application* or the *institutional appropriation* of ideas around 'decolonisation' became a crucial part in understanding the poignant harm easily perpetrated when we take up the seductive but politically-doomed role of Harney and Moten's 'critical academic'.[26]

But the extent to which the word 'decolonisation' has been turned on its head in the past few years goes beyond even this phase of appropriation and re-instrumentalisation of individual activists' work. My most recent and most disturbing experience of 'the newest decolonisation' occurred last year at the University of Pretoria, South Africa, at a conference entitled *Unsettling Paradigms: The Decolonial Turn and the Humanities Curriculum*. In a sinister programmatic choice, Wits Vice Chancellor Adam Habib had been invited to speak as part of a panel of VCs from a number of South African universities in a discussion entitled 'Decolonising the African University: Inspiration from Without the Ivory Tower'. Habib, having been responsible for the deployment of excessive police force (rubber bullets, in some

Diagram E: footnotes for vice-chancellor panel at 'Unsettling Paradigms' conference, 11 July 2019

instances at close range, military vehicles, teargas, stun grenades) against FeesMustFall protestors and their comrades at Wits University between 2015 and 2017, has since written a book entitled *Rebels and Rage: Reflecting on #FeesMustFall* in which he assumes an authoritative position in an exploration of the movement. His book, somehow framed by him simultaneously as a subjective memoir and as 'setting the historical record straight', has been criticised not only for historical inaccuracies but also as an irresponsible piece of writing demonstrating a lack of academic rigour in reductive framings of fallist politics, name-calling of academic staff who aligned with the movement and unethical inclusions of names and personal correspondence without the necessary permissions.[27]

In this turn – a colonial one, par excellence – we see Habib, a footsoldier of colonial reproduction in some of its most basic forms of physical violence and strategic misnaming, assume the role of epistemic authority over the meaning of the very labour that his agency, in collaboration with police, violated, traumatised and squashed. Not only should we hold Habib personally accountable for causing pain and fear to a decolonial student movement, but we should listen to and study his work on the subject of decolonisation itself. Herein, we can recognise the forceful and insidious undoing of this word, suddenly able to denote the very structures of violence and power that it, at a certain stage, contested and disrupted. At the panel discussion itself, a small, silent and open protest was organised by former RMF member Kealeboga Ramaru and her comrades, disturbing the event's bizarre perform-

ance of business as usual with signs detailing Habib's use of force against FMF activists. Despite the fact that information about Habib's application of force was made explicit by the action, the panel continued unhindered, with Habib speaking from behind silent protestors. The only acknowledgement of our presence was in one panelist's attempt to analyse it in real-time. In a severely infantilising moment, she congratulated us, going on to collapse the recent, tangible histories of trauma and violence that the protest highlighted into an added 'symbolic' layer of 'complexity' and 'nuance' that served to flavour the conversation. In this seemingly innocent seizure of authorial power over the act of disruption we can note another kind of institutional gesture of *lift and removal*.

In my own field of the visual arts, it is not unusual to encounter discussions or roundtables about 'decolonisation' at commercial galleries or even art fairs – centres of the racist, exploitative, capitalist exchange that roots the 'art world'. In these discussions, one often encounters a curious shift in the word's employment, whereby 'to decolonise' something no longer implies a structural and enacted critique of conditions through which knowledge production or exchange takes place, but rather involves a series of speculative, vague assertions that are perpetually relegated to the future. This drastic re-reading of the word – perhaps echoing the failures of historic decolonisation – is by no means an error. By taking it up in bewilderingly reductive questions like 'how do we decolonise arts practice?', or 'how do we decolonise education?', and situating it in the parameters of capitalist space-time, the discussants and listeners' sensory attention in these contexts is shifted from the immediate presence of coloniality or of the neoliberal structures that determine the rules of exchange in the first instance. In these polite intellectual overhauls, the likeliness of radical intervention is reduced, insurgency collapsed by forced conflation of the word and the meaning or application of 'decolonisation'.

New/Old Ruptures

> Official discourse seeks to accustom us to thinking about state violence as a warranted part of the social order. For them the security of belonging accompanies the re-racialisation of whiteness as the intensification of anti-blackness. The police elaborate the grounds for the extension of a renewed and reconfigured white supremacist political economic order.[28]

In the destruction-work that has followed the hypervisible brutality of George Floyd's murder by the US state, a radical conscientisation, echoing the likes of Jared Sexton, Steve Martinot and many others, is immediately observable, accelerating the meaning of BlackLivesMatter (BLM) from something like 'police must be held accountable under the law for killing black people', to something like 'policing's very mechanism is as a terrorist wing of the white supremacist state'.[29] Whilst Sexton and Martinot's use of 'black' in 'anti-black' cannot be regarded as the same Black in Black Consciousness, I cite this quote to highlight its critique of the police, which figures policing in general as an operation with the function of perpetually sustaining the 'white supremacist political economic order', in their words (with further comment on my conception of black-Black relation to come.)

In BLM's call for the defunding of the police, I speculatively suggest that we may be witness to the bouncing of meaning across space. This is to say that this newly amplified call of BLM directly refuses, on a mass scale, the capture of the movement's intention by a singular cosmetic act, by a *lift and removal*, or good PR, in the form of arrest and punishment of a single officer. Instead, policing as structure is recognised as a system whose 'honest work' is the reproduction of (b)lack criminality and thus ongoing forms of enslavement. A BC elaboration on this would necessarily have to extend the understanding of policing's white supremacist expressions beyond their active role in the reproduction of the (b)lack slave, to

also include the continued theft and destruction of Indigenous peoples' land, Islamophobia, increasingly violent anti-immigration and bordering policy, anti-Palestinian workings of the US state, re-marginalisations of Africa and the 'global South' in (b)lack American conceptions of (b)lack history, culture and theory, and countless other instances of *racism*, as premised on the notion that race in general is formed through a binary relation to whiteness.

The destruction of Confederate, religious and imperial symbols, often described by diverse media as 'vandalism' or 'graffiti', highlights the dissonance between the violence of normative colonial systems, such as those described above, and the radical refusal in the impulse variously named as 'decolonial', 'anti-racist', Queer, Black, and so on. If we are to analyse this in a BC frame, in keeping with the fundamentals of this text, we could note that such metaphysical resistance work, of pulling, tying, drowning, burning and hanging – *Black work* – could never appear to be generative within coloniality's logic. I say this inasmuch as Black work, as labour unalienated from itself, cannot be understood as labour at all (in its essential manifestation in racialised capital, labour is only labour because of the sustenance it provides to the reproduction of white supremacy). Thus, in the relative illegibility of Black insurgency, in its refusal of the correct channels and its determination to use its own connective technology, we find some common aesthetics, all vulnerable to the misnomers of a colonial imaginary: Edward Colston, a seventeenth-century slave merchant is toppled and then drowned by BLM *vandals* in Bristol; two Confederate statues are pulled down with ropes, dragged through the streets, with one strung up on a lamppost, by *radicals* also associated with the BLM movement in Raleigh, North Carolina; religious statues are mysteriously beheaded in the middle of the night by an unknown *extremist* in Sudbury, Northern Ontario; Columbus suffers the same fate in Boston at the hands of an anonymous *cultural worker*; and recently, the bust of Cecil John Rhodes in Cape Town, whose nose was sawn off in 2015, is decapitated overnight by an unknown *rigorous aesthetic critic*.

The notion underpinning all such intervention irrespective of how it gets named is that Black lives, within the wide parameters of policing that constitute life in racial capital, *cannot* matter. Thus, the affirmative declar-

Diagram F: lynched, beheaded, drowned

ation that they do, even in the ongoing celebrated presence of slave merchants, colonialists and genocidaires, is a kind of sci-fi action, a violent seizure and induction of another world that actually recognises, and so loves, Black life. This action is necessarily deeply destructive of the values underpinning *this* world, and will thus inevitably be the subject of attempts to render it into abstraction, inaction and depoliticisation.

Lifts and removals, in many forms.

I propose here that solidarity and love (Black, Queer) operate in a metaphysical realm – where the *meaning*, the necessity for rupture, is sincere, consistent and held, and words like 'decolonisation' are changeable and temporary tools, important inasmuch as they facilitate this meaning temporarily. In the aesthetic possibilities presented by bodies acting against coloniality – the aesthetics of decolonisation, in one moment – we note a possible carriage of radical Black critique across space and time, a force that will continue to be taken up, regardless of the continued co-option of its vocabularies.

Thulile Gamedze is a cultural worker from Johannesburg, involved in a mixture of art criticism, art history education and art production.

Notes

1. My interest in the aesthetics of insurgency draws on a number of recent politically-oriented writings that study the tonal, stylistic, textural, auditory and visual choices that have marked modes of contemporary Black protest or resistance in South Africa, reading these as portals through which subversive historical references, political alternatives and radical positions

might be read. Athi Mongezeleli Joja, 'Bolekaja Aesthetics', *AS-AP/Journal* 5:2 (May 2020), 248–256; Kelly Gillespie and Leigh-Ann Naidoo, 'Between the Cold War and the Fire: The Student Movement, Antiassimilation, and the Question of the Future in South Africa', *South Atlantic Quarterly* 118:1 (2019), 226–239.
2. RhodesMustFall Writing and Education subcommittees, 'RhodesMustFall Statements', *The Johannesburg Salon* 9 (2015), 6.
3. Racial disparity in ownership of land has not only remained unaddressed following the end of apartheid but also deepened with ongoing government evictions, destruction of shacks and confiscation of building materials belonging to Black people living on unused government or private land. The issue gained attention during the COVID-19 crisis as evictions continue even though the country's lockdown regulations render them illegal. Lucky Makhubela, 'The plight of unlawful evictions in South Africa', *News24*, 8 July 2020, https://www.news24.com/news24/columnists/guestcolumn/-opinion-the-plight-of-unlawful-evictions-in-south-africa-20200708.
4. Patrick Bond, *Elite Transition: From Apartheid to Neoliberalism in South Africa* (Pietermaritzburg: University of Natal Press, 2000).
5. 'Azania' is the Pan-Africanist name for South Africa. The name has radical socialist connotations and calls for the nationalisation of land and resources.
6. On the 9th of March 2015, UCT student Chumani Maxwele threw a bucket of faeces at the Rhodes statue, whilst wearing a placard reading 'Exhibit White Arrogance @ U.C.T.' The faeces were collected from open toilets in Khayelitsha, a Cape Town township, with Maxwele's intervention drawing connections between the white middle class institution and the ongoing impoverishment, exploitation and indignity of a working class Black majority, living in the urban margins. 'Chumani Maxwele ignites the RhodesMustFall movement at UCT', *South African History Online*, accessed 23 July 2020, https://www.sahistory.org.za/dated-event/chumani-maxwele-ignites-rhodesmustfall-movement-uct.
7. The key textual elements guiding these areas were Kim-

berlé Crenshaw's work on intersectionality, Steve Biko's work on Black Consciousness as well as histories of BC student organising in the South African Students Organisation (SASO), and African histories of independence struggle from the Mau-Mau uprising to the Algerian War and the work of FRELIMO in Mozambique. The Fanonian vocabulary was relentless as was other work from the Black Radical Tradition, in particular, early DuBoisian conceptions of double consciousness as well as Orlando Patterson's – and later Afropessimism's – conception of the slave.

8. W. E. B. Du Bois, *The Souls of Black Folk* (New York: New American Library, 1995).

9. Thembinkosi Okonko, 'On Afrophobia', *The Johannesburg Salon* 9 (2015), 32–33.

10. Internally, the movement struggled against patriarchy under Black men, although this may be better articulated as 'white patriarchal mimicry'. In mimicry, we see the dehumanising effects of race, where the racialised subject is not granted western identificatory features – like gender – in the same way that white people are. To speak of mimicry is to suggest that Black patriarchy is the enactment of a colonial imperative and a deepening of the project of white supremacy, where Black men themselves do not benefit from the abuse they reproduce, but uncritically play out their colonial role. This reproduction of power was harmful to RMF members and made the space unsafe for many of us. The movement was deeply criticised by the UCT Trans Collective, whose protest-intervention in an RMF photographic exhibition at the beginning of 2016 highlighted the erasure of the labour of trans bodies from its images and halted the show. This intervention extended into a structural critique of the movement's patriarchy and lack of meaningful inclusion of trans people. Additionally, the intervention critiqued the movement's seeming acceptance and representation of sexually violent Black men in its photographs. Yusuf Omar, 'Trans Collective Stops RMF exhibition', *UCT News*, 10 March 2016, https://www.news.uct.ac.za/article/-2016-03-10-trans-collective-stops-rmf-exhibition.

11. Paolo Freire, *Pedagogy of the Oppressed* (New York: The Continuum International, 2005), 87–124.

12. There were deep failures of solidarity with disabled comrades at the institution that meant that for many, the physical space of occupation and the mostly physical manifestations of protest reproduced the inaccessibility of the university that they had long been addressing. As for those who were able to participate, the mental health crisis that erupted following the year of intensity and trauma of RMF participation – particularly amongst Queer and trans people, and cis women – was left largely untreated by the community; only those with the financial means were able to access the medical help that they needed. These are instances of a multitude of shifts from the status quo that RMF was not able to make, although there has been much work on these fronts since then.

13. Fred Moten and Stefano Harney, *The Undercommons: Fugitive Learning and Black Study* (New York: Minor Compositions, 2013). Whilst this text did not enter into popular RMF discourse,

I believe its conception of 'the undercommons' – and notions of debt, the neoliberal university and the academic 'critical professional' – offers a useful theoretical reading of the movement's politics.

14. Walter Rodney, *How Europe Underdeveloped Africa* (Washington, DC: Howard University Press, 1981), 209.

15. Steve Biko, *I Write What I Like: Selected Writings*, ed. Aelred Stubbs C. R. (Johannesburg: Heinemann, 1987), 97.

16. Rodney, *How Europe Underdeveloped Africa*, 203–280.

17. The hymn outlines a radical Pan-African solidarity that spans 'from Cape to Cairo, Morroco to Madagascar', describing a coming revolution in which there will be an armed seizure of the land, Azania, energised by the work of the Freedom Charter.

18. Biko, *I Write*, 97.

19. Edouard Glissant, 'For opacity', in *Poetics of Relation* (Ann Arbor: University of Michigan Press, 1997), 189–194; Jack Halbersatm and Tavia Nyong'o, 'Introduction: Theory in the Wild', *South Atlantic Quarterly* 117:3 (2018), 453–464.

20. RhodesMustFall Writing and Education subcommittees, 'RhodesMustFall Statements', 13.

21. Michael Safi, 'Racist Gandhi statue removed from University of Ghana', *Guardian*, 14 December 2018, https://www.theguardian.com/world/2018/dec/14/racist-gandhi-statue-removed-from-university-of-ghana.

22. RhodesMustFall Writing and Education subcommittees, *The Johannesburg Salon* 9 (2015), 128; RhodesMustFall & National Education, Health and Allied Workers' Union (NEHAWU), '#Outsourced', Youtube video, 7 October 2015, https://www.youtube.com/watch?v=-pu_pm5g3Ao.

23. 'Cecil Rhodes loses his nose', *News24*, 22 September 2015, https://www.news24.com/news24/mynews24/cecil-rhodes-loses-his-nose-20150922; Mpho Raborife, 'Cecil John Rhodes statue in Cape Town vandalised, head chopped off', *News24*, 14 July 2020, https://www.news24.com/news24/southafrica/news/cecil-john-rhodes-statue-in-cape-town-vandalised-head-chopped-off-20200714.

24. First mobilised in October 2015 at Wits University, FeesMustFall protests sparked a series of shutdowns of South African universities and protest marches putting pressure on individual institutions as well as on the state to address the still unfulfilled constitutional right to 'free education', twenty-one years into the new South Africa.

25. Jenna Etheridge, 'We want a #Shackville TRC', *News24*, 15 September 2016, https://www.news24.com/news24/-southafrica/news/we-want-a-shackville-trc-uct-students-20160915.

26. Moten and Harney, *The Undercommons*, 25–43.

27. 'An open letter to the readers of Adam Habib's "Rebels and Rage"', *Mail & Guardian*, 1 April 2019, https://mg.co.za/article/-2019-04-01-an-open-letter-to-the-readers-of-adam-habibs-rebels-and-rage/.

28. Jared Sexton and Steve Martinot, 'The Avant-Garde of White Supremacy', *Social Identities* 9:2 (2003), 176.

29. Sexton and Martinot, 'The Avant-Garde', 169–181.

Problem and solution

Occupation and collective complaint

Ethiraj Gabriel Dattatreyan and Akanksha Mehta

In the spring and summer of 2019, a group of Black and PoC students from Goldsmiths, University of London formed Goldsmiths Anti-Racist Action (GARA) and occupied Deptford Town Hall – a key administrative building on campus – to push back against the institutional racism they experienced in the university. We, two junior academics situated in different departments in the university (Anthropology and Media, Communications & Cultural Studies, respectively), were struck by how British and 'international' Black and PoC students, as well as British white students, collectively created a multiplatform set of demands that placed discriminatory labour practices towards cleaners, reception staff and security guards in the university (a majority of whom are Black and PoC), and the institution's complicity in gentrification of a Black and PoC working-class neighbourhood, in the same frame as a complete curricular review, overhaul of complaints procedures and anti-racist training for all staff.[1] These demands, taken together, were the result of years of unresolved and bureaucratically managed complaints that lived, siloed from one another, as discrete conversations in the university that often could be sidelined or forgotten because of the inevitability that students who raised these issues would move on after they graduated. GARA's work was, in part, to link these complaints to one another and to other struggles within and outside the university and to show how they formed a larger set of enduring problems in an institution that purports to be radical and progressive.

As each of us began to work with GARA's key members, we learned that their broad range of demands – some that could be rolled out as sanitised diversity initiatives by the institution itself (mandatory anti-racist training, for instance), others that appeared to challenge the literal foundations of the university (taking down the frescoes of slave owners on the edifice of Deptford Town Hall, for instance) – were the result of a careful consensus-based decision-making process that GARA had initiated within its loose leadership structure. As students came together to challenge the university that they experienced and conceptualised differently, they had to configure an organising platform that was non-hierarchical and gave each core member an equal voice.[2] Because GARA didn't narrow its engagement to the 'BAME' student experience, but, rather, connected issues of racialised and unequal labour conditions in the university, the endurance of colonial landmarks and the experience of Black and Brown students in classrooms, its demands seemed to confuse management. The institution initially responded to these demands by framing GARA students as unreasonable, irrational and politically naive.

As the occupation continued, stretching from weeks into months, we saw the university's senior management struggle to come to terms with the fact that GARA simply wasn't going to go away and that it could not successfully spin the public narrative about what was happening.[3] The institution's leadership concluded that it would have to 'publicly' listen to GARA and rely on it for potential 'solutions' to end the occupation. These solutions, of course, were encoded in the multiple demands themselves. GARA wanted management to listen to and address these demands on its own terms. However, even as the university leadership conceded that GARA offered a diagnosis and a concrete set of solutions to various issues in the university that fell under the broad banner of racism, it continued to assert that the students remained a problem as long as they occupied the town hall building. Senior management emphatically refused to comply with GARA's requests to provide written responses to its demands until it vacated the building.

Eventually, three months into the occupation, management relented and agreed to negotiate with GARA

– first providing written (if terse) responses to each demand, then setting up two days of negotiation facilitated by an external mediator, a community activist from Lewisham agreeable to both parties. However, as was revealed in the last few days of the occupation, and soon after the face-to-face negotiations concluded, management was simultaneously building and filing a legal case against GARA. Just as GARA was coming to a final agreement with management, it found pinned on the door of Deptford Town Hall a large envelope with over 500 pages of documents charging trespass and filled with social media 'evidence' of GARA members' involvement in the occupation. Rather than a simple injunction, senior management threatened to prosecute core individuals involved in the occupation if they didn't vacate the building immediately. In the end, after 137 days of occupation, GARA vacated Deptford Town Hall. Before ending the occupation, it succeeded in getting management to sign a document agreeing to fulfil all of its demands.[4] These demands, at the time of this writing one year after the occupation, remain unfulfilled.

GARA's occupation, as an endeavour to create a shared space of learning and care for students, staff and community members in Lewisham in the heart of the Goldsmiths campus, whilst putting pressure on the institution to address structural issues, taught us several important lessons. As each of us became increasingly involved in GARA's activities, we found its approach to organising, collaborative decision making and communality a powerful and novel example of creative and generative resistance to institutional racism that produced a vibrant, if temporary, undercommons. We also saw how GARA's engagements with the university administration, the campus trade unions and our colleagues revealed important lessons about how Black and PoC students and faculty (ourselves, in this case) are received and channelled by the university administration and staff when they collectively identify potential ways to address racism within the institution. In this essay we discuss one lesson that we've learned – the ways in which participants in GARA's actions have been individualised and positioned between being/offering potential solutions to issues of racism in the university and being intractable problems precisely because they/we participated in generating a collective complaint that publicly shamed the institution and its staff.

Sara Ahmed pushes us to think carefully about complaints as a way to strategically reach an institution's ears.[5] Complaints, in Ahmed's reading, disrupt the workings of the institution by revealing its inability to see and serve those who are systematically marginalised within it. Complaints, however, are easily individualised and domesticated in the university's workings. They traverse institutional circuits that limit their capacity to become anything other than singular problems to be managed. We are interested in how complaints become public demands when they emerge out of collective action, and the ways in which these demands work to make those that enunciate them both problems *and* solutions for those charged with managing the university. In other words, we are interested in how collective complaints (and the demands they generate) position those who participate in making them public. On the one hand, those who participated in GARA have had to experience the affective weight of counterclaims, denial and angry scrutiny from staff and leadership in the university, both publicly and privately. They have had their Otherness amplified. On the other hand, they have been asked, often by the very people that problematise them and the claims they embody, to offer additional ways to fix problems or to sit at the table in working groups, task forces, steering committees and more to deliberate on how to 'action' the original GARA demands. Here, we discuss how senior management and university colleagues, in their approach to students and staff involved with GARA, demonstrate how issues of racism and racial inequality (and the possibility for institutional remediation) become firmly located in the bodies of Others.[6] We argue that in the white public space of the university, this move to make racial difference the problem of those who purportedly embody it and to place the institutional labour of solving it on them is inevitable. This doubling creates a political and ethical dilemma for those who are involved in struggles for racial justice in the university around whether to take on the enormous labour of attempting to change the institution and whether it will, ultimately, change anything.

What does it mean to call the British university a white public space? Whiteness, as Helán Page and R. Brooke Thomas remind us, becomes a taken for granted condition of possibility because there is an assumption that the implicit and explicit practices, beliefs and values within a space are shared.[7] The space of the British uni-

versity remains white, in large part, because whilst the student body has diversified over the last twenty years, its staff, curriculum and teaching practices have not necessarily reflected these demographic changes. Indeed, the whiteness of British Higher Education comes into relief as the sector has diversified its enrollment since the late 1990s. The 1998 Teaching and Higher Education Act and, later, the Widening Participation Programme had a part to play in this process of diversification, particularly as the latter offered a monetary incentive to universities in the UK to enroll 'BAME' students and provided a nominal state sanctioned route towards mobility for the 'most deserving' individuals who hail from the UK's ethnic minorities.[8]

The shift towards fees, loans and the internationalisation of recruitment has also diversified the student body in UK higher education institutions, whether in the Russell Group universities, the post-1992 institutions that were formerly polytechnics, or in smaller, niche art and humanities colleges like Goldsmiths.[9] The story of

neoliberal strategies to diversify and monetise the sector over the last thirty years is too extensive to do justice to here. Suffice to say that in the present moment, British higher education institutions can now publish images of the university that show smiling Black and Brown faces against the backdrop of an idyllic campus green while also counting on tuition fees from these students. These Black and PoC students (and the few faculty of colour who have been hired on permanent contracts in this thirty year period), whilst positioned quite differently from each other on various axes, all share the experience of stepping into the white university and having to strategise about how to navigate it.[10]

As Ahmed argues, seeing whiteness is 'about living its effects.'[11] Seeing whiteness is, of course, easier to do when one sits outside of it. Conversely, it is curiously difficult to see whiteness and the ways in which it shapes space, location and relations if one embraces its framing vision or doesn't question one's inclusion in it. As a result, as Audre Lorde suggests, race and race talk has a tendency to locate itself in the bodies of those who are not white, particularly those who are marked as Black.[12] Which is to say, race becomes the 'baggage' of those outside of the liberal enclosure of whiteness.[13] Whiteness, as such, can disappear as a foundational, anchoring social, cultural and racial category for those who find or actively locate themselves within it. Or, perhaps, it doesn't so much disappear as become hidden in plain sight.

Discussions of racism in the university and the university as white space, thus, are more likely than not engendered by those who sit outside whiteness. When Black or PoC students or faculty arrive at the university and confront whiteness, locate it in institutional practice or embodied habitus, a common tactic, resorted to by those who can't and don't wish to see its effects, is to evoke the spectre of 'identity politics'. This move serves to reify racism as a problem of the 'Other' who has a deep investment in their racialised identity rather than open up an engagement with whiteness and its intersectional effects as constitutive of institutional life. Seeing and describing whiteness, locating its scripts, its locutionary force and its edifices has consequences. It generates a reaction from those who feel seen in its naming. Naming whiteness is taken personally. As DuBois observes, 'this knowledge makes them now embarrassed, now furious'.[14] An oscillation between the structure and individual opens up – discussions regarding structural whiteness are responded to with angry demands to name the 'bad apples' and absolve the rest of racism. Conversely, identifications of individuals implicated in power structures of whiteness are met with defiant cries to focus on the structural.[15] That these consequences emerge in and as affects doesn't take away their material force. We would argue that it is not just reactive 'white fragility' that plays out in these moments of interaction.[16] These affects, rather, are the animating spirit that begets various forms of violence directed at Black and PoC students and staff in the institution and, as such, reproduce structures of power. Many of the students who were involved in GARA narrated experiences, prior to the occupation, of being positioned relentlessly as problems when they, in one way or other, named whiteness and its effects on them as students.

The university typically responds to the complaints made by those who sit outside of whiteness – if they don't go away on their own or can't be managed through institutional reporting systems but accumulate and intensify – by hiring professional diversity workers.[17] Since GARA's occupation, the institution has hired a team of diversity workers to look into issues of racial inequality in the university.[18] These workers, some of whom have worked across public and private sector institutions, are charged with doing research, writing reports and organising working groups or committees with the goal of eventually making recommendations for change in the institution. What is ironic in this case, of course, is that GARA, with its well-researched demands, had already done much of the work to provide substantive solutions to some of the long standing problems of inequality for the institution.

At present, GARA members – some who have graduated, some who are still students in the institution and both of us as staff members – are asked to sit on committees led by diversity workers who have been put in charge of seeing some of the demands through to implementation. GARA's time and labour in these spaces is unpaid and its interjections in the meetings are seen as a problem for the functioning of these groups and committees by those that convene them. Many GARA students have wryly observed that they are invited to these meetings simply because the institution fears that failing to do so could reignite GARA's public protest in ways that would further tarnish it. In this case, the threat of student protest is generative of student activist participation in management strategies to maintain the white university.

The diversity workers that institutions like Goldsmiths hire, more often than not, inhabit positions marginal to normative conditions of classed, gendered, ableist whiteness. They are charged with narrating problems in their specificity and reducing them to issues that can be addressed without upsetting the foundational premise of the university as white space. Take for instance the 'Insider/Outsider' report, written and published by Goldsmiths in October 2019, a few months after the GARA occupation ended.[19] The document touches upon but ultimately skirts the issue of white institutional space. Rather, it focuses on Black and PoC student testimonies of trauma within the university to make a case for harm reduction. We might consider, based on this report, that GARA's demands – which located the white university as the problem – required diversity workers to return the problem of difference onto its Black and PoC students. If diversity workers had diagnosed and narrated the problem as one of a failure of the institution to see its own foundational (white) logics then perhaps this report wouldn't have been published. Indeed, an earlier version of the report which included a foreword written by a GARA core member (who was also the Welfare and Liberation Officer of the Student Union) that markedly pointed to the broader problems of university stewardship under the current management regime and pushed, once again, for the university to meet its demands, was rejected by the senior diversity officer. Major edits were introduced to make the foreword (and the report) a palatable set of recommendations. Several GARA members were furious and tried to force the issue but the report was nevertheless published without their contribution.[20]

As Ahmed describes, diversity workers' recommendations translate well into non-performative solutions that bring to a close the diversity workers' tenure in the institution.[21] Ahmed defines non-performativity as speech acts that don't do much of anything. If we consider performative speech acts as, per Austin, consummate action, non-performatives foreclose the possibility for action by becoming the action in and of themselves.[22] What follows is rote. The institution makes public promises of various kinds and continues on, just slightly different from what it was before the solution raised itself as a problem. During the occupation, management offered many such non-performative speech acts, expressing deep sympathy for the cause of the occupation and publicly articulating their desire to sit at the table and talk with GARA. However, it didn't want to do the one thing GARA asked of it: offer a written response to each of its demands. Putting words on paper, it seemed, veered dangerously close to making language do work. Especially, it seems, if those written words are in direct conversation with students' complaints, demands and solutions, rather than routed through the filter of diversity worker reports.

GARA's occupation comes on the back of several student movements that have, in their own ways, attempted to push institutions to address their endemic structural inequalities. Since the 2010 tuition fee protests, there has been a growing disquiet amongst Black and PoC students and staff in the UK. Rumblings about the need

for change became rallying cries that borrow from student movements elsewhere, for instance Rhodes Must Fall in South Africa or the 'I am' movement that started in the United States.[23] These collective and publicly visible protests, actions and occupations, for the university, require different (or additional) solutions. The same institutional actors who previously outsourced the management of problems that diversity brings by hiring diversity workers, develop other techniques to manage the problem. Invitations are issued to students and staff who have raised issues of racialised disparity, hostility and exclusion, to provide solutions to the very issues they raised in diversity and, more recently, anti-racism committees. Black and PoC academics are asked to lead these committees or, at the very least, participate meaningfully in them. Black and PoC students are asked to provide input. Complaint and grievance, in the eyes of management, become the grounds to cultivate participation while dampening collective rage.

If you are one of the students or staff members who finds themselves invited or even expected and obligated to provide solutions to the intractable problem of racism by sitting on (or even chairing) a department anti-racism or diversity committee, you find yourself enmeshed in affects of whiteness. Remorse, regret, rage, surprise and a strange sense of righteousness oscillate and produce insistent counter-demands to those who have raised problems to subsequently solve them, all the while maintaining decorum. If you show irritation or any sign of emotion, you again become a problem.[24] To be clear, these oscillations don't just come from management. Even amongst colleagues who claim a radical politics there is no agreement on what constitutes meaningful critique. Faculty (and in some cases, students) who are raising issues regarding racial disparity and who are amplifying GARA's message have been accused of unconsciously doing liberal diversity work rather than offering substantive critique of the neoliberal university.

GARA students and the two of us, as we've been invited into these forums, are then left to work through the range of feelings they (we) are exposed to. We (are forced to) try to chart a course that takes the opportunity to offer solutions to the problems that have been raised in the hope of making the university (even slightly more) survivable for ourselves and the students and faculty of colour who come after us. But even as we do so, we struggle to reject the compulsion to provide this labour freely, especially given the lack of recognition of the emotional toll it takes to do the work of explaining how tenets of liberal whiteness are embedded in every process, the imperative of doing so without causing upset or anger, and the possible detriment to our careers and future prospects as a consequence of doing this work. All the while, there remains a scepticism that offering one's labour in this way will result in substantive institutional change. We do it nonetheless in the knowledge that if we don't, Black and PoC students (present and future) in the institution will, ultimately, suffer. But the process drags on. Semantic railroading disrupts or delays the promise of any substantial change. Ahmed's non-performative solutions take on new meaning. They are now framed as dialogues without end and without result.

The fight that GARA began in 2019, one that spread to other institutions,[25] has once again reignited. George Floyd's murder in the US and the uprisings and calls for abolition in its aftermath coupled with the devastating effects of COVID-19 on Black and PoC populations in the UK, has pushed students and staff to ask why the demands that GARA made over a year ago haven't been met. These public queries have again created a public image problem for an institution touted for its progressive politics in a moment when it is already teetering as a result of financial deficits. In turn, the university has once again begun to reach out to those who raised the problems in the first place, for solutions. Both of us, certainly, have been invited onto various committees and even bids for grants dealing with structural racism in British higher education, in large part, we would argue, because of our involvement with GARA. Participation in GARA has ironically created a kind of fraught institutional capital for each of us. Others in the university seem to have grasped this 'opportunity'. Some who were strong critics of GARA for various reasons – that it wasn't radical enough, that it played identity politics, that it didn't know how to negotiate with the university, that racism wasn't a big enough problem in a progressive institution – have now begun taking up GARA demands (particularly the sexy, decolonial ones such as the removal of colonial statues on Deptford Town Hall) or positioned themselves close to Black and PoC students in the institution to curate events with them. Somehow, aligning oneself close to the problem without necessarily having done the work of engaging with, listening to, and supporting students in GARA, seems to be becoming a viable strategy to accrue academic capital.

Acknowledgements

We presented a version of this essay at the Sixth Annual ACGS Conference – Racial Orders, Racist Borders – in Amsterdam in October 2019 and are grateful for the feedback we received. Thanks are also due to our student community at Goldsmiths, with whom we've held many spaces of (un)learning, organising, collective writing and care (including the teachouts during the 2019 and 2020 UCU strikes and during the occupation of DTH) that have been crucial to shaping this work and surviving/fighting the institution. We remain forever inspired by, grateful for and accountable to our GARA community and the worlds of care we have nurtured. We stand together in continuation of our collective struggles within and outside the institution.

Ethiraj Gabriel Dattatreyan is a teacher, writer and filmmaker based at Goldsmiths, University of London. Akanksha Mehta is a feminist educator, researcher and writer based at Goldsmiths, University of London. Photo credits: GARA.

Notes

1. This document, part of a larger archive that details GARA's actions and activities, elaborates on GARA's initial demands: https://docs.google.com/document/d/1I6Jn-q8TLqnZtEGiEjEtOd_egF70q2ENcOmwJyk5uIM/edit.
2. The adoption of this consensus-based model of decision-making within the collective was in part inspired by local grassroots organisations such as Sisters Uncut UK.
3. The 'public' narrative of GARA's occupation was, on the one hand, fashioned by the university's PR team and, on the other, articulated by students in GARA on social media and through pieces in a variety of publications including the *Guardian*, *galdem*, *EastLondonLines*, *The Independent*, etc. GARA also made all correspondence with senior management public on social media (see https://www.facebook.com/goldsmithsanti/notes/). Throughout the occupation, GARA invited journalists to report on its struggle, which it linked to larger issues of systemic racism in UK higher education.
4. External mediators were brought in to facilitate the signing of the contract so that the institution could save face and GARA members could leave the building feeling that they had won an important victory.
5. Sara Ahmed, 'Complaint and Survival', 23 March 2020, https://feministkilljoys.com/2020/03/23/complaint-and-survival/.

6. On diversity and its limits, see Ellen Berry, *The Enigma of Diversity: The Language of Race and the Limits of Racial Justice Work* (Chicago: University of Chicago Press, 2015). On diversity talk in the university, see Roderick Ferguson, *The Reorder of Things: The University and its Pedagogies of Minority Difference* (Minneapolis: University of Minnesota Press, 2012). See also Tariq Modood and Stephen May, 'Multiculturalism and education in Britain: An internally contested debate', *International Journal of Education Research*, 35:3 (2001), 305–317.

7. Helán Page and R. Brooke Thomas, 'White Public Space and the Construction of White Privilege in U.S. Health Care: Fresh Concepts and a New Model of Analysis', *Medical Anthropology Quarterly* 8:1 (1994), 109–116. See also Karen Brodkin, Sandra Morgen and Janis Hutchinson, 'Anthropology as White Public Space?', *American Anthropologist* 113:4 (2011), 545–556.

8. These policy initiatives were preceded by efforts by the Labour government of the late 1960s. For example the 1965 and 1968 Race Relations Acts were implemented to improve 'race relations' through localised initiatives to educate white populations about new immigrant labour and to help integrate Caribbean and Asian immigrants into white British life. BAME (Black, Asian and Minority Ethnic) or BME (Black and Minority Ethnic) is a British bureaucratic racial category that surfaced in public discourse in the 1970s and 1980s. For more information on widening participation, see Debbie Weeks-Bernard ed., 'Widening Participation and Race Equality', Runnymede Perspectives, https://www.runnymedetrust.org/uploads/publications/pdfs/WideningParticipation-2011(Online).pdf.

9. See https://www.hesa.ac.uk/data-and-analysis/students for information on the diversification of British higher education since the early 2000s.

10. Whilst the university has diversified student recruitment over the last twenty years, it has not done the same for staff. See for example Richard Adams, 'Fewer than 1% of UK university professors are black, figures show', *Guardian*, 27 February 2020, https://www.theguardian.com/education/2020/feb/27/fewer-than-1-of-uk-university-professors-are-black-figures-show.

11. Sara Ahmed, 'Declarations of Whiteness: The Non-Performativity of Anti-Racism', *Borderlands* 3:2 (2004), http://www.borderlands.net.au/vol3no2_2004/ahmed_declarations.htm.

12. Audre Lorde, *Sister Outsider: Essays and Speeches* (New York: Crossing Press, 1984).

13. For a discussion of how liberalism shapes race consciousness, see Barnor Hesse, 'Im/plausible deniability: racism's conceptual double bind', *Social Identities* 10:1 (2004), 9–29.

14. W. E. B. Du Bois, *Darkwater: Voices from Within the Veil* (New York: Harcourt, Brace and Howe, 1920), 29.

15. Sara Ahmed, *On Being Included: Racism and Diversity in Institutional Life* (Durham: Duke University Press, 2014); see also 'Selfcare as Warfare', 25 August 2014, https://feministkilljoys.com/2014/08/25/selfcare-as-warfare/.

16. Robin DiAngelo, *White Fragility: Why It's So Hard for White People to Talk about Racism* (New York: Beacon Press, 2018).

17. Ahmed, *On Being Included*.

18. See Goldsmiths letter of response, in which it promises to fight for racial justice, in part by assembling a consulting team to do so: https://www.gold.ac.uk/racial-justice/commitments/dth-protest-college-response/.

19. Sofia Akel, 'Insider/Outsider: The Role of Race in Shaping the Experiences of Black and Ethnic Minority Students', October 2019, https://www.gold.ac.uk/media/docs/reports/Insider-Outsider-Report-191008.pdf.

20. In October 2020, *The Guardian* published a piece on the report; see David Batty, 'Goldsmiths racism report finds BME students feel unsafe on campus', *Guardian*, 10 October 2019, https://www.theguardian.com/world/2019/oct/10/goldsmiths-university-to-tackle-racism-after-damning-report. After speaking to GARA students and the writer of the foreward, it published another piece the very next day that reported the watering down of the report: Rachel Hall and David Batty, 'Students accuse Goldsmiths University of watering down racism report', *Guardian*, 11 October 2019, https://www.theguardian.com/education/2019/oct/11/students-accuse-goldsmiths-university-of-watering-down-racism-report.

21. Ahmed, 'Declarations of Whiteness'.

22. J. L. Austin, *How to Do Things with Words* (Cambridge: Harvard University Press, 1962).

23. For a discussion of the Rhodes Must Fall and Fees Must Fall movements, see Kelly Gillespie and Leigh-Ann Naidoo, '#MustFall: The South African Student Movement and the Politics of Time', *South Atlantic Quarterly* 118:1 (2019). For a discussion of the impact of the Fallist movements in the UK, see Amit Chaudhuri, 'The real meaning of Rhodes Must Fall', *Guardian*, 16 March 2016, https://www.theguardian.com/uk-news/2016/mar/16/the-real-meaning-of-rhodes-must-fall.

24. This process is also inherently gendered. The naming of Black women and women of colour as 'problems' and the negative reactions to them are often quicker and more intense. This was visible in the ways in which senior management spoke to and tone policed Black women from GARA and also in the difference in treatment we, a WoC and a man of colour, receive from our colleagues.

25. See the Warwick Student Union statement on their occupation, which began in November 2019: https://www.warwicksu.com/news/article/warwicksu/SU-statement-on-student-occupation-2019/.

Spirit of the Bauhaus in electronic sounds

Florian Schneider-Esleben, 1947-2020

David Cunningham

'There is no beginning and no end in music . . . Some people want it to end but it goes on'

Florian Schneider, 1975

Not long after the death of Florian Schneider was announced in May of this year,[1] I re-watched the 1979 film *Radio On*, directed by Chris Petit, and co-produced by Wim Wenders. A singular attempt to graft a Wenders-inspired German version of the US road movie onto a bleak, run-down, black and white English landscape during the dog days of the Callaghan government, the film opens with a long tracking shot that creeps slowly around a dimly-lit flat in Bristol, before coming to rest on the feet of a suicide in his bath. Structured, like most of *Radio On*, as much by its late 1970s' musical soundtrack – in this case the English-German version of David Bowie's six-minute *Heroes/Helden* recorded at Hansa Studios in Berlin – as by any conventional narrative drive, the opening shot lingers, briefly, on a handwritten sign pinned to a bedroom wall:

> We are the children of Fritz Lang and Werner von Braun. We are the link between the '20s and the '80s. All change in society passes through a sympathetic collaboration with tape recorders, synthesisers and telephones. Our reality is an electronic reality.

The words come from Kraftwerk, the group which Florian Schneider founded with Ralf Hütter in Düsseldorf in 1970 – a fitting reference, given *Radio On*'s larger fixation on German music and cinema as an alternative to the hegemony of Hollywood's dreamworlds and an increasingly desiccated Anglo-American rock still in thrall to the mythos of 'the sixties'. Petit has claimed in interviews that he became a music journalist solely with the intent of meeting Kraftwerk. And certainly their music

has an unusually prominent role in the film. Before setting out to drive from London to Bristol, through an England shadowed by terrorism and the war in Ireland, the film's protagonist is introduced opening a package from his dead brother containing three tape cassettes of the band's 1970s albums, *Radio-activity* (1975), *Trans-Europe Express* (1977) and *The Man-Machine* (1978): sounds and images of a modernity starkly at odds, the film suggests, with the nostalgia of the pub rock which makes up the bulk of the British part of the film's soundtrack.

This sense of Kraftwerk as an embodiment, musically and existentially, of the very image and *idea* of the new is, of course, one which resonates not only through their extraordinary influence on the 'electronic reality' of the music emerging from the industrial towns of Manchester and Sheffield around the same time as Petit's film, but more strikingly, and far more peculiarly, in the black metropolises of the South Bronx, Miami and Detroit. Partly this was, in the seventies and early eighties, a function of their very otherness as Germans working in a cultural form still very much defined by an Anglo-American identity – *Trans-Europe Express* was, the New York DJ and rapper Afrika Bambaataa recalled, quite simply 'one of the weirdest records I ever heard' – an otherness which is not only foregrounded by *Radio On*, but which was deftly mobilised by Hütter and Schneider themselves in their self-presentation throughout the period. But it also connects with a certain idea, or ideal, of pop music itself, as that artistic form which, in its inextricable dialectical relations to a mass technological culture mediated through the form of the commodity, has made the excitement of the 'new' intrinsic to its very historical dynamic and artistic meaning. It is not surprising, then, that, in seeking to describe a sense of the inertia of the musical present, for which the idea of pop as a privileged vehicle of the new has apparently come itself to be an object of nostalgia, the late Mark Fisher should ask specifically, 'Where is the 21st-century equivalent of Kraftwerk?'[2]

What is certainly true, as the flood of tributes that followed Schneider's death reminded us, is that few if any artists of the latter part of the twentieth century so emphatically embraced (and realised) a demand to be 'absolutely modern' as *the* defining axiom of their work. In part this was a function of the unusual degree to which they conceived of their own artistic logic in terms of its immanent engagement with the latest technological means of musical production; something which seems to have been particularly pushed by Schneider himself. (Largely responsible for the group's use of electronic vocal synthesis, in 1990 he was co-applicant for a patent at the European Patent Office for the Robovox 'system for and method of synthesising singing in real time'.[3]) 'The music of a technicised world can only be made on instruments that have been devised by a technicised world', as the press release for their 1981 album *Computer World* asserted. Yet, as the handwritten sign in the opening scene of *Radio On* implies – with its references to the 'link between the '20s and the '80s', to 'tape recorders, synthesisers and telephones', as well as to Fritz Lang and Werner von Braun – the specific articulation of the modern generated by their art was a complex one, tied up with a return to past motifs as much as with a creative destruction of the 'old', and with the discontinuous and conflictual legacies of twentieth-century German and Central European history from which they emerged. How pop's specific affirmation of the new in the wake of the rupture of fifties' rock 'n' roll – a fundamentally modern conception in its broadest and most basic sense – relates to what is customarily taken to be signified by that more loaded term *modernism* remains thus a difficult question, particularly where Kraftwerk are concerned. Yet it is also what makes their music so important, as an unlikely meeting point of the legacies of European modernism and the historical avant-garde with what Paul Gilroy calls those 'countercultures of modernity' embodied in the sonic experimentalism of the Black Atlantic.

Born in 1947 in the French occupation zone in southern Germany, before moving to Düsseldorf at the age of three, Schneider was part of the generation of Germans born immediately after the Second World War, and hence of what his musical partner Hütter, born a year earlier, called a 'generation with no fathers'. The duo's conception of Kraftwerk as 'the link between the '20s and the '80s' must obviously be understood in this light. As Hütter put it in a 1982 interview for an Austrian TV documentary: 'The culture of Central Europe was cut off in the thirties, and many of the intellectuals went to the USA or France, or they were eliminated. We are picking it up again where it left off, continuing this culture of the thirties'.

While the specific words here are those of Hütter, everything suggests that it was probably Schneider who first initiated this identification. In the photograph for the front cover of their third album, *Ralf und Florian*, from 1973, a boyish-looking Hütter is long-haired and dressed in the standard bohemian uniform of the early seventies, but the short-haired Schneider is already wearing a well-cut suit and tie that is more Thomas Mann than Mick Jagger. (Visconti's *Death in Venice*, the middle part of his 'German trilogy', had appeared two years earlier.) As bandmate Wolfgang Flür, who joined in the same year, recalled, by the time of *Autobahn*, released in 1974, the group as a whole had 'adopted the "German" image at Florian's suggestion … The Discreet Charm of the Bourgeoisie'. Just as importantly, musically, while *Ralf und Florian* still has one foot firmly planted in the forms of lengthy 'open' improvisation and tape manipulation characteristic of their first two albums, often centred around Schneider's own heavily electronically-treated flute playing, and exemplary of much German experimental rock of the period – works that Schneider would later dismiss as mere 'archaeology' – one can hear in tracks like

'Kristallo', with its pulsating synthesised bass and simple *romantische melodie*, a shift towards a very different idea of the modern than that pursued by existing models of 'art rock'.

Son of Paul Schneider-Esleben, a prominent post-war modernist architect, Schneider's own 'fatherless' status was evidently complicated. Schneider-Esleben senior – Florian began omitting the 'Esleben' around the mid-1970s – was himself instrumental in the recovery of *Neue Sachlichkeit* and Weimar-era design practices in buildings such as the Mannesmann head office in Düsseldorf – the first steel frame structure with a curtain wall to be built in Germany – and later collaborated with a new generation of neo-avant-garde artists including Joseph Beuys (then a Professor at the Kunstakademie Düsseldorf), who was a frequent visitor to the Schneider-Eslebens' villa. Of Schneider's father's wartime activities, the *Neue Deutsche Biographie* says simply that he 'participated' in the war from 1939-45, suspending his studies at the University of Applied Sciences in Stuttgart. Michael Rother, guitarist in an early three-piece incarnation of Kraftwerk with Schneider and Klaus Dinger – who played a series of remarkably aggressive concerts while Hütter was absent from Düsseldorf completing his own architectural studies[4] – recalled him as 'a nasty, famous and rich guy ... very unpleasant, bullying'. Whatever the truth of this, Schneider's wealthy background certainly contributed not only to Kraftwerk's capacity to acquire the most advanced musical technology during their early years – as Flür observed: 'Ralf and Florian ... always had to have the newest tools' – but also the unprecedented autonomy that they managed to ensure for themselves once they had established their own Kling Klang studio in a rundown area of Düsseldorf.[5]

Generationally, Schneider and Hütter's connection of their work to a culture 'cut off in the thirties' identified them with a number of German artists working, across a range of different media, from around the mid-1960s. As John Patterson has written of the contemporaneous films of Wenders, Rainer Werner Fassbinder, Werner Herzog, and others (all born in the early to mid-1940s), for an immediate post-war generation in particular, seeking to reinvent a German cultural identity in the wake of Auschwitz, there was little choice but to self-consciously assume the role of representatives of an artistic 'culture with no fathers (except the Nazis), only grandfathers (Murnau, Pabst, Lang)'.[6] From New German Cinema's declaration that '*Papas Kino ist Tod*', to the search for pre-World War Two artistic models in the works of artists from Alexander Kluge and Gerhard Richter to Berndt and Hilda Becher (one of whose photographs of an electric transformer adorns the inside cover of Kraftwerk's first album), this motif of a 'fatherless' generation dominates much West German art of the 1960s and 1970s. As Hütter put it: 'In the war Germany was finished, everything wiped out physically and also mentally. We were nowhere. The only people we could relate to, we had to go back 50 years into the '20s. ... [W]e certainly represent the generation with no fathers'.

Famously, Wenders' 1976 film *Kings of the Road*, dedicated to Fritz Lang, ends with a half-lit neon cinema sign reading *Weisse Wand*: white wall or screen, blank canvas, *tabula rasa*; what, in other works of the time, was termed a *Nullpunkt* or *Stunde Null* (zero hour). In this Malevichian demand for a radically new beginning, the question of 'what it means to identify oneself as a German, what it means to say "*ich*" and "*wir*" in a Germany that still finds itself under the shadow of the Holocaust', also becomes, however, a search for what Eric Santer has termed such 'stranded objects' as might yet be re-collected from 'a cultural inheritance fragmented and poisoned by an unspeakable horror'.[7] It is this that gives the search for a series of modernist 'grandfathers' of the 1920s and '30s its singular historical dynamic:

> To be able to feel any bonds at all, we had to go back to the Bauhaus school. It sounds strange but to continue into the future we had to take a step back forty years. The Bauhaus idea was to mix art and technology. An artist is not an isolated creature that creates for the sake of creation, but as part of a functional community. In the same way we are a kind of musical workers. The spirit of Bauhaus in electronic sounds ... Our roots were in the culture that was stopped by Hitler.

Such 'stepping back' has often been characterised as a kind of 'retro-futurism', a nostalgia for the lost futures of early twentieth-century modernism and utopian fiction in Kraftwerk's work.[8] Yet it can also be construed as continuing a project to reconnect post-war culture in the new German Federal Republic with a pre-war modernism that began almost as soon as the war was ended, and which is exemplified in both the foundation of the Darmstadt International Music Institute in 1946 and the establishing of Documenta in Kassel in 1955. Whereas, however, the emphasis in such immediate Cold War institutions was on securing German artists' reintegration into a purposely 'depoliticised' mode of formal(ist) abstraction – rigorously stripped of any pre-war associations with socialism or investment in mass culture – as part of what Ian Wallace calls a general 'cultural rehabilitation process' against both the Nazi past and the form of Stalinist Communism being established in the GDR,[9] the cinema and music emerging in the late 1960s marked an attempt to reconnect with a rather different modernism, and, hence, a significantly different cultural politics *per se*.

The 'idea to mix art and technology' played an evidently central role here, and it is no coincidence that it is specifically in those forms definitive of an era of mass technological reproducibility – recorded music and cinema – that this is most productively played out in much West German art of the 1960s and 1970s. In itself, this has often suggested parallels with the Weimer era and its dominant interests in the technological arts of radio, film, photojournalism and documentary. Indeed, such is a key aspect of not only Kraftwerk's specific retrieval of 'the spirit of the Bauhaus', but also of a far more general emphasis on art's immersion in the everyday that runs throughout their work:

> We just find everything we do on the streets. The pocket calculator we find in the department stores. The autobahn we find in the first five years of our existence, when we travelled 200,000 kilometres on the autobahn in a grey Volkswagen. So everything is like a semi-documentary. 'Autobahn' we made with the image that one day our music would come out of the car radio. 'Radioactivity' came about from the combination of radiation and radio.

Musically, this 'semi-documentary' relation to the social and technological forms of quotidian modernity is manifested in particular, from *Autobahn* onwards, by the increasing incorporation of directly mimetic everyday sounds into the structure of such pieces: the Geiger counters and radio static of the album *Radio-activity*, the engine and car horn noises that punctuate the 'motorik' beat of 'Autobahn', the electronic bleeps of 'Pocket Calculator' (generated by Schneider's Casio fx-501P programmable calculator), the synthesised moving train and bicycle chain noises used as the basic rhythm tracks of 'Trans-Europe Express' and 'Tour de France'. Exem-

plary of a Baudelarian lineage of modernism dedicated to the capturing of 'the special nature of present-day beauty', here, the sound-worlds generated by technology are shaped as a means of immanently registering and mediating fundamentally new modes of *social* experience as characteristic of a technicised modernity more broadly. Through reflecting upon these as form, they are thus made constitutive of the artwork's own historical meaning and value.

It is this that characterises, among other things, what both Hütter and Schneider described as the 'travelling form' of much of their music: 'Just keep going. Fade in and fade out rather than being dramatic or trying to implant into the music a logical order … In our society everything is in motion'. Formally, from the title track of *Autobahn* onwards (although already presaged in pieces like 'Kling Klang' on *Kraftwerk 2*), this conception manifests itself in a musical form dominantly built around overlapping patterns of repetition constructed through the layering or montage of short sequences of material, whether arpeggiated chords, 'riff-like' basslines or more abstract textures of electronic sound. Liberated from the standard verse-chorus structures of 1960s pop, such layering – made increasingly possible in the late 1970s by new 'sequencing' technology able to mechanically reproduce such sequences and sync them together – generates an impression of potentially infinite machinic form that is signalled in the titles of pieces such as 'Europe Endless' (1977) or 'Musique Non-Stop' (1986), and which has become a basic template of much electronic dance music since the 1980s.

Kraftwerk's unique foregrounding of the technological time and space of recorded sound on albums from

Autobahn onwards, and the programmed use of drum machines, computers or sequencers as motors of musical production, is easily readable, from this perspective, as something like a historical equivalent to the 1920s 'New Vision' affirmation of the industrialised eye and techno-human hybrids of photography and cinema – not only as compositional logic, but as a whole aesthetic of 'machine age' objectivism. 'We are the robots', as the opening track of *The Man-Machine* from 1978 most famously has it. Yet, to the degree that this self-consciously repeats a pre-war critique of, say, the subjectivist idealism of early Expressionism carried out by the *Neue Sachlichkeit* or by the Bauhaus post-1923, it is also, just as importantly, fundamentally *altered* via its re-inscription as a determinate negation of what was in the mid-1970s a very contemporary idea of the musician as expressive virtuoso, soul-baring troubadour or romantic rebel. This is why, to adopt a Benjaminian terminology, it is precisely the constellation of a specific *Now* – the 1970s of West German consumer capitalism – and a specific *Then* – the 1920s of avant-gardism and 'the first machine age' – that assumes such singular importance in Kraftwerk's work. It is the conjunction of a democratic and liberatory conception of the fusion of art and technology with a contemporary use of *new* technologies in pop that, above all, underpins the major works of the 1970s and early 1980s. To put it another way: if modernism as a general temporal logic of artistic production is embodied through the artwork's specific dialectic of newness and negation, then Kraftwerk's modernism is a function not so much of their references back to Constructivism or Bauhaus *per se*, important as these were, as it is of the ways their own music from around 1974 to 1981 can be understood in terms of its radical determinate negation of a whole series of existing constructions of 'rock': synthetic production *contra* gritty or confessional authenticity, cool detached objectivism versus libidinal passion, European planning versus American libertarianism, and so on – something which was intuitively grasped in their journalistic reception in the mid-1970s, if in usually negative terms.

Of course, such complex recovery and re-purposing of pre-war motifs as a means of intervening within a specifically post-war cultural field is also given an added geo-cultural dimension in what is, in this case, a self-consciously European reworking of an essentially North American history and vocabulary. In an interview from 1991, Hütter noted: 'We woke up in the late '60s and realised that Germany had become an American colony. There was no German identity, no German music, nothing. It was like living in a vacuum. The young people were into the American way of living; cars, hamburgers and rock 'n' roll' – a comment that echoes a famous moment towards the end of *Kings of the Road*, in which, as the two men at the centre of the film get drunk in an abandoned U.S. army post, with 'Rock 'n' roll is here to stay' graffitied on the wall, one boozily complains 'The Yanks have colonised our subconscious'.

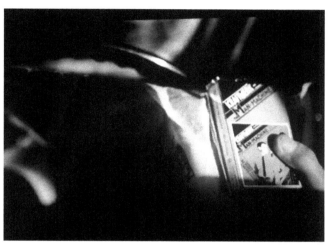

As a response to such a culture of the 'colonisers', with their cars and their rock 'n' roll, Kraftwerk's art was an obviously ambiguous one (as, indeed, was Wenders'). For to the degree that this was marked by an oft-expressed desire to re-establish a specifically modernist German or Central European identity – effaced once by the Nazis and then again in its displacement by 'the American way of living' – the medium through which it sought to do so came by way of cultural 'colonisation' itself. By seeking to create its own new constellations both with and *between* a 1920s avant-garde and a transfigured post-war form derived from imported North American popular culture, Kraftwerk sought thus to produce a form of post-war European modernism that would reclaim something of the radically democratic ambitions of a culture 'cut off' by fascism. But, in doing so, the contradictions inherent to capitalist mass culture also inevitably manifested as problems of form immanent to the artworks themselves.

Nowhere is this more apparent than in the self-conscious paradoxes inherent to Kraftwerk's frequent depiction of their music as a kind of *industriell Volks-*

musik, or an 'ethnic music from the Rhine-Ruhr region', as Schneider once playfully put it (much to the delight to David Bowie, among others). Musically, this is reflected in the avoidance of those blues-based modes characteristic of Anglo-American rock music in favour of what Michael Rother termed 'distinctly European harmonic and melodic contours' derived from *Volkslieder* and from romantic art music.[10] On *Radio-Activity*, for example, the closing track, 'Ohm Sweet Ohm', with its gentle opening vocodered vocal refrain, may have an electronic beat derived from the 4/4 rhythms of rock, but its elegiac melody has more in common with Schumann than the Rolling Stones, while, most blatantly, the main melody of the later 'Tour de France' single is directly filched from the 1936 *Sonata for Flute and Piano* by Paul Hindemith, a composer who himself moved from an advocacy of the *Neue Sachlichkeit* in music to the incorporation of folk songs; a piece that Schneider was presumably familiar with from his original training as a flautist.

Schneider's characterisation of Kraftwerk as an industrial 'ethnic music' may thus be profoundly tongue-in-cheek, but, here, the point seems very much to be the paradox itself: that it is the very forces of industrial production which necessarily destroy the nostalgic world of the *Volk* imagined in romantic and conservative *Heimat* culture (of which 'Ohm Sweet Ohm' is an obvious parody), transforming it instead into a 'homeland' exemplified, for Kraftwerk, by the modernity of the heavily industrialised Rhineland and pop's deterritorialised and technicised mass culture. If this recalls the Bauhaus' own struggles to reconcile the reinvention of craft traditions with the destructive energies of capitalist modernisation, as much to the point it also defines the contrary pushes and pulls intrinsic to the development of post-war pop music itself: a form born from the vanishing traditions of American folk music and the blues, but born into, and propelled by, the modernity of the industrial dynamics of mass commercial production and the new media landscapes of consumer culture.

Crucial as Kraftwerk's identification with the early twentieth-century avant-gardes may have been then – as a prism through which to critically situate themselves within mid-1970s pop culture – it was their ambition to work with and through specifically *contemporary* mass forms, from a (quasi-autonomous) site inside the spaces of industrialised popular culture, that has made them so

important to the music of the late twentieth and early twenty-first century.

Any attempt to understand Kraftwerk's extraordinary and seemingly improbable influence on black music – and on those black cultural forms that are, as Gilroy puts it, themselves 'both modern and modernist' – should no doubt have to start from here. Nowhere is this better exemplified than on the album *The Man-Machine* – as it happens, the first LP I remember buying, in a branch of Our Price records in Essex, sometime in the early eighties. Released in May 1978, less than a year after the bloody end to the so-called 'German Autumn' of attacks by the Red Army Faction, the album design, with its iconic cover photo of four dark-haired men dressed in red shirts and black ties standing diagonally on a suitably modernist staircase, is, the inside sleeve informs us, one 'inspired by El Lissitzky'. Emblematic of the short-lived hopes for an International Constructivism forged between Soviet Russia and Weimar Germany, the allusion to El Lissitzky's art accords with Hütter and Schneider's frequent conjoining of their music to the Bauhaus. But, alongside its references to early twentieth-century technological utopianism and the cult of the machine, *The Man-Machine* is also the first of Kraftwerk's works to engage explicitly with those forms of contemporary black musical expression that their earlier recordings (particularly *Trans-Europe Express*, released in the previous year) had begun to influence, in a kind of reciprocal exchange that would continue through the remarkable *Computer World* (1981) to their contacts with the Detroit techno collective Underground Resistance in the 2000s. Among *The Man-Machine*'s credits is, significantly, one to Leonard Jackson, a black mixing engineer from LA, also known as Colonel Disco, who worked with ex-Motown luminary Norman Whitfield, and who was hired to give the record some extra sonic punch for dancefloor play. (Supposedly, Kraftwerk were in two minds about adding such an obviously non-Germanic name to their album credits, while Jackson, until he actually met Hütter and Schneider, was convinced, on the basis of its rhythm tracks, that the group must be black.) Most importantly, musically, one can hear in a piece like 'Metropolis', which closes the album's first side, Kraftwerk's incorporation – alongside its vocal allusions to Fritz Lang's film and the timbres of the *mensch-maschine* – of the metric rhythms of disco in its relentless sixteenth-note electronic bass and 'four-on-the-floor' drum pattern. (Not coincidentally, Donna Summer's 'I Feel Love', produced by Giorgio Morodor, an Italian based in Munich, and released a year earlier, is its closest cousin in the disco of the period, to which it is probably indebted.) This is a useful reminder both that Kraftwerk's relationship with the sonic experimentalism of black popular music was a two-way street from early on, and that it was in the synthetic sounds and libidinal impulses of disco that their music first exerted an influence on U.S. dance music. *Trans-Europe Express* was awarded 'disco crossover of the year' in the *Village Voice* critics poll in 1977, and was repackaged for play in New York clubs as part of the 12"promo *Kraftwerk – Disco Best* in 1978, which included 'Showroom Dummies' and the title track from *Trans-Europe Express*, as well as 'The Robots' and 'Neon Lights' from *The Man-Machine*.

Such connections were developed further in the increasingly sophisticated syncopated layering of drum machine and synthesiser sequences on the 1981 album *Computer World*, in pieces like 'Home Computer', 'It's More Fun to Compute' and 'Numbers'. The latter, in particular, has probably been Kraftwerk's single most influential track on the music of the last forty years, built on Karl Bartos' drum programming but composed, in part, around Schneider's experiments with a frequency shifter and the new Texas Instruments hand-held translator from which the syncopated counts in various languages that structure the track are generated. (Rendering abstraction somatic, indeed danceable, the piece thereby amounts to a revenge of Kracauer's mass produced Tiller Girls in popular art itself.) Combined with the melody from 'Trans-Europe Express', it is a recreation of the rhythm track to 'Numbers' that famously propels Afrika Bambaataa's 'Planet Rock', released in 1982; a record whose own influence reverberates through the electro of the early 1980s to the magnificent 'Trouble Funk Express' (1984), by the Washington go-go band Trouble Funk, to the R&B of the 2000s. But the sounds of *Computer World* turn up everywhere in house and techno, from the proto-Detroit techno of 'Shari Vari' (1981) by a Number of Names to Cybotron's 'Clear' (1983), both of which borrow heavily from 'Home Computer', to innumerable later pieces by Juan Atkins, Derrick May, Carl Craig, Underground Resistance, Drexciya, and others.

Of course, placing a group of (very) white, privileged, Mitteleuropean men at the centre of what are profoundly African-American forms carries with it some obvious dangers – to say the least. And plenty of other precedents can be found in the likes of Funkadelic and Parliament, as well as in disco itself. But the contrary impulse to downplay this influence, as well as denying the rather obvious evidence on the part of the musicians themselves, can be equally problematic, where it assumes a certain essentialised identity of black music or experience into which Kraftwerk's modernism couldn't possibly fit. ('I don't think they even knew how big they were among the black masses in '77 when they came out with *Trans-Europe Express*', Bambaataa has remarked.) Indeed, it was the very 'futurism' of a rich vein of existing black music, from Sun Ra to George Clinton, that probably made Kraftwerk's modernism resonate to a black urban audience in a way, tellingly enough, that they rarely did for a white mainstream rock audience in the U.S. At the same time, unashamedly Eurocentric as Kraftwerk may have been in the 1970s (for all their love of the Beach Boys and James Brown), this otherness or what Bambaataa terms their 'weirdness' was also surely part of the appeal. (A similar point might be made for the more or less contemporaneous fascination of another disco-funk band, Chic, with the 'art rock' of Roxy Music.) Indeed, despite the political and artistic radicalism of second-generation producers like Drexciya and Underground Resistance, the original Detroit techno artists – the so-called Belleville Three of Atkins, May and Kevin Saunderson – associated their own attraction to Kraftwerk (unlike the hip hop audience in the housing projects of the South Bronx) partly with their suburban *distance* from Detroit's inner city and an aspiration to an imagined European elegance and chic.[11] The 'Shari Vari' referenced in the title of A Number of Names' 1981 track is itself a reference to the Charivari clothing store that championed European and Japanese designers.

Given this complex and multiple influence, it is not surprising perhaps that Kraftwerk have often been compared by journalists to the Beatles in their impact upon popular music since the 1980s. But a more apt comparison in this respect would probably be with a figure like Chuck Berry, and not only because of a shared artistic obsession with the social and technological forms and experiences of modernity. Just as Berry's lexicon of guitar riffs and textures is so ubiquitous across 'rock', from the Rolling Stones and Jimi Hendrix to the Sex Pistols and

Pere Ubu, as to become almost unnoticeable, so Kraftwerk's music has, particularly via digital sampling, become akin to a kind of collective electronic database of rhythms and timbres disseminated throughout recent music. This has to be set against the relative lack of productivity of the group themselves since the 1980s. Released in 2003, *Tour de France Soundtracks* is a better sounding and more interesting album than *Electric Café* (1986), with its largely ill-advised attempts to incorporate early digital technologies and 1980s' pop song structures, and its vague invocations of a pre-war European café culture. But it is also the only more or less genuinely new music that Kraftwerk have released in more than three decades. Since Schneider himself left the group in 2008, Hütter has concentrated on what has become effectively an archival project devoted to updating the technological presentation of the existing material and on performing the back catalogue live. Schneider meanwhile surfaced only once before his death with the charmingly slight 'Stop Plastic Pollution' in 2015, produced with Dan Lacksman of the Belgian group Telex, in support of an environmental charity. Ralf and Florian had been divorced for some time when the latter died, but the definitive end to what Hütter once called their 'electronic marriage' also brings to an end a certain idea of pop music as modernism itself.

David Cunningham is a member of the Radical Philosophy *editorial collective.*

Notes

1. Schneider died of cancer on 21 April 2020. The following tribute draws in parts upon an earlier essay: David Cunningham, 'Kraftwerk and the Image of the Modern', in *Kraftwerk: Music Non-Stop*, eds. Sean Albiez and David Pattie (London: Bloomsbury, 2011), 44–62. Albiez and Pattie's collection as a whole remains the best overview of Kraftwerk's work.
2. Mark Fisher, *Ghosts of My Life: Writings on Depression, Hauntology and Lost Futures* (Winchester: Zero, 2014), 9. For a different but not unconnected genealogy of an idea of rock or pop as modernism to that sketched here, see David Cunningham, 'Rock as Minimal Modernism: Lou Reed, 1943-2013', *Radical Philosophy* 183 (January/February 2014), 69–72.
3. Buried away on youtube one can also find Schneider's 30-second vocoder ode to the Doepler A100 synthesiser entitled 'Electronic Poem': https://www.youtube.com/watch?v= pLRgjzEjFkM

4. One can find on youtube some live 1971 recordings of Schneider, Rother and Dinger, which, on pieces like 'Heavy Metal Kids', develop the sound of 'Ruckzuck' from the first Kraftwerk album while pointing heavily in the direction of Rother and Dinger's future band, Neu!: https://www.youtube.com/watch? v=D8emDpWEBzE and https://www.youtube.com/watch?v= lTP-Clo62Dg
5. By contrast to most Anglo-American groups of the era, the rich period of German experimental rock in the early 1970s – including the likes of Can, Faust, Tangerine Dream, Popol Vuh, and others – often relied on access to similar resources for self-production. Like Kraftwerk at Kling Klang, Can, for example, began to produce their own recordings, with bass player Holger Czukay (a former student of Stockhausen) acting as engineer and technician, in a castle called Schloss Nörvennich, before building their own Inner Space studio in a cinema in Weilerswist outside of Cologne.
6. John Patterson, 'A film without a cinema', *The Guardian*, 2 October 2004, https://www.theguardian.com/books/2004/oct/ 02/featuresreviews.guardianreview13
7. Eric Santer, *Stranded Objects: Mourning, Memory and Film in Postwar Germany* (New York: Cornell University Press, 1990), xiii. In the case of Kraftwerk, the kinship with Fassbinder, who would frequently drive his actors crazy by playing *Autobahn* and *Radio-activity* on repeat while filming, was particularly strong. The title track of the latter album, for example, soundtracks a key scene in the film *Chinese Roulette* (1976).
8. See, for example, the recently published biography by Uwe Schütte, *Kraftwerk: Future Music From Germany* (London: Penguin, 2020).
9. Ian Wallace, *The First Documenta 1955* (Berlin: Hatje Cantz, 2012 [1987]), 5. As Wallace notes, Documenta in the 1950s 'crystallised and consolidated' a larger process in this sense (5): 'The identification of modernism with individualism and freedom of expression, and abstraction with internationalisation, was a common [Cold War] language of legitimisation for liberal factions in both the U.S. and Germany' (7). Missing from the first Documenta's presentation of modernist continuity were thus the Constructivists, Berlin Dada, much of *Neue Sachlichkeit*, the Weimar revolutionary left, and, indeed, the more political elements of the Bauhaus.
10. Quoted in Rudi Esch, *Electri-City: The Düsseldorf School of Electronic Music* (London: Omnibus Press, 2016), 70. See also, for example, David Bowie's comment in a 2001 interview that: 'What I was passionate about in relation to Kraftwerk was their singular determination to stand apart from stereotypical American chord sequences and their wholehearted display of a European sensibility through their music'.
11. See Dan Sicko, *Techno Rebels: The Renegades of Electronic Funk* (New York: Billboard, 1999); Kodwo Eshun, *More Brilliant Than the Sun* (London: Quartet, 1999); Sean Albiez, 'Post Soul Futurama: African American Cultural Politics and Early Detroit Techno', *European Journal of American Culture* 24:2 (2005), 131–52.

Reviews

Witchcraft and magic among the Marxists

Paul Mattick, *Theory as Critique: Essays on* Capital (Leiden: Brill, 2018; Chicago: Haymarket, 2019). 288pp., £110.00 hb., £19.99 pb., 978 9 00436 656 5 hb., 978 1 64259 013 5 pb.

Paul Mattick, *Social Knowledge: An Essay on the Nature and Limits of Social Science* (Leiden: Brill, 2020). 142pp., £86.00 hb, 978 9 00441 480 8

Paul Mattick Jr.'s compact book on the 2008 economic crisis, *Business as Usual: The Economic Crisis and the Failure of Capitalism* (Reaktion 2011), placed the events of that year in the context of the decades-long dynamic of the advanced capitalist economies since the end of World War Two. Mattick focused on two key questions: the role of business profitability in determining the ups and downs of the business cycle, and the contradictions and dilemmas specific to the post-war 'mixed economy', in which a substantial share of economic activity is state-financed and exists side-by-side with the private business economy. His own account of the crisis is contrasted with the inadequacy of the *post hoc* chronicles of the crisis (speculation, deregulated financial markets, policy missteps) proffered by economists in its aftermath and prevalent in the business press and halls of power.*

In *Business as Usual*, Mattick paid special attention to the blunders of the profession in the run-up to the crisis, throughout which Nobel Prize-winning neo-classical economists touted the self-equilibrating features of the system that were said to assure an optimal distribution of social resources through the elegant simplicity of the price signal. Whisked off-stage momentarily by the fast unfolding of the crisis they failed to anticipate or even conceive of, the door was opened to their apparent guild rivals, the Keynesians, who were thrust forward in the crisis' aftermath. This school ran the profession for the first three decades after the war, claiming to have mastered the business cycle by means of counter-cyclical interventions, using state expenditures to boost effective demand in downturns. Yet, as Mattick recalls, this once-hegemonic

wing was itself routed in the late 1970s by *its* crisis, the so-called 'stagflation' crisis (economic stagnation combined with a surge in inflation) that it could neither explain analytically, nor help surmount by means of its once-trusted policy prescriptions. Why, then, Mattick asked in *Business as Usual*, does this specific group of intellectuals, academics and governments advisors, whether neoclassical or Keynesian in allegiance, continue to enjoy such prestige and institutional power despite its utterly dismal record of failure during these post-war decades?

Though the ineptitude of the economics profession is writ large in periods of crisis, Mattick has been pondering the discipline's enduring credibility, despite its recurring debacles, for decades now. Its invulnerability is a central concern of Mattick's first book, *Social Knowledge: An Essay on the Nature and Limits of Social Science*, originally published in 1986 and just re-issued by Brill. Written in the aftermath of the crisis of the Keynesian school in the late 1970s, Mattick sets out in *Social Knowledge* to examine why Marx understood his own theoretical labours as a critique of, rather than a contribution to, the discipline of economics. Doing so, however, requires an exploration of what Mattick calls the broader 'epistemological conditions' of Marx's critique of economics. A revised version of a 1981 dissertation advised by Hilary Putnam, *Social Knowledge* grasps this critique through the lens of contemporary debates in the philosophy of science, which had to that point completely neglected Marx's work.

Social Knowledge revisits the disputes raised by E.E. Evans-Pritchard's 1937 study of witchcraft of Azande

* The author would like to thank Jacob Blumenfeld and the New Institute for Social Research (https://isr.press/) for their thoughtful comments and criticisms on an early draft of this review.

people of central Africa, taken as an exemplary case study for its exploration of the methodological issues specific to the philosophy of the social sciences. Mattick strikingly compares Evans-Pritchard's treatment of witchcraft in Azande culture and Marx's approach to the discipline of economics in his own. From this starting point, Mattick argues, we can conceive of Marx's own undertaking as *anthropological* in nature, a study of his own society as alien and other: a premise that makes his use of the category of 'fetishism' in *Capital* something other than a literary flourish or rhetorical device. The critique of political economy must not only explain the essential relations that regulate and set in motion the process of accumulation, it should also explain how these relations appear to the 'inhabitants' of capitalist society.

In *Witchcraft, Oracles and Magic Among the Azande*, Evans-Pritchard sets out to explain why the beliefs and behaviours constituting the practice of witchcraft remain central to this society's functioning, despite the logical incoherence that surfaces the moment these beliefs and behaviours are scrutinised; in the same way, Mattick argues, Marx offers an 'explanation of a conceptual scheme that is functionally indispensable to the life of a culture despite its inconsistencies and absurdities.' In Evans-Pritchard's study, witchcraft's theoretical incoherence in no way affects the Azande's assessment of its place in their society; in capitalist societies, the role of economists remains invulnerable despite the discipline's confusion over and inattention to the fundamental axioms of its discourse as well as a track record of analytical and policy failures few other 'sciences' could survive or surmount. In *Theory as Critique*, Mattick cites Jerome Radetz on mainstream economics as largely a 'folk science' in this vein, that is, 'a body of accepted knowledge whose function is not to provide the basis for further advance but to offer comfort and reassurance to some body of believers.'

Mattick's decision to write a dissertation in philosophy in the late 1970s was not unusual for someone with his personal and political background. As the social movements of the 1970s decomposed, and the labour movement faced a ferocious counter-attack in a context of unrelenting economic crisis, Mattick, like many others, migrated into other, more traditional fields: law, NGOs, Democratic party politics, social work and academic study. Active in the student and anti-war move-

ments, in 1969 Mattick formed a small collective with Jeremy Brecher, Stanley Aronowitz, and others, Root & Branch, which developed analyses of contemporary workplace struggles, while drawing lessons from historical episodes. Unlike other currents on the New Left, dominated as they were by party-building sectarianism, Root & Branch was committed to revisiting the lessons of the workers' council movement of the inter-war period, in view of promoting struggles for direct worker control over production and society. After completing his graduate work, Mattick pursued studies in the philosophy of language; later, he would publish two books on aesthetics, all while publishing occasional pieces on art and politics for periodicals like *Art in America*, *The Nation* and *The Brooklyn Rail*.

Having exhumed the epistemological conditions for Marx's critique of economics as well as its anthropological nature in *Social Knowledge*, Mattick set out in the mid-1980s to examine more closely Marx's method of theory construction in *Capital*. The result of these studies became Mattick's *Theory as Critique: Essays on* Capital. Written over three decades, these essays, like *Business as Usual*, analyse recent economic events – an entire chapter on the 2008 crisis, several pages on the Asian crisis of 1997-98 – in the context of broader discussions of Marx's crisis theory, with a special attention to the relation between his method of abstraction and empirical economic events. But the bulk of the essays deal in great detail with the (often false) problems of interpreting Marx's text raised by Marxists and critics of Marx alike. No attempt, according to Mattick, has been made to present these essays' findings in a systematic manner, so as to offer an all-encompassing exposition of Marx's theory. Yet a scan of the book's contents reveals that *Theory as Critique* is devoted to many of the key *topoi* in Marxist debates: questions of method, intricate reconstructions of Marx's value theory, reconsiderations of the so-called 'transformation problem', the reproduction schemas of Volume Two, Marx's truncated theory of class, and of course the crisis theory presented in *Capital, Volume Three*, rooted in what Marx calls the 'tendency' of the rate of profit to fall.

As with his earlier works, *Theory as Critique* scrutinises the shortcomings of the economics profession. What sets Mattick's more recent book apart, however, is not simply its textual probing of Marx's critique of

political economy, but the way it takes aim at a peculiar tendency within contemporary economics: what Mattick calls 'Marxist economics'. The emphasis is on the impossible conjunction of these two terms (Marxism and economics): the critique of political economy is not an alternative version of it. Yet this bastard formation has a by-now protracted history, dating at least as far back as Rudolf Hilferding's 'modernisation' of Marxist theory in *Finance Capital* (1910), in whose preface it is claimed that the propositions of Marxist theory have the same impartial status as those emitted by the bourgeois positivist sciences. This marginal current has more proximate roots, especially in its prevailing academic form, in the efforts of Paul Sweezy in the 1940s, who helped legitimate para-Marxist styles of analysis by warping its concepts and methods in conformity with those predominant in the profession. It would come into its own, however, only in the 1970s, as ex-activists of social movements poured into the academy to study history, sociology and economics at the very moment the post-war Keynesian consensus crumbled in the face of the stagflation crisis.

What is Marxist economics? In some variants of this trend, according to Mattick, Marx is fancied a prize pupil of the Ricardo School, adopting with minor tweaks the latter's theory of value, while for others it is possible to be a Marxist while abandoning the theory of value alto-gether; in still others, a version of the factor theory of production, the subject of Marx's relentless and mocking criticism, prevails. Many mistakenly construe Marx's value theory as an attempt to explain the formation of individual prices, rather than the historical emergence of an entire social form. All converge in their shared use of economic data collected using the profession's methods and concepts (e.g. national income accounting) to prove or confirm this or that feature of Marx's theory. The notorious Cambridge 'controversy' of the fifties and sixties, then the neo-Ricardian criticisms of Marx in the early seventies – debates Mattick strategically revisits in *Theory as Critique* – played an outsized role in shaping the preoccupations of Marxist economists. The economic crisis of 2008 revived interest also in Marx's crisis theory. Yet, here too, the adulterations of Marx's theory put forward by self-identified Marxist economists were typically compromised by the grafting of Keynesian concepts (e.g. insufficient effective demand) onto it, or devolved into explanations rooted in non-Marxist frameworks (sectoral imbalances, 'financialisation', etc.). Among those who claim to follow Marx's crisis theory more narrowly, there is almost universal consensus that data collected by government statisticians and economists can be used or adapted to measure with precision the rate of profit at any given point in time. A recent survey of these analyses by Deepankar Basu and Ramaa Vasudevan showed, however, widespread disagreement regarding the trajectory of the profit rate itself in the run up to the crisis, with as many claiming – on the basis of the same data used by other economists – the profit rate was rising as those who insisted it fell. Such disarray in the field of Marxist economists, Mattick argues, mirrors the debacle within its parent discipline.

The reason why 'Marxist' economists cannot agree on the most basic interpretative or analytical matters is that they have paid scant attention to the method of Marx's critique of their discipline, and in particular to 'Marx's use of abstraction and idealisation in theory construction'. The perennial debates within Marxist theory, Mattick argues, have generally arisen on the basis of a fundamental misunderstanding of the structure and the object of Marx's theory. Commentators of all stripes, for example, assume that the construction of Marx's analytic over three volumes gives rise to a 'problem' between the value theory presented in the first two volumes and the theory of production prices in the third. Critics of Marx see an intractable contradiction between these moments of his system, while Marxists vie with one another to construe its most plausible solution. What they share is a blindness to the method by which Marx constructs his theory, in which the idealised model of capitalism's invariant 'laws of motion' presented in the first two volumes is, in the final volume, made more concrete in order to account for specific historic features of the system as it evolves (a process Henryk Grossman, an important touchstone for Mattick, calls 'approximation').

When, in the first two volumes of *Capital*, Marx, by analogy with the founding principles of modern physics, opposes the 'laws of motion' of the capitalist mode of production to what he calls its visible or 'real process' (or 'actual movement'), he supposes that commodities exchange at their values. He makes this assumption not, as even many Marxist economists contend, so that he can explain the formation of particular prices, but because he wants to describe as rigorously as possible a number of 'long-term trends' in the development of capitalism. Such trends run through the history of this social form, even as its specific component parts vary or mutate. These structural features are outlined primarily in the first volume: increasing mechanisation of production, concentration and centralisation of production, the po-

larisation of class relations, the nature of the business cycle and the recurrence of crisis. It is only with the third volume that Marx sets out to describe the actual movements visible on the surface of society, assuming now that commodities exchange not at their values but at their market prices, that individual capitalists compete with one another for maximum shares of surplus value, that profit rates tends to equalise across sectors, and so on. This process of approximation or de-idealisation is what makes Marx's theory useful not only for understanding the structural trends organising and driving forward the development of the system as a whole, but for particular, variable features of that system, be it the transition from gold as commodity money to fiat money and the credit system, the historical emergence of so-called 'monopoly capital', changing class configurations, and so on.

What bourgeois critics of Marx – those who claimed he did not supply 'proof of the concept of value' (Böhm-Bawerk), those who found his 'whole construction of prices useless' (Bortkiewicz), and so on – share with defenders of an imagined Marxist orthodoxy, then, is an incomprehension in the face of Marx's methodological approach, which he explicitly modeled on the practice of the natural sciences. This method deploys not only, as Marx himself famously observes, 'the power of abstraction', but what Mattick calls, following the Polish philosopher Leszek Nowak, the method of *idealisation* as well. Abstraction merely entails the exclusion of many features of empirical reality while remaining a literally true description. Idealisation, on the other hand, not only methodically suppresses features of reality, it fictionalises (or deliberately falsifies) them as well, in order to better clarify a given structure and its laws of motion. In modern physics, examples of such idealisations are frictionless planes and perfectly rigid bodies; in Marx's theory, the assumption, in the first two volumes of *Capital*, that commodities exchange at their values rather than at market prices. The philosophy of science calls such an idealised representation of a system a 'model'. In Mattick's reconstruction, Marx's theory is said to be composed of two models, a more idealised model in the first two volumes of *Capital*, a more concrete (but still idealised) one which accounts for features of the system like competition, the equalisation of profit rates, and so on, in the third.

The high degree of idealisation entailed in what Mattick calls Marx's 'Model I', required for the exposition of the labour theory of value and the capital system's 'laws of motion', introduces an unbridgeable gap between the inapparent agency of these laws and the price patterns empirically observable on the surface of society. Both classical political economy and Marxist economics, in Mattick's assessment, consistently conflate or confuse the value relations formalised in abstract models with the economic phenomena reported in business statistics. Indeed, Marx's criticism of political economy, and in particular the exemplary form it assumed in Ricardo's theory, often centres on the way these writers prematurely flatten distinct structural levels, or are forced into explanatory errors when confronted with value-price deviations or with the apparent conflict between the theory of value and the tendency for profit rates among competing capitals to equalise. Mattick applies a similar analysis to the self-identified Marxist economists he addresses in *Theory as Critique*, particularly in the book's concluding chapter ('Value Theory and Economic Events'). Whether they are attempting, once again, to solve the so-called 'transformation' problem which bourgeois economists in the early twentieth century claimed to have identified in Marx, or are amalgamating the more concrete but still idealised model of capitalism presented in *Capital, Volume Three* with the actual workings of the (global) economy, the impulse is to 'jump across the explanatory chasm between the value analysis and empirical data' that Marx's theory rigorously maintains. When these Marxists resort to the uncritical use of statistical data to confirm or test the validity of the system's laws of motion first formulated by Marx, they not only end up with embarrassingly divergent results, they fundamentally misconstrue the nature of these laws altogether. Unlike Newton's laws of motion – here the analogy ends – the developmental laws of the capitalist system are not subject to empirical and quantitative verification. Their combination forms instead what Mattick calls a *qualitative* theory, one that cannot be 'tested in any exact-quantitative way'. This theory is confirmed, not proven, in the increasing recurrence of economic crises, just as it is corroborated in the broad tendency toward the centralisation and concentration of capital, in the tendency to replace labour with machines and the concomitant accumulation, over time, of a reserve army of the unemployed. Marx's value theory allows us to describe these long-term patterns with incredible accuracy, but it can neither verify them, quantitatively, at any single point in time, nor can it predict the timing of their occurrence or the tempo of their unfolding.

When, in the earlier *Social Knowledge*, Mattick characterised Marx's critical approach to capitalist society and its specific form of 'witchcraft' as anthropological in nature, this claim forces upon us the inevitable question: how can Marx assume a position outside of his own culture or society, a situation assumed as given for the anthropologist? What made Marx's act of self-alienation viable, he speculates, were the deep divisions already running through capitalist societies, its splintering into opposed interest groups, classes and 'subcultures'. One nineteenth-century subculture stands out: the socialist movement, to which Marx belonged for most of his adult life. Not all class societies are capitalist; but the class divisions in capitalist society are such that one class, defined by its exploitation at the hands of the dominant class, can be said to represent or embody the negation and overcoming of that society. This class anticipates the founding of a new society, organised on the basis of the abolition of wage labour and the free association of producers. Insofar as the socialist movement 'expressed', as Mattick puts it, these distinguishing traits of the working class, it created a vantage point from which Marx could analyse his own culture from the perspective of another society, one 'yet to be created'.

Mattick's explanation for why Marx's study of economics as a field is anthropological in nature – as a member of the socialist movement, Marx could assume a perspective 'outside' of the society he critically analyses – is elliptical and somewhat tentative, yet fascinating in its implications. It calls for two related observations.

The first is that Mattick's polemical account of the shortcomings of Marxist economics closely resembles an earlier account of the degeneration of Marxist theory first proposed by Karl Korsch in 1923. In *Social Knowledge*, Mattick speculates on the conditions that gave rise to Marx's scientific breakthrough, his involvement in the vibrant socialist movement of the nineteenth century; in *Theory as Critique*, he reconstructs the trend he names Marxist economics backwards from its recent resurgence through Sweezy to the 'modernisations' carried out by the leading theoretical lights of German Social

Democracy. What he leaves still implicit in this latter account, however, is why the revisionist current in Marxist theory gained the upper hand in the early twentieth century, at the very moment the socialist movement secured political legitimacy, on the very eve of its successful integration into the inner workings of capitalist society.

In 'Marx and Philosophy' (1923), Korsch traced what he called the historical 'degeneration of Marxist theory into vulgar Marxism'. He is referring specifically to the consecrated 'Marxism' of the Second International in the period roughly from the death of Engels, in 1894, to the outbreak of the First World War, two decades later. For Korsch, this tendency's exemplary figure is Hilferding. His use of the epithet 'vulgar' to characterise a sophisticated modernisation of Marxist theory is modeled on Marx's own distinction between classical political economy and its 'scientific impartiality and love of truth' – this is how Marx speaks of Ricardo – and the decomposition of Ricardo's school into a vulgar discipline concerned primarily with justifying the current order of things, on the basis of that order's own self-understanding. For Mattick, this same Hilferding represents a key inflection point, after which Marxism will be construed as a contribution to economics, rather than its critique; it will soon be understood not as a science of the eventual destruction or overcoming of its object, but as an alternative method of managing 'the economy'.

Mattick depicts the consolidation of 'Marxist economics' in the aftermath of the unwinding of the social movements of the 1970s. It originates, however, with what Korsch deemed vulgar Marxism. A properly dialectical materialist conception of this development, in Korsch's estimation, will attribute the emergence and hegemony of the vulgar Marxism of the Second International neither to the theoretical weakness nor to the historical perfidy of individual authors or currents, but rather to mutations within the 'general class history of the proletariat'. The degeneration of Marxist theory, in Korsch's analysis, is 'for dialectical materialism a necessary expression of parallel changes in the social practice of the proletarian struggle.' Vulgar Marxism, in all its variations from Bernstein to Hilferding, therefore 'appears as an attempt to express in the form of a coherent theory the reformist character acquired by the economic struggles of trade unions and the political struggles of the working class parties.' Unlike bourgeois economics, Marxism in Korsch's conception – and, I would argue, in Mattick's as well – must be the theory of its own practice, by which he means, the critique of political economy must be able to theorise not only its own genesis, as a rupture with the classical political economy of Ricardo in particular, but also *its own subsequent decomposition* into apologetics. The devolution of Marxist theory as a critique of economics into a leftist folk science can take myriad political forms, be they social democratic demand management or Bolshevik planning manuals.

The fact that Marx's participation in the socialist movement (or 'subculture') afforded him sufficient distance from his 'own' society to carry out a scientific analysis of it should be tempered, this is my second observation, with the consideration that his relations with that movement were often embattled and antagonistic. He was a forceful and relentless critic of its dominant tendencies, be they Proudhon and his followers in France or, at the end of his life, the confusions and compromises of Lassalle and his devotees in Germany. It is Marx's relentless criticism of and alienation from the main currents of thought within the socialist movement, as much as his participation in it, that lays the groundwork for his scientific 'breakthrough' in the late 1850s and beyond. And yet, his contentious relation to this movement is perhaps a less significant condition for the breakthrough than the historical action of the working class itself in the years preceding his scientific study: the worker insurrections of 1848 and just after. These events project forward, if fleetingly, the possibility of a rupture with capitalist society. Fleetingly, indeed. It was only with the eventual routing of these insurrections that Marx undertook his long study of capitalism and political economy, in an atmosphere of defeat and withdrawal. The construction of his theory depended as much on the sudden breaches opened in the walls of capitalist society by the worker legions, thrown unexpectedly into battle, as on Marx's sustained, critical assault on the prevailing errors within the socialist movement. If science is made in the painful intervals between these uprisings, its possibility is caught sight of when the working class dominates, for a time, the workshops and the avenues.

Jason E. Smith

Tools for a political psychiatry

Frantz Fanon, *Alienation and Freedom*, eds. Jean Khalfa and Robert J. C. Young, trans. Stephen Corcoran (London: Bloomsbury, 2018). 816pp., £30.00 hb., 978 1 47425 021 4

It is often taken for granted in the psychiatric field that the time for contestation has passed. Terms like 'anti-psychiatry' and 'institutional therapy', as well as discussions of the image of the patient or 'madman' in society now seem outdated. This is partly due to a change of paradigm in the social and political sciences, and is partly the result of broader societal changes. However, to a large degree, it can be explained by a corollary change of paradigm in psychiatry itself: from an approach that tried to criticise our modern society from the viewpoint of the disenfranchised (which had roots in psychoanalytic and phenomenological traditions) to the rise and subsequent near-hegemony of the neurosciences. In the eighties, discourse around psychiatry progressively introduced ideas of the hidden potential relating to so-called 'mental disorders' and that of neuroplasticity (e.g. 'resilience' under pressure). This transformed what had functioned as a criticism of modern capitalist societies of control into normalised behaviours; mental illnesses became assimilated into circuits of production and consumption. As a result, we are now living in an era in which mental illnesses are increasingly being stripped of their societal significance.

This shift is one of the reasons why the publication of previously unpublished materials by revolutionary psychiatrist and political activist Frantz Fanon is so important today. Although constituted of fragments (including two plays, various scientific articles and a memoir on neuropsychiatry, letters, political articles and – last but certainly not least – Fanon's library), this volume helps to bring cohesion to an often fragmentarily read oeuvre. In it, we can clearly see an evolution of Fanon's thought and his increasing political engagement. The volume should serve as a definitive antidote to essays seeking to dim his call for collective liberation and other defenses of social peace under current circumstances.

As a doctor myself officiating in a psychiatric hospital in Belgium, I am confronted on a daily basis with extremely complex situations, whether in consultations, in the ER or with hospitalised patients. Forms of social rejection and economic distress are often intertwined with psychiatric illnesses, which makes this job, as a social worker colleague remarked, a weaving enterprise, slowly putting back threads such as the patient's current experience of the world, their traumatic past, their social exclusion, their familial relationships (if they are still existent) into a slowly reappearing personality and individuality. All of this is done in increasingly shorter periods of time, due to institutional and societal pressure, and more often than not we are confronted with failures resulting in frustration, of the patient, of course, but also of ourselves as healers. Fanon helped me go into this profession knowing that another psychiatry is possible, one that would question and tackle societal and not only individual issues. He taught me that the clinical was often a reflection of the social. But more importantly, Fanon taught me that another world is possible, one in which the exploitation is finally over. And he taught me to fight for it.

One should start by mentioning the richness of this volume, the number of doors it will open for Fanon enthusiasts everywhere, and it should be said that part of this richness is due to the tremendous work put in by the editors, Robert JC Young and Jean Khalfa. Their introductions to each section provide us with very useful material and in-depth research into the themes explored by Fanon; their notes provide context that allows for sometimes very interesting dialogues between Fanon and a number of his contemporaries (including Henri Ey, Foucault, Le Guillant and Merleau-Ponty). Many of the texts collected intersect with and answer each other from different perspectives: poetic, psychiatric and political.

The psychiatric writings represent the bulk of the book, which opens with Fanon's dissertation on mental alterations in Friederich's ataxia, a neurological disease in which patients often show psychiatric symptoms. It is his first major text, written at the same time as *Black Skin, White Masks*, but published the year before to obtain his medical doctorate. Here, Fanon explores the conditions of possibility for mental illnesses and makes the argument that such illnesses could never emerge solely from ontological (or genetic) alterations. Instead he argues that it is necessary to integrate said differences dynamically with the patient's social interactions, which will make him or her grow to become a very different human being according to his or her social context:

> I do not believe that a neurological disorder, even when inscribed in an individual's germplasm, can give rise to a determinate psychiatric symptom cluster. Instead, my aim is to show that all neurological impairment damages the personality in some way. And that this open crack within the self becomes all the more sensitive whenever the semiology of the neurological disorder is severe and irreversible.

This dissertation should be seen as integral to his canon and is essential to understand the ground for his later takedown of the primitivist psychiatry of the Algiers School. The latter based its racist theory on the idea that the 'other', the Arab, was genetically inferior to white people and had a biological propensity to crime and violence (which were and still often are understood as pathological behaviours). By shifting the scientific gaze from the genetic to the social in his dissertation, Fanon prepared tools that equipped him to understand and dismantle this theory.

Concepts such as sociogeny (the influence of the social and societal context on the making of the personality) or the body schema (a person's mental bodily image) not only become central in Fanon's work, they also become essential to understanding his theory of liberation for colonised people, evident in later essays such as 'Algeria Unveiled' for instance.

'Day Hospitalization in Psychiatry' (1959) is another major text, which could be seen as Fanon's testament to institutional psychiatry. Based on his experience of managing Africa's first neuropsychiatric daycare hospital in Tunis, he tackles public mental health issues and defends the day hospitalisation model against what he calls the 'monsters', the giant psychiatric hospitals that still exist to this day:

> The point is ... not to remove patients from the circuitry of social life, but to set in place a therapy that is part of the setting of social life. From the viewpoint of psychiatric assistance, this amounts to an attempt to disengage from the apparently secure atmosphere bestowed by the existence of the asylum.

By dispensing with the carceral logic of the asylum, day hospitalisation changed the relationship of the patient to the institution, and hence changed the relationship between the patient and their own experience:

> The patient no longer experiences his possible discharge as the product of the doctor's benevolence. The a minima master/slave, prisoner/gaoler dialectic created in internment, or in the threat thereof, is radically broken. In the setting of the day hospital, the doctor-patient encounter forever remains an encounter between two freedoms. That condition is necessary for all therapy, but especially in psychiatry.

In this innovation, Fanon was, ahead of his time, a precursor to Franco Basaglia's Law 180 in Italy. (Basaglia, who is known to have been influenced by Fanon's work, wrote a significant commentary on his letter of resignation to the French Algerian Governor in 1956.) It is important to not only read Fanon's article in relation to our present decaying institutions, but also to connect them to the revolutionary decolonial climate in which he operated, and which provided the conditions of possibility for his project to succeed.

The psychiatric section of the collection also highlights his pedagogical engagements, both through the collection of many of his 'psychoeducative' editorials from the internal journal of the Blida Psychiatric hospital that he founded in 1953, and through the class he taught at the University of Tunis in 1959-1960 on Psychiatry and Society. (Unfortunately, a third body of pedagogical work has been lost: a class on Sartre's *Critique of Dialectical Reason* that he taught to cadres of the FLN (the Algerian National Liberation Front).) In the former, he tried to teach both the nursing staff at Blida hospital and his patients socialtherapy, through tackling daily issues that would occur in the hospital; issues that arose mainly from resistance to the introduction of his new methods. The latter was an ex cathedra course aimed to introduce psychiatry to an audience of young intellectuals, both in its mainstream repressive use as well as in his own reformulation of it in a revolutionary setting. Both texts are easy to read (one of them is penned by a student of Fanon's) and contrast with the rest of the volume in their simplicity, proving Fanon's point that 'To write is to want to be read. It is then also to want to be understood', as he says in one of the editorials.

Another group of his psychiatric texts aim to introduce his concept of sociogeny in the psychiatric field. By analysing the local customs and social characteristics of North Africans, and integrating them into his psychiatric practice, Fanon undermined the School of Algiers' claim that the North African is congenitally mentally deficient and highlighted the limitations of his own school of thought: 'social therapy'. His biographers describe the period in which he wrote these articles as extremely productive: Fanon was spending day after day treating patients at the hospital and night after night out and about in the region with his intern and acolyte Jack (later Jacques) Azoulay (who co-authored his article regarding the limitations of socialtherapy). In this period, Fanon was getting acquainted with local customs and with a culture of which he was ignorant before he arrived to Blida in 1952. This allowed him to identify the elements that were central to the Arabic/Berber culture and that could in turn be incorporated into a hospital unit in order to make it a meaningful place ('*un lieu de sens*') for the patients. The cultural relativism and overall perspicacity that such a methodology entailed were completely new in the socialtherapeutic field and, obviously, at odds with primitivism.

Finally, the volume comprises texts concerned solely with clinical trials, some of which are co-authored. These texts reveal how deeply implicated Fanon was in medical research, despite the scarcity of resources he had at hand. They explicitly show that Fanon didn't see psychiatry as an isolated discipline, but instead wanted it to have close relationships with other medical specialities. Although profoundly philosophical and political, his work was nonetheless medical, in that it centred on the lessening of patients' suffering.

The earliest texts of this collection are in the first section of the volume: two plays written in 1949, when Fanon was 24 years old. Both plays are valuably indicative of what would become two central themes of Fanon's oeuvre: while the question of the body is omnipresent in *The Drowning Eye*, the problem of the legitimacy of violence in bringing about a 'new man' is at the heart of *Parallel Hands*. A third play, 'La Conspiration', if Fanon ever completed it, is unfortunately lost.

The most striking aspect of *The Drowning Eye* is its language: an exuberant, symbolistic poetic style, reminiscent of Glissant and Césaire, where bodily sensations and perceptions are pushed to the extreme. The explosive vitality of the language used is heightened by the contrast it offers to the sobriety of the plot: two brothers (not so much unlike Fanon's brother Joby and himself) are rivals in seducing a young woman. Although deeply influenced by the negritude movement, Fanon was already distancing himself from it, avoiding essentialising the Black experience in any way. Instead his use of the semantic field of the 'body' prefigures his own developments on the body schema and the breaking into pieces of the colonised body. While *The Drowning Eye* may be read as Fanon's inventory of the pieces, several essays of *A Dying Colonialism* may be considered as attempts to bring these fragments back into a cohesive whole.

Parallel Hands powerfully preempts *The Wretched of The Earth*, both in the sense that it asks the question of the appropriation of power (with its related question of the legitimacy of violence) and in the way it tackles the need for a new humanity to rise, a concern that is present in the emphatic call of the later book's last pages. The influence of Nietzsche is pervasive, through the dramatisation of that new rising, a theme explored in Fanon's oeuvre by Jamaican philosopher and critic Sylvia Wynter.

The political writings in the collection are mostly articles from *El Moujahid*, the FLN's newspaper, to which Fanon contributed from 1957 until 1960. Those familiar with his posthumously published articles collected in *Towards An African Revolution* will recognise his astute political and psychological analysis of the colonial machine and its propaganda, with much still relevant to this day in colonial contexts such as Palestine (e.g. the first article 'The Demoralised Foreign Legion', which describes the psychological conditioning of the colonial army). An article that stands out is his denunciation of Patrice Lumumba's assassination in 'Africa Accuses the West'. The emotion in this text makes it clear that Fanon considered Lumumba as nothing short of a brother: 'Patrice Lumumba died knowing that his sacrifice would contribute to his people's victory. May he live forever in the hearts of fighters for a free Africa.'

The section ends with a short letter to Iranian revolutionary Ali Shariati, which discusses religion and the place it could hold in the decolonisation process, a theme rarely tackled in Fanon's oeuvre. As he wrote to Shariati: 'I would like to emphasise, more than you do yourself, your remark that Islam harbours, more than any other social powers of ideological alternatives in the third world (or, with your permission, the Near and Middle-East), both an anticolonialist capacity and an anti-western character.' This is unfortunately only one of four letters he exchanged with Shariati, the rest of them are lost to us. It underlines the need for further research on, and publication of, Fanon's correspondence.

The fourth section can be read like an epistolary novel. It contains letters exchanged between Fanon and his publishers François Maspero and Giulio Einaudi (assisted by Giovanni Pirelli). Those letters show the difficulties encountered and the risks faced by his publishers during that period, as well as the will of Fanon to have his last book, *The Wretched of The Earth*, published and disseminated as widely as possible, especially in African countries.

The last section, as alluded to earlier, is a real gift. Not only is it an inventory of the books said to have belonged to the author, but the editors have also transcribed significant annotations made in the books by Fanon. Although these additions provide no big surprises, one can relish reading Fanon's violent comments added in the margins of racist allegations by famous psychoanalysts. For example, Fanon wrote 'Bastard' in the margin of Freud's *Introduction to Psychoanalysis*, alongside the sentence 'the primitive man made work acceptable at the same time as he used it as an equivalent and substitute for sex-activity', and 'Shit, and when I think that there exists a psychoanalysis based on this psychology' in the margins of a book by Jung. Most revealing are the notes on his philosophical and political influences (Sartre being the most annotated author). This makes this section a very compelling read.

The concept of alienation is central to this volume and Fanon didn't separate the psychiatric from the political. The alienation he was fighting within the psychiatric setting, through aiming to restore the patient's agency and control of his or her own life – their disalienation – by using tools from social therapy as well as from his own research, was the same alienation he fought in the political field, by dissecting the colonial machine and joining his forces to the revolutionary effort of the Algerian People (and thereby the whole African continent and beyond). He saw both alienations as one, stemming from a capitalist and racist society that found the peak of its development and its barbary in colonialism, and in the enslavement of human beings to what he called elsewhere 'the abjection of those who want to make of the Man a machine'. He articulated the entanglement of the social and the psychic and hence of the political and the psychiatric in a letter to the Resident Minister in Algiers in 1956:

> If psychiatry is the medical technique that sets out to enable individuals no longer to be foreign to their environment, I owe it to myself to state that the Arab, permanently alienated in his own country, lives in a state of absolute depersonalisation …. The extant social structure in Algeria stood opposed to any attempt to put the individual back in his or her place.

Fanon's work is essential in that it represents the most fruitful meeting of psychiatry and politics to this day and provides us 'technicians of practical knowledge', or intellectuals, with a deeper purpose than to protect and replicate our current institutions.

Ibrahim Khayar

Revolutions of the past and future

Rachel Douglas, *Making The Black Jacobins: C. L. R. James and the Drama of History* (Durham, NC: Duke University Press, 2019). 320pp., £83.00 hb., £20.99 pb., 978 1 47800 427 1 hb., 978 1 47800 487 5 pb.

In the same way that there are poets' poets and communists' communists, Rachel Douglas is a C.L.R. James scholar's C.L.R. James scholar. *Making the Black Jacobins* synthesises the many versions and marginalia of James' work on the Haitian Revolution. By taking account of each separate rendition of the story, it has done scholars of Caribbean revolutionary history an immense service. Attention to the torsions of history as drama and drama as history have been the basis for a number of studies of James' *The Black Jacobins* in recent years, in particular Jeremy Glick's *The Black Radical Tragic*. Adding to this wave, Douglas reminds us that written history not only aligns or experiments with generic conventions, but is also an act undertaken by an author in a social context and under specific political conditions. In James' case, real life contingencies are preserved in manuscripts, papers, archives, notes and ephemera. They are not epiphenomenal to the author's published work but allow us to understand books as provisional and unfinished objects.

The Black Jacobins, a book of history published in 1938, is the most famous work of the great Trinidadian historian and theorist, but Douglas introduces us to its predecessor: the 1936 play *Toussaint Louverture*. Then, following the 1963 updated edition of *The Black Jacobins* – whose additions are the subject of David Scott's monumental study, *Conscripts of Modernity* – we learn of the second stage play written by James in 1967, also called *The Black Jacobins*. Douglas observes that most scholarship has conflated or neglected the multiplicity of texts and genres at work in James' Haitian preoccupations. Reading across history and theatre while using an intellectual-historical methodology based in the material archive, Douglas' transparent prose finally lays textual conflation to rest. *Making the Black Jacobins* examines the many revisions that exist in both genres over the course of four decades, in order to interrogate how drama and history inform each other across James' life, and, in many ways, across the arch of twentieth-century anticolonial thought.

In Scott's now famous argument, the narrative of the 1938 version of *The Black Jacobins* can be described as a romance, according to Hayden White's theory of historical emplotment, while the 1963 version is written as a tragedy. What Douglas shows most powerfully in her analysis is that the transformations to which James subjected the history of the Haitian Revolution chart a series of important clarifications in his conception of emancipatory politics in general. Because these transformations are not unique to James, but represent broad tendencies within the international socialist movement as a whole, the story of James' mutability as a historian is ultimately a story about the mutability of the past and its relationship to future histories. It was James' goal in 1938 to write about the 1804 revolution in Haiti in order to bolster coming revolutions elsewhere. Douglas writes, 'From the overall pattern of historical developments that James outlines throughout his narrative, he repeatedly stresses their special significance for the coming emancipation of, and anticolonial revolution in, Africa ...' When those revolutions came and went, James' 1960s revisions were shaped in order to adumbrate new insurrections and new forms of self-determination that have not yet come to pass. These emphases offer still-relevant tools for understanding the relationship between revolutions of the past and revolutions of the future.

Following Jeremy Glick's argument that 'that tragedy is there all along already in 1938', Douglas counters the claim of historical emplotment by situating James' work in its political time. Drawing on the history of Marxism, Douglas shows how the tragic elements of James' 1938 study occur as 'the tension and gap between the individual and the mass base.' This tension grows over the course of several decades, brought about by James' own political activity and involvement with world-historical events. The revisions made in the sixties concern, therefore, theoretical changes that correspond to the increasingly important rejection of traditional notions of party, vanguard and authoritarian leadership within James' thought in the second part of the twentieth century. *The Black Jacobins* texts of the sixties, especially the 1967 stage play, underscore the revolutionary character of 'ordinary' people and prioritise what James called 'the question of power', hinging on the spontaneity of the masses. If Toussaint Louverture, as revolutionary leader and military mastermind, occupies the central place in the story of Haiti's independence for James' work of the thirties, he will fade more and more into the background with later versions. James will move 'obscure leaders' and dissidents to centre stage, both metaphorically and literally, in line with his own shifting conceptions of popular power and workers' democracy. James' rejection of the vanguard model of revolution came through the elaboration of new Marxist theories of struggle produced among comrades in the Johnson-Forest Tendency and later in the Correspondence Publishing Committee and Facing Reality. These new approaches to contemporary struggle effectively drew historical figures (such as Moïse) out of the shadows of Haitian history and pulled Toussaint 'The Opener' down from his pedestal in the literature of Afro-diasporic revolt. Having taken certain cues from Daniel Guérin's study of the French Revolution, James fades the spotlight on the Black Jacobins, pivoting it to illuminate the Black Sansculottes.

Douglas shows us the lengths to which James deployed 'quarreling' against racist historians as an important mode in his writing process. In this, James is not only setting things straight, so to speak. Rather, he is returning to the revolutionaries of 1804 their heroism *and* fear, their failures *and* their brilliance. By following the principles of quarrelling, rewriting and collaboration, Douglas embarks upon a tale of revisions, friendships, transitions and experiments. This tale contains political concerns such as the American occupation in Haiti (1915-1934) and the invasion and brutal colonisation of Ethiopia by Mussolini's army in 1935. It also contains collective projects such as James' antifascist and anticolonial organising with George Padmore in the International African Friends of Abyssinia (IAFA) and later the African Service Bureau. James' collaboration with communist actor Paul Robeson, who starred as Toussaint in James' 1936 stage play, is shown to have transformed the Trinidadian's ideas about presenting 'the image of history as theatre.' Essential for scholars of anti-imperialist Marxism is Douglas' treatment of the communication between James' history of the Haitian Revolution and Trotsky's *History of the Russian Revolution*. Douglas uncovers the research and writing contributions of Eric Williams to *The Black Jacobins* history book, and examines links to Williams' famous study, *Capitalism and Slavery*. We are also offered a candid portrait of James in Paris in the mid-1930s, undertaking his Haitian research and making important contacts, such as Pierre Naville and Léon-Gontran Damas.

In her analysis of the addition of the appendix to the 1963 version of the history, we learn about the role played by the Cuban Revolution in James' reimaging of 1804, focusing on the vital significance of 'the past and future of the islands' of the Caribbean in relation to the history of the present. James' rewriting for the 1963 version captures not only his renewed vision for Caribbean emancipation, but underscores his 1938 forecasting in order to render the 'logical and historical' connection between Dessalines' Haiti, Castro's Cuba and the future revolutions that promise to transform the region. Douglas concludes the book by exploring the afterlives of James' Haitian works, demonstrating how they moved across borders, languages and expressive forms. Producing historical accounts as political solidarity is not unique to James, as Marxist historians across the twen-

tieth century often united partisan inheritors with the specific political pasts that formed them. But in James' case, the theatre became an equally important tool for writing history against the 'imperial archive', exploiting its particular capacities and freedoms in order to enact the 'history from below' that his 1963 revisions had begun.

As the late Michael Dash noted in 1974, 'one feature of Third World writers which distinguishes them as a distinct literary fraternity is the fundamental dialogue with history in which they are involved.' In each new textual rendition of the Haitian event, James was set on defeating the 'imperialist treachery and hypocrisy' of historical reception, but, in doing so, he accentuated the changeability of the past, putting onto the table questions of historical movement and non-synchronicity. Douglas, in developing a deeply historical view of the writing of political history, continues the specifically anticolonial conversation on revolutionary temporality, its plurality and untimeliness. Marxist theory has seen a renewed interest in the politics of untimely temporality, as scholars revisit these notions in the work of Bloch, Gramsci and Althusser. However, the most robust meditation on this theme has arguably been had among Caribbean political

intellectuals of the twentieth century and scholars of these thinkers in recent decades. Indeed, the Haitian Revolution has been called a 'prophetic vision of the past' by Édouard Glissant, and was the basis for Aimé Césaire's ruminations on the proleptic eruption of the past into the future, generating a sort of 'now-time' reminiscent of Walter Benjamin's theses 'On the Concept of History'. What Douglas describes as the 'positive untimeliness of *The Black Jacobins*' is best understood when situated in the changing history of James' political positions and collective engagements; it is necessarily subject to modifications produced by its reception beyond James' lifetime.

Scott's 2004 intervention against the romance of anticolonial revolution was made in a 'time of postcolonial crisis in which old horizons ha[d] collapsed or evaporated and new ones ha[d] not taken shape.' The pessimism of the interregnum is based in the very real failures of nation-states and dependent territories throughout the Caribbean in the twenty-first century. But if *The Black Jacobins* has again recently become a source for nourishing the 'longing for revolution', to use Scott's phrase, perhaps it is because new horizons of transformations have become apparent. As the United States enters a historical moment in which the call for the abolition of police has taken on certain mainstream dimensions, we must ask if this non-trivial shift in the white imagination deserves a healthy dose of revolutionary optimism. Uprisings of the last five years alone – including in Haiti – show that the aspiration for comprehensive social transformation *is* constant.

This is not to deny the resilience of reactionary formations or to downplay the harrowing plasticity of racial capitalism but there is every reason to believe that any time history could give itself over to a conjuncture as radical as decolonisation. Despite its shortcomings, James saw the destruction of 'eternal' European empires and the restoration of Third World sovereignty as an event that 'shattered the foundations' of the Old World. If *The Black*

Jacobins projected itself, as a 'prophetic vision of the past', into a decolonial future in which 'the world ushered in by Christopher Columbus and Martin Luther' ceased to exist, what kind of revolutions will James' sixties revisions foresee? There is a mass longing for integral and systemic change, which recognises the primary of race and racialisation in structuring contemporary existence, from the materiality of our labour to the immateriality of our desires. This is not a romance. It is simply the willingness to believe, as people have historically believed, desperately and euphorically, in something beyond the boundary of the present.

Jackqueline Frost

Discriminatory data

Ruha Benjamin, *Race After Technology: Abolitionist Tools for the New Jim Code* (Cambridge: Polity Press, 2019). 172pp., £60.00 hb., £14.99 pb., 978 1 50952 639 0 hb., 978 1 50952 640 4 pb.

If you've ever listened to *Pod Save America,* the voice of centrist Democratic politics presented by a crew of former Obama staff, you might have noticed that the show is sponsored by Zip Recruiter, a recruitment website designed to appeal to both job seekers and employers. The site supposedly scans thousands of resumes for every vacancy, its 'powerful matching technology' connecting job seekers with the perfect openings. Such processes, an excited October 2018 article on CNBC's website explained, are 'removing human biases that can hold back some applicants'. According to CNBC, the prospect that 'your next job interview could be with a robot' should be welcomed.

The reality of artificial intelligence, as Ruha Benjamin outlines in her latest monograph *Race after Technology*, promises no such automatic liberation from human prejudice. On the contrary, she claims, 'your next interview could be with a racist robot'. Benjamin is a scholar of the social dimensions of science and technology. *Race After Technology* is a work of politics and sociology that explores how social relations, particularly of race and power, shape the digital landscape, by inquiring into the design practices of the tech industry. Borrowing from the legal scholar Michelle Alexander, Benjamin argues that we live in a new era, a space where the data divide mani-

fests as 'the New Jim Code'. As Benjamin notes, 'Codes are both reflective and predictive. They have a past and a future'. The extent to which the tech industry is racially coded is what *Race After Technology* explores.

How does a digital code become racist and when did it first begin to integrate itself into the technologies we use? The coding problem, for Benjamin, is the problem of how 'race as a form of a form of technology' is engineered by the humans who design the machinery. It begins with an archetypal nineteenth-century technology – the camera. With the invention of the first permanent camera by Joseph Nicéphore Niépce in 1825 in Paris, the race to develop a commercially successful camera for the mass market was independently being contested by French, British and American innovators. By the 1880s, George Eastman, the developer of Kodak film, was able to create an industry closely tied to the film industry, which would revolutionise how still and moving images were seen. Years later, it was revealed that the colour film used in the photo industry was racially biased, distorting the appearance of Black skin tones and lightening the skin of women of colour. These discrepancies were not an accident but derived, as Lorna Roth has noted, from the film industry's use of solely white subjects as the prototypes for their calibration. The genealogy of racial bias in analogue and digital images can also be traced to the algorithmic practice of classifying humans in the nineteenth century.

As Benjamin argues in her third chapter, 'Coded Exposure', racial coding is not new but the means of recording it have changed. Nineteenth-century coding was visual. It created coding structures that neglected Blackness, in some cases, and made it hypervisible in others. Using accounts from social media and race critical code studies scholars, Benjamin tries to unpack how society constructs technology and notes that the development is 'not just *what* we study but also … *how* we analyse, questioning our own assumptions about what is deemed high theory versus pop culture, academic versus activist, evidence versus anecdote'. She implements this methodology in her chapter 'Default Discrimination', when she presents us with a screenshot from Twitter on 19 November 2013 in which a Black woman with the handle @alliebland stated: 'Then Google Maps was like, "turn right on Malcolm Ten Boulevard" and I knew there were no black engineers working there'. The glitch in the technology that translated Malcolm X's last name into the Roman numeral 10 could be understood as a random occurrence, but Albla's point is that a Black person would have recognised the error and corrected the technology accordingly.

Benjamin shows here how people use social media to actively debate the racial codes in tech design. At the same time, Benjamin demonstrates that these malfunctions expand beyond computer algorithms and exposes the tensions between inclusion and accuracy. Digital documentation straddles both the invisibility and hypervisibility of marginalised groups. One example of invisibility is the case of Polaroid camera's underexposure of dark skinned people, whereas hypervisibility is evident in cameras tied to surveillance, which disproportionately monitor dark-skinned people. Contemporary society is highly dependent on procuring digital identity through biometric inputs, which are parallel to stratified human differences. At the core of her book is the insight that digital glitches are merely an extension of the societal glitches that stratify human life. In this way, Benjamin maps out the genealogy and archaeology of racist virtual space that engineers inequity.

One of the most interesting elements of *Race After Technology* is that it moves us from the fantasy world of the allegedly neutral robot into a world where we have to reckon with the unintended consequences of digital discrimination. Robots have become ubiquitous in our lives as electronic devices that are instructed upon command. When a person instructs Siri to call a friend or Alexa to play a song, there is a servitude that its owner expects. What one gathers from these technologies is that they create vertical realities that offer convenience for some and surveillance for most. Electronic technologies that act on command can be freeing and luxurious, yet they also tie into what Shoshana Zuboff has described as surveillance capitalism.

Digital technologies are extensions of the carceral state and do the work of monitoring the masses, through their mobile phones, computers and more. In the context of the United States, where policing and prisons are paramount, artificial intelligence has metamorphosed into an instrument of surveillance, and electronic monitoring is an extension of mass monitoring. For anti-racist prison abolitionists who want to use technology benevolently, electronic monitoring offers an alternative to incarceration. Advocates claim that it improves community safety and allows for people in the correctional industrial complex to be integrated into working and living conditions within the free world. This is a point at which the reader is confronted with the ethics of monitoring systems: where does this information get stored and who tracks it? The type of collection and the extent to which the data is housed by private or public entities plays a big role in the political output. Some private companies, as Benjamin points out, use their ethno-racially coded databases as proxies for predicting individuality. Understanding the depths of the New Jim Code entails not merely an engagement with discrimination but with how capital tries to define, categorise and make a profit from people. Unfortunately, private and governmental data collection has become ubiquitous for everyone. And what Benjamin shows is the way that racialised technology can make deep-seated interventions and intrusions into people's lives. Personhood is something that is constituted into data. Data appropriates life for capitalism, and, with the New Jim Code, its power is instantiated even further and shapes people's life spans. Data collection constructs the hierarchies of humanity.

While *Race After Technology* sketches the obvious points of tension between technology and society, Ben-

jamin's integration of media activist Mia Mingus's text 'Moving Toward the Ugly' explores how aesthetics features in virtual space. Mingus's text is a manifesto that hopes to move people away from society's obsession with beauty; a work that tries to turn away from ableism, racism and classism. This has great implications for Eurocentric perceptions of beauty, but it is not always clear how far technology can or does codify beauty. Benjamin unpacks the history from a visual perspective and shows how the late twentieth- and early twenty-first-century camera is one of the many ways in which skin bias is reproduced, leaving darker skin complexions underexposed. Yet, the problems of technology are not merely skin deep but can determine who gets hired and the conditions under which hiring happens. AI technology is streamlining discrimination and is now deployed in recruitment technology. In *The Enigma of Diversity*, Ellen Beny explains how people who have a superficial conception of diversity use technology to celebrate cultural difference. Nancy Leong shows how institutions commodify racial diversity for their own benefit. It appears that some people are able to overcome this through code switching. As Benjamin notes, standard English is a code of power that can overcome the problems of AI racism.

The book's last chapter tries to offer a sense of reprieve or hope. The author moves from describing discriminatory design to abolitionist tools that challenge the New Jim Code. This entails resources that can be directed to releasing people from jails or implementing empathy through 'design thinking'. A driving question is how we transcend divisive technology when the relevant power structures seem omnipresent and oppressive. Although codes are informed by a racist past, a radical imagination can help us create a just future. This entails accountability for tech designers and advancements that create innovative alternatives. As Britt Rusert's *Fugitive Science* shows, there is a long history of Black scientists, scholars and artists resisting and subverting racist science. In the twenty-first century, racism is a classification practice that bears new life in technology. *Race After Technology* ends with a growing list of tech and social initiatives that are not only committed to understanding AI-based technologies and digital coding, but people who are committed to creating alliances, collectives and archives that concretise tech literacy for working class people of colour. In this way, Benjamin's work and the communities she lists open up the possibility for the inclusion of more Black people in the tech industry. It does so by honouring the lived experiences of people who have traditionally been left out of the field but who are now seeking to design an unbiased digital space.

Edna Bonhomme

The Logic of Critical Theory

Robert B. Pippin, *Hegel's Realm of Shadows: Logic as Metaphysics in* The Science of Logic (Chicago: University of Chicago Press, 2019). 322pp., £34.00 hb., £24.00 pb., 978 0 22658 870 4 hb., 978 0 22670 341 1 pb.

In one of Lenin's most famous lines, he notes that 'it is impossible to understand Marx's *Capital* ... without having thoroughly studied and understood the *whole* of Hegel's *Logic*.' This might seem an odd starting point for a review of Robert Pippin's most recent book, a highly technical treatise that might best be understood as an explication of what Pippin regards as the *Logic*'s single-most radical thesis: that logic and metaphysics 'coincide'. For Pippin, the *Logic* shows that an account of being or 'what is' (metaphysics) cannot be successful or avoid begging questions without also including an account of the intelligibility or 'thinkability' of such an account (logic). To make sense of things (the task of metaphysics according to Aristotle, one of the two heroes of the *Logic*), we must make sense of the very idea of 'sense-making', the basic forms of thought.

To put this point in the terms of one of the book's key interlocutors, Wittgenstein: if 'being' is understood as the most capacious language-game we play, then what Hegel is asking is what it would mean to give a coherent account of the rules of the game, as well as of the general notion of rule-governed games. For something to be, it must be intelligible, conceptually articulable. There are not unknowable things outside of the bounds of sense, but no things at all, only sheer nonsense.

Pippin's book provides a *tour de force* reading of the *Logic* in terms of the 'logic-as-metaphysics' thesis and the related notion of the 'apperceptive' character of thinking, a career-long preoccupation of Pippin's. He also brings Hegel's work – both the greater *Logic*, published in its final form in 1832, and its 'minor' counterpart, the *Encyclopedia Logic* (1817) – to bear on a number of current philosophical topics, including Frege's distinction between the force and intelligibility of a proposition, Wittgenstein on the limits of sense, the relationship between concept and intuition, and Aristotle and Kant on the mechanical inexplicability of living organisms. Given Pippin's rather esoteric set of concerns, the suspicion might be that *Hegel's Realm of Shadows* is the ultimate exercise in analytic scholasticism, the culmination of a

century-long process of depoliticising Hegel, and thus the polar opposite of Lenin's *Conspectus* (1929), his compiled notes for a reading of the *Logic* in the service of advancing Marx's critique of capital. Yet, despite appearances to the contrary, Pippin's book is actually one of the most important contributions to the tradition of critical theory since he began publishing in the 1970s. Aside from its evident contributions to Hegel scholarship, engaging as it does with a host of contemporary analytic idealists, from McDowell to Brandom to Houlgate to Longuenesse, *Hegel's Realm of Shadows* is also a crucial philosophical intervention in critical theory with radical implications for our understanding of social critique.

Pippin's book is divided into two parts and comprises nine chapters. The first four chapters which make up Part I establish the frame for the reading of each of the three books of the *Logic* (the Logic of Being, the Logic of Essence and the Logic of the Concept) undertaken in Part II. In the introductory chapter, Pippin argues for the general significance of Hegel's *Logic* by pointing to its status as the 'science of "reasons", of ways of giving reasons in rendering anything genuinely or properly intelligible'. Part of the revolution inaugurated by Kant – the other key figure for the *Logic* – lay in his famous distinction between general and transcendental logic, between the rules of thought in abstraction from objects and the rules of thought that make the experience of objects possible. Famously, Kant provides a 'transcendental deduction' meant to demonstrate the applicability of such rules – the pure categories of the understanding – to the distinctly human form of sensibility, space and time. What was supposed to be a general account of knowledge turns out to amount to no more than a rather modest account of how things appear to 'us' humans, constrained as we happen to be by these spatial and temporal forms of intuition. How things are 'in themselves' is unknowable, beyond the bounds of (our) sense. Hegel radicalises Kant (to borrow a phrase from John McDowell) by rejecting the need for such a demonstration of the world-directedness or 'objective purport' of the categories and by claiming that an examination of the forms of thought themselves, properly executed, will just thereby yield knowledge of the forms of things. (Pippin provides multiple discussions of how Hegel fully prosecutes what Kant merely sketches, a 'metaphysical deduction', throughout the book.) General logic will no longer be separable from transcendental logic, and logic and metaphysics will 'coincide'.

Pippin begins to explain what such an examination of pure thought involves in the second and third chapters ('Logic and Metaphysics' and 'The Significance of Self-Consciousness'), by turning to the deep influence exercised on the *Logic* by the Kantian notion of the unity of apperception. According to Pippin, Hegel inherits Kant's claim that the basic unit of thought is not the concept but rather the judgement, of which concepts are possible predicates. The meaning of concepts is determined by use – by how they are used in practical and theoretical judgements. To master the concept of 'blue' is to know how to use it, to know to which sorts of things one can apply it (to cubes and flowers but not to gravity or love) and to know what other concepts its application excludes (red, green) or entails (coloured). All thought is apperceptive, for Kant as for Hegel, in that it is not a mere registering of perceptions, desires, beliefs, and so on, but an attentiveness to what one has *reason* to desire or believe.

The *Logic*, on Pippin's account, is the record of thought's apperceptive attempt to think the thought of itself, to ask the question what it means to think. The fourth chapter prepares us for the exemplification of this dialectic in Part II through an account of the self-negating, self-correcting character of any thinking – including thought's thinking of itself ('thinking thinking thinking', in the Aristotelean phrase quoted several times by Pippin). In an important discussion in the penultimate section of the chapter, Pippin contrasts his own reading of Hegel with that of Robert Brandom, whose own understanding of 'determinate negation' in terms of 'material incompatibility' (something's being reptilian specifically excludes its being mammalian) is criticised by Pippin as appropriate only to the first of the three books of the *Logic* and as insufficient to grasp the form of self-negation that functions as the moving principle of the work as a whole. As chapter five demonstrates, in trying to think the thought of pure being, thought has committed itself

to thinking something entirely indeterminate, and hence to thinking 'nothing' at all. Such indeterminacy is not just an indifferent fact about pure being, but a failure *of* thought that it must resolve, if it is to truly think being as it ought to be thought. What Brandom fails to grasp, on Pippin's account, is the *a priori* openness of thought to its own possible negation, just by virtue of the norm-governed character of any act or belief.

Throughout the first five chapters, especially in the notes, Pippin takes great pains to correct common misunderstandings prompted by infelicitous formulations in his first path-breaking work on Hegel (*Hegel's Idealism* (1989)), while also working to distinguish his clarified position from the 'ontological' reading of the *Logic* popularised by Stephen Houlgate. In brief, if for Houlgate one can infer directly from the categories of the *Logic* to how things in themselves are, then, for Pippin, the *Logic* articulates how being must be thought for things to be intelligible as what they are. This is a difficult thought and one could be forgiven for thinking that Pippin is just splitting hairs, as early reviews of the book have often suggested. But in actuality, how one comes down on this issue is a matter of absolute importance: if one does not frame Hegel's 'science of pure thinking' in terms of thought's reason-responsive attempt to think being *rightly*, as it ought to be thought, one risks assimilating Hegel to the pre-Kantian rationalist tradition – represented by Descartes, Spinoza, Leibniz and Wolff – he himself criticised and will thereby miss what is truly distinctive about the Hegelian option.

Pippin's book culminates, as the *Logic* does, in an account of the categories of Life and the True and the Good. Pippin offers a powerful defense of Hegel's account of life as a non-empirically derived, logical category, not just required heuristically by 'us', for the empirical study of nature (as Kant thought), but required by thought itself, for the full conceptual specification of possible being. Yet if there is a weak spot in *Realm of Shadows*, it is here, where Pippin mostly passes over in silence Hegel's understanding of life not just as a distinct category of judgement, but as itself the most primitive form of judgement and of practical spontaneity: living individuals strive to reproduce themselves through negotiation with an external environment in light of species-specific generic constraints.

In a remarkable passage, Hegel even notes that pain – the normative sense that one's condition is deficient and requires one to act – is the 'prerogative of living natures'. Life is thought's first attempt to specify what it means to be the kind of being that thinks; but given the apperceptive requirement underscored by Pippin, life fails as such an account, since life alone is insufficient for grasping what it means to be a living being. That will require an account of a form of life that *knows* itself to be alive, an account of the *rationally* living. In the Subjective Logic, thought's account of sense leads it to provide an account of the kinds of beings that can *make sense*, living members of a species and, eventually, members of historically evolving societies, with changing conceptions of what counts as true and what counts as good. Hegel shows, in other words, that a determinate conception of being must include an account of the kinds of historically self-realising, materially dependent living beings that

render the world intelligible. It is this 'logic' of historical and social self-actualisation that completes the *Science of Logic*, as Pippin shows us in his daring final chapter.

Pippin's book gives new meaning and urgency to Lenin's old chestnut about Hegel's *Logic* and *Capital*. As Pippin writes, 'Hegel's diagnosis of the fix we have gotten ourselves into consists in the claim that we have not properly understood how to understand ourselves and the social and natural world in which we dwell'. As he has also suggested in a recent article, written during the same period as *Realm of Shadows*, unless we 'understand what is to understand anything', we will be poorly equipped to understand our historical form of life, let alone to properly diagnose its deep, structural failings.

This reflects something of a shift in the thinking of Hegel's most important contemporary reader: in his earlier book, *Hegel's Practical Philosophy* (2008), Pippin had noted that 'Marx was right about Hegel', for whom 'the point of philosophy is to comprehend the world, not change it; and this for a simple reason that Marx never properly understood: it can't'. According to Pippin's recent work, by contrast, the point of philosophy is to change the world *by* comprehending it. Indeed, especially if we take into account Hegel's radical understanding of spirit as a higher form of life (rather than something other than or 'added to' the living), the reading of the *Science of Logic* that Pippin makes available could provide a new philosophical foundation for that other famous German science, often (and mistakenly) counterposed to idealism – a 'historical materialism'.

As Hegel demonstrates with his concept of life, the idea of a historically mutable 'life process' (what we might call a 'mode of production') is partly constitutive of any possible spiritual existence. And if we fail to grasp what it means to be spiritually alive, the *Logic* wagers, we will be unable to grasp what it means for anything to intelligibly *be* at all. Consequently, with *Hegel's Realm of Shadows*, Pippin not only makes another invaluable contribution to Hegel scholarship; he changes the world – if only a little bit – by helping us to understand how we ought to understand ourselves.

Jensen Suther

Ruined resentments

Wendy Brown, *In the Ruins of Neoliberalism: The Rise of Antidemocratic Politics in the West* (New York: Columbia University Press, 2019). 264pp., £62.00hb., £22.00 pb., 978 0 23155 053 6 hb., 978 0 23119 385 6 pb.

Wendy Brown has been one of the foremost critical theorists and political commentators on the left since the publication of *States of Injury: Power and Freedom in Late Modernity* in 1995. Her work has many virtues; its clarity of exposition, its willingness to blend high theory with topical examples, and its admirable interest in examining theory produced by people on the other end of the political spectrum. But its defining feature is Brown's fascination with modernity and an effort to keep alive the kind of grand critique of the age, which many scholars in her generation – often under the influence of poststructuralist philosophies – shied away from. Unlike authors with similarly epochal ambitions, such as David Harvey or Slavoj Žižek, Brown has also engaged in this critique without ultimately appealing to a comprehensive theoretical framework such as Marxism or Lacanian-Hegelianism. This gives Brown's work a democratic quality, as her many sources of authorial inspiration dialogue and wrestle with one another throughout her texts. At its best this makes for thrillingly erudite reading. Her new book *In The Ruins of Neoliberalism* demonstrates all of the virtues Brown brings to her best work, while displaying a new level of focus and synthetic acumen.

In the Ruins is the culmination of a decade of theoretical reflection on the nature of neoliberal societies. Brown's short 2010 book *Walled States, Waning Sovereignty* now seems prophetic in its insistence that with the destabilisation of national and individual identities brought about by global capitalism, the idea of walls takes on a new symbolic resonance. Brown argued that modern governments seek to shore up communal homogeneity by erecting legal and psychical barriers against an invasive 'other' responsible for this destabilisation while insulating capital from reform. The election of Donald Trump in 2016, around the rallying promise to build a wall along the Mexican border, makes the book look extremely acute in hindsight. Brown's 2015 book *Undoing the Demos: Neoliberalism's Stealth Revolution* continued the analysis in a more systematic manner. Here, she interprets neoliberalism as a governing rationality which economises everything while corroding forms and institutions of democratic opposition. *Undoing the Demos* is a more empirically driven work which examines the impact of neoliberal reforms on the ground. Both books are rigorous, but lack a decisive engagement with the rationality of neoliberalism understood on its own terms. *In the Ruins* completes the overall project, while also enriching and demanding reexamination of the earlier works, by responding to the arguments of major neoliberal thinkers, while showcasing the failings of their ideas in practice. The conclusions link these failures to the rise of Trumpism in 2016 and its resentment-driven politics.

F.A Hayek emerges as the chief intellectual foil of the book. Looking at the nuances of his work takes up the major parts of *In the Ruins*'s opening chapters. Brown's ambition is to show how many of the failings of neoliberalism which are currently being lamented by its proponents were latent in the theoretical and political ambitions of intellectuals like Hayek from the beginning. She pushes convincingly against efforts to paint Hayek as a proto-libertarian thinker who emphatically rejected all forms of social hegemony and traditionalism. Of course Hayek himself occasionally implied such a rejection, as in his classic essay at the conclusion of *The Constitution of Liberty* with the ambiguous title 'Why I Am Not A Conservative'. But Brown points out that throughout Hayek's life he continuously stressed the importance of traditional morality, alongside capitalist markets, as generative of uncoerced order. This traditional morality 'cannot be submitted to rational justification' but emerges 'spontaneously' to organically hold society together. Individuals submit themselves to the imperatives of traditional morality without reflecting on it too deeply. This is just as well, since such reflection might prompt rationalising efforts to deconstruct traditional morality in theory and thence democratic agitation to reject it in practice. As Brown puts it:

> Freedom for Hayek is not emancipation, it is not power to enact one's will. Indeed, it is not even choice. Importantly it is also not independence of the traditions

generating rules of conduct and the habits of following them. Hayek writes in one of his notebooks 'restraint is a condition, not the opposite of freedom.' ... Hayekian freedom, then, has nothing to do with emancipation from accepted social norms or powers. Rather it is the unco-erced capacity for endeavour and experimentation within codes of conduct generated by tradition and enshrined in just law, markets, and morality. Schooled by Edmund Burke, whom he modernises via Darwin, Hayek marvels at the capacity of tradition to produce social harmony and integration along with a means of change, all without recourse to the coercive agency of institutions or groups.

For Brown, this point is key to understanding the entire neoliberal project and why it appealed to many contemporary conservatives. It also demonstrates why the apparent break between neoliberalism and reactionary Trumpism is less stark than it might initially appear.

For Hayek and other neoliberals, morality and the markets operate in tandem to generate order and prosperity for all. But they will always be threatened by those who rationally seek to justify and then criticise the seeming arbitrariness and hierarchical stratification produced by moralistic capitalism. Often these progressives march under the banner of social justice; in particular by demanding the devolution of sovereignty to the demos so that it can redistribute power and wealth more equally. For Hayek and other neoliberals this would be an appalling development. But how then to push against ongoing progressive demands without lapsing into authoritarianism and silencing dissent? As is well known, some neoliberals, including Hayek himself at points, were willing to bite the bullet by flirting with authoritarian regimes which enforced moralistic capitalism and halted the emergence of socialist democracy. Pinochet´s Chile and apartheid South Africa are prominent examples, but such instances were obviously not ideal since they exposed the limitations to freedom that neoliberalism was supposed to overcome. Instead, Brown claims the neoliberals deployed three techniques to maintain the status quo without resort to strict authoritarianism. Firstly, they sought to limit legislative power by halting efforts to deliberate and pass laws related to regulating the market or encouraging emancipation from traditional morality. Secondly, neoliberals discredited all talk of 'social justice' as nonsensical and potentially totalitarian. And finally, the law was to be used to provide protections for personal morality beyond the private sphere. This last technique

was especially important, and Brown goes on to unpack its ramifications at length, providing an explanation for why many neoliberals were willing to support the efforts of employers to regulate the moral behaviour of their employees or provide protections enabling socially conservative women´s groups to spread false information about the health 'dangers' of abortion.

Brown´s analysis clarifies a great deal while challenging much conventional wisdom. Few critical theorists have managed to showcase the connections between the many different strands of neoliberal and conservative thinking and praxis so expertly, while still taking its main proponents seriously as intellectual opponents. Many of us (guilty as charged) have long been tempted to regard neoliberalism as a kind of super-liberalism or libertarianism, which created considerable puzzles in explaining why many traditionalist conservatives were attracted to its doctrines. The typical argument given is strategic rather than ideological; many strands of traditionalist conservatism supported unbridled capitalism and their alliance with neoliberals was therefore one of political realism rather than ideas. More probing commentators like Corey Robin in *The Reactionary Mind* took great efforts to show that there was a good deal more ideological overlap in the mutual desire to pushback against democratisation and preserve social hierarchies. Brown goes a step further in presenting the intricate connections between neoliberalism and traditionalism which far too many of us underestimated when reading *The Road to Serfdom*. This also helps highlight the connection between neoliberalism and the emergence of Trumpism.

The book's last chapter returns Brown to the politics of resentment she has been probing since *States of Injury* decades ago. If the book's first three chapters owe a big debt to critiques of neoliberalism from the left, Chapter Five operates on a more Nietzschean basis. She observes that, despite the rosy sublimations of neoliberal theorists and conservative traditionalists, the economisation of neoliberalisation led to a deepening nihilism and the desublimation of values. This creates a paradoxical reaction in conservative figures, who simultaneously resent the 'disenchantment of the world' while feeling liberated to unleash their anger against the Other they feel is responsible for the condition of nihilism. Invoking Marcuse´s theory of 'repressive desublimation' Brown characterises the Trumpist right as defined by exercises of an increasingly unconscionable and resentment-driven aggression to reinforce prejudice, violence and traditional values. Rather than deal with the social conditions which desacralise the world, generate inequality and create feelings of power in the face of capital, the Trumpist right directs its energies against the weak to support the strong. This is because its resentment is of a very different type than Nietzsche predicted; rather than being fired upwards against the masters it punches down towards those groups who are trying to use democratic agitation to level the social playing field. In particular, white middle-class men who feel increasingly disempowered by nihilistic economisation and inequality despise this democratising development, seeing it as a serious threat to their relatively esteemed status in the hierarchy. Many therefore put their faith in a racist, misogynistic President who seems unbound by discursive norms and is willing to offer a retrenchment of power against those who demand a fair share.

Brown´s reading in this concluding chapter impressively blends critical theory, economics, psychoanalysis and Nietzschean philosophy. Nonetheless, there are some limitations to her analysis. Perhaps the most important is that, crucial as Nietzsche is to her work, Brown largely ignores religious concerns about the importance of transcendent meaning and the challenges posed by secularisation. Indeed, not only does she largely ignore it, Nietzsche himself is chided for being 'limited by his preoccupation with God and morality as they were being challenged by science and reason.' A comprehensively critical project must put Nietzsche and Marx in dialogue by examining both material conditions and their ideologies *and* the dialectic of secularisation. There is good work being done in this area, such as in Jefferey Nichols´ interesting book *Reason, Tradition, and the Good: MacIntyre´s Tradition Constituted Reason and Frankfurt School Critical Theory*, but there is still much further to go. One hopes that Brown´s next work takes secularisation theory more seriously to weave it into the fascinating theoretical perspective she is developing.

Matthew McManus

Agents of change

Lilia D. Monzó, *A Revolutionary Subject: Pedagogy of Women of Color and Indigeneity* (New York: Peter Lang, 2019). 290pp., £95.59 hb., £36.74 pb., 978 1 43313 407 4 hb., 978 1 43313 406 7 pb.

History is usually taught through a white, Eurocentric, male lens, erasing the contributions of women. Women of Colour and Indigenous women, specifically, have consistently been erased from history; at best, marginalised to a footnote. In *A Revolutionary Subject*, Lilia D. Monzó situates Women of Colour and Indigenous women as revolutionary subjects who have played a pivotal role in revolutionary movements and who continue to do so in the present. Tracing her own path toward political consciousness, and providing the stories of revolutionary women through history, Monzó's book situates these protagonists as critical agents of change, proposing that the revolutionary subject is 'made in the process of struggle'.

Establishing the genesis for the subject of her book, Monzó examines the work of Karl Marx and Raya Dunayevskaya to situate Women of Colour and Indigenous Women as revolutionary subjects. The book begins with an intersectional reading of Marx, one that considers the ways gender and race, alongside class, have particularly impacted Women of Colour and Indigenous Women. As Monzó moves back and forth in her reading of Marx, she covers coloniality, slavery and white feminism. Acknowledging interpretations that problematise Marx, Monzó nonetheless challenges analyses that characterise Marx as Eurocentric and sexist, offering an inclusive reading that encompasses Chicanx and Latinx movements.

Monzó's text acknowledges and names women as key players in revolutionary events in history in order to combat the ways in which Women of Colour, as she writes, to 'varying degrees'

> have internalised deficit narratives, disdain for our ways of being and thinking, deep seeded fears of our physical and emotional safety, guilt for succeeding in a dominant White male world, and an uncritical gratitude for everything, including for being allowed to breathe. I want

to argue that it's time we challenge the narratives, ideologies, and normalised gendered and racialised practices that are meant to keep us 'in line'.

By considering Women of Colour and Indigenous women as central figures in revolutionary change in history, Monzó portrays what is still possible today. In addition to listing the many critical contributions by Women of Colour during moments of, or movements for, revolutionary transformation such as the Cuban Revolution, the Black Panther Party and the Zapatistas, Monzó also details her own path toward political consciousness.

Monzó writes that her 'book is about the revolutionary history and potential of racialised women', and the strength of her text lies in those sections where she introduces revolutionary Women of Colour and outlines their path toward political consciousness and political radicalisation. In Chapter 4, 'In Search of Freedom: My Road to Marx', Monzó walks the reader through experiences in her life that led her toward becoming a Marxist humanist feminist. Anticipating the reader's query, she addresses the question: 'So how did a Latina Cuban "exile" come to question and challenge all that she had grown up hearing and find her way to Marx?' Her political awareness largely stemmed from her family's move to the United States, specifically the family's move from Miami to Los Angeles. In California, away from the Cuban community, the family was left with little to no resources or connections. During their time living in California the family endured economic hardships and setbacks, which, in turn, allowed Monzó to see that the U.S. economic system treated the worker as 'subhuman'. Her awakening to feminist thought is less formed for the reader, but Monzó suggests witnessing and questioning gender roles in and outside of the home was part of that journey. Her experiences growing up frame her critique of social class and capitalism, clarifying the book's genesis and goal.

Following her description of her personal political trajectory, she moves on to list revolutionary women across history and throughout the world, providing an analysis of women such as Assata Shakur, Ding Ling, Celia Sanchez and Zhao Yiman, which situates them as pivotal players within their respective historical and revolutionary events. For example, in highlighting Shakur's role within the Black Panther Party, Monzó points out that her 'story reveals grippingly how the personal is always political and how Black revolutionaries are not born but

made in the context of Black exploitation and oppression'.

In the same chapter, she briefly explores contemporary women-centred movements such as Zapatistas, the Women's Protection Units in Rojava and Black Lives Matter. Acknowledging that these groups are women-centred, and naming the 'three self-identified Queer Black women' who founded the Black Lives Matter movement (Alicia Garza, Patrisse Khan-Cullors and Opal Tometi), is a strong step toward an inclusive pedagogical analysis that positions women as revolutionary subjects in present-day movements, but Monzó could have delved a bit deeper here.

Appropriately given the subject of the book, the voices of women *en la lucha* are represented in Chapter 6, co-authored with Anaida Colón-Muñíz, Marisol Ramirez, Cheyenne Reynoso and Martha Sanchez. Within this chapter, the four women mentioned share their narratives and reflect on the economic and gendered oppression that led to their political consciousness as revolutionary subjects, with one narrative provided in Spanish with the English translation offered as an appendix. Each woman is involved in a local organisation. Colón-Muñiz, for instance, is a coordinator of el Centro Comunitario de Chapman University, which offers education programs to the Latinx immigrant community. Sanchez is an undocumented woman who is an organiser for the Alliance of Californians for Community Empowerment, which helps low income families. It is within these stories that Monzó provides the pedagogy suggested in her title. The women detail how they arrived at political consciousness, how their experiences in poverty and as women informed how they would interact with their community. The narratives serve as a lesson on what is possible, in spite of structures of oppression: their poverty, their undocumented status and the racism they experienced from a young age.

By contrast, in the last chapter on the 'Pedagogy of Dreaming' Monzó seemingly shifts the direction of her book from the materiality of political struggle to the realm of dreams. Dream here indicates a potential for imagining a new way of being and living. She begins with a discussion of the ways Christianity and Jesus's teachings can be seen as communist, making connections through the phrase 'walking with grace'. At first, this chapter seems to deviate from the previous chapters,

which focus and delineate a Marxist humanist reading of women's contributions to revolutionary change. However, Monzó's attempt with this section, which borrows from Peter McLaren and Jose Miranda, to argue 'the communist teachings of Jesus Christ … had nothing to do with the savagery and barbarism of the colonial being that claimed to draw inspiration from Christianity to engage in a project of mass genocide against Indigenous peoples to dispossess them of land and resources' is an attempt to be inclusive of the ways in which religion and / or spirituality is central to many articulations of a need for change. While this argument seems gratuitous and underdeveloped, it sets up one of the themes of Monzó's chapter: the power of dream. A dream is a vision of what is possible. Consequently, Monzó connects religion to 'political grace', which she argues, 'draws upon our spirituality to unearth and develop these lost subaltern epistemes toward a liberatory praxis'. Monzó contends that Women of Colour and Indigenous women must see ourselves, first, as fully human and that our 'dreaming must not only reflect our desires but also be connected to how we truly see ourselves in the world today'.

Monzó offers a 'pedagogy of Women of Colour and Indigeneity'. She also provides a pedagogical approach to history by suggesting what might be learnt from women's roles in revolutionary events:

The oppression of Indigenous women and Women of Colour is clearly a function of a complex interplay between gender, colonialism, race, class, and other antagonisms. It is my contention that this violence against Indigenous women and Women of Colour will not be eradicated unless we develop a struggle that is anti-capitalist, anti-imperialist, anti-sexist, anti-racist as well as against all other forms of oppression.

Monzó's contention is a timely one. Her book serves as a guide to the past and as a blueprint for what could be possible in the future. Read during this pandemic, as uprisings against police brutality continue across the United States, *A Revolutionary Subject* provides some reflection on the ways capitalist society treats the worker, especially the worker of colour, and reminds the reader of the power of the collective. Monzó shows that minoritised women as a collective have the power to shift present day conditions just as they have participated in revolutionary movements throughout history. The hope, or the dream, as Monzó would argue, lies in the collective struggle against a capitalist system. One can only imagine the agents of change today's systems of oppression are creating.

Lydia Saravia

Ghosts in fishnets

Elizabeth Otto, *Haunted Bauhaus: Occult Spirituality, Gender Fluidity, Queer Identities, and Radical Politics* (Cambridge, MA: The MIT Press, 2019). 282pp., £28.00 hb., 978 0 26204 329 8

I once heard the artist David Shrigley remark that the reason he became an artist was due to an adolescent fascination with art students, particularly those at the Glasgow School of Art in the late 1980s. He wanted not so much to pursue a career in art production as to briefly inhabit the outré confines of art school, with its outsider posturing, outlandish fashion, tactile classrooms, potential for sexual liberation, and, above all, the embrace of that seemingly ageless genie-in-the-bottle: cool. In a panel discussion in the early 2000s with several other artists at the ICA, in London, he suggested that the only real task of the art student was to serve the drive for experimentation, whether it results in blurry photographs, plasticine teapots or paintings of questionably brown armchairs. For Shrigley, to be an art student in Glasgow was to be free of the normies, forever at the fringes of the work-a-day conformity of religion and politics that emanated from some creaking church hall in the Scottish suburbs.

Reading Elizabeth Otto's admirable book, *Haunted Bauhaus*, I was put in mind of Shrigley's characterisation of what it means to be part of a student collective, and the conflicting impulses that mark out its territory, variously governed by the personal, pedagogical, spiritual and architectural. The myth of art school experience as an embodied experiment is often traced to the Bauhaus's iconic activities, to which, despite its brief life between 1919-1933, many contemporary art schools with collaborative studio disciplines (like the Glasgow School of Art) can mark a direct line.

Otto's project here is to unpack this myth by deemphasising the objects generated by its more prominent members, Paul Klee, Wassily Kandinsky, Oskar Schlemmer and Joseph Albers, in favour of celebrating the 'life experiments' of a number of lesser known students and teachers. She focuses particularly on the *Bauhäusler*'s work with photography and photomontage, drawing on ghostly double-exposures to argue that the school was haunted by a repressed sexual counterculture. The school's legacy, now one hundred years old, is apparently ready for a ghost tour. Otto wants to prise open the closet and allow the spectral other to roam the halls, free to spook the 'rational modernism' of the austere chairs, tea infusers and nesting tables that have made its name. Her attempt to reintegrate these ghostly presences into the school's history is guided by what Freud in 'Notes Upon a Case of Obsessional Neurosis' (1909) called 'unlaid ghosts': 'In an analysis, a thing which has not been understood inevitably reappears; like an unlaid ghost, it cannot rest until the mystery has been solved and the spell broken.'

The foundation of the *Bauhäusler*'s life experiments was Walter Gropius's 'Program of the Staatliche Bauhaus in Weimar', published in April 1919, where he collapsed the hierarchy between teachers and students, calling for all members to pursue a utopian future that would 'rise toward heaven from the hands of a million workers like the crystal symbol of a new faith.' But while Gropius was animated by the prospect of an eclectic and quasi-spiritual vision, as Otto reveals, it required another figure, Johannes Itten, the charismatic teacher of the school's preliminary course, to embed an unorthodox pedagogy. Itten helped convert students to a hybrid religion called Mazdaznan, which combined Zoroastrianism, ayurvedic medicine, tantric Hinduism, Christianity and ancient Egyptian philosophy. Its practice required strict vegetarianism, extended fasting, hot baths, breathing exercises and a near-constant program of singing and smiling. He had students wear ornate ceremonial robes and, after assuming the medieval character of the ratcatcher from Hamelin, led them to the roof where they disrobed for gymnastics, encouraged to imagine themselves as a piece of stained glass. Itten often told his class: 'Before you can draw a tiger, you have to learn to roar like a tiger.' One of the student converts to this esoteric religion was Paul Citroen, who in a 1922 drawing titled *Mazdaznan Regime*, documented an exercise that showed practitioners shaking, defecating and vomiting while wrapped in bandages, anticipating Hermann Nitsch's Viennese Actionism of the 1960s.

Otto writes that one of the reasons Mazdaznan was embraced with such fervour was due to the ambivalence over industrialised technology many students felt in the wake of World War I. Adolf Koch, the founder of German nudist camps and exercise schools, echoed the prevailing sentiment at the Bauhaus when he wrote that citizens required an urgent balm for 'the misery of our times'. In privileging the body over the object, the body over the machine, students were able to circle back and create objects with inflections of the body. Influenced by Mazdaznan's sun exercises, László Moholy-Nagy created *Light Prop*, a mechanical sculpture in the form of Baroque-era water fountains intended to create immersive spectacles through light. Moholy-Nagy reflected on the sculpture as if it could generate spirits: 'I felt like the sorcerer's apprentice. The mobile was so startling in its articulations of light and shadow sequences that I almost believed in magic.' According to Otto, the material object here is infused with the modern experiences generated by the Mazdaznan exercises, uniting the sensory and spiritual to transcend the impetus for capitalist production. It's a powerful rewrite of how we have long seen these objects, as products of a rational modernism that reshaped the market for utilitarian design.

In the middle section of *Haunted Bauhaus*, Otto shifts away from reintegrating school spirits into the official history to focus on its 'shadow masculinity' and 'femininities in transformation'. The guide here is Michel Foucault's critique of the concept of sexual identity as unified and fixed in *The History of Sexuality*. In place of what Foucault calls the 'austere monarchy of sex', one should think of an open structure of 'bodies and pleasures'. The political right-wing's fetishisation of armoured masculinity permeated the Weimar Republic, and the Bauhaus offered a shadow-site in which to renegotiate the status of the male body.

Profiles of Marianne Brandt and Marcel Breur reveal photomontages that doubled, mocked, undercut or made impotent the seemingly impenetrable fascist physique. These speculative attempts to reconstruct masculinity were part of a broader utopian project oriented away from war. Conversely, work by *Bauhäusler*'s Ré Soupault and Gertrud Arndt embraced emergent femininities, exploring new ways of living and being, exemplars of the Bauhaus's spirit of New Womanhood, a concept generated by the suffragettes and consolidated by interwar

cinema, such as in Marlene Dietrich's star vehicle, *The Blue Angel* (1930).

Building on these explorations of emergent bodies, *Haunted Bauhaus* moves into a higher gear making a striking claim about queerness at the school. Otto suggests that much of Bauhaus activity was attended by a 'present-yet-hidden spectre of queer desire independent of their makers' sexualities.' Given the Weimar Republic's restrictive laws around homosexuality, abortion and birth control, Otto reads experiments with photography as evidence of quiet illegality, with the *Bauhäusler* as resistance fighters against the strictures of gender binaries. The argument is that eccentric modes of being that challenged normative gender roles qualify as encoded queerness, but the code is so opaque as to be invisible.

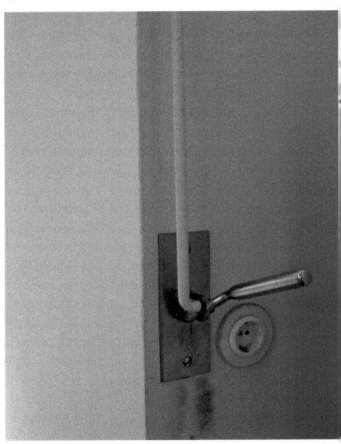

While it might be a diverting exercise to project gender fluidity onto these photographs, however, retrospectively assigning the past an understanding of gender and sexuality of the kind espoused by Judith Butler seems not only anachronistic but prescriptive. What is read here as encoded queerness could be interpreted simply as the clownish theatricality that emerges at a party. While this theatricality was informed by the chaotic social milieu of the school, men in drag do not necessarily indicate some emergent fluidity. It could, indeed, signify the reverse, where playful theatricality serves to reinforce the gender binary.

Otto offers close readings of numerous photographs, such as Florence Henri's nude wearing a leather belt and Max Peiffer Watenphul's portrait of art-dealer Johanna Ey, but one consequence of the objects' intense material scrutiny is that they become less convincing territory on which to map gender fluidities. Sexual identity may not be fixed, but is it always unfixed? Are the open borders always being crossed, or on the *verge* of being crossed? The photographs, however dusty from the archive, appear to reject Otto's readings, which seem lost on the road from the lecture hall to the neat campus office (where grant applications await). To embark on a project to solve the mystery of these images, as Otto gives as her aim, takes for granted that their mystery exists, but *joie de vivre* does not always mean gender trouble. If this sounds reductive, or out of tune with Otto's desire to upend the Bauhaus's official narrative, it's because the objects used as evidence do not sufficiently demonstrate her claims. The reader requires more than painted moustaches and fishnets to be convinced the Bauhaus was a site of contingent sexual identities.

We are on less shaky ground in the final chapter, which explores the radical politics that consumed the Bauhaus's later years. In 1930, when Mies van der Rohe took over as director of the Dessau site from Hannes Meyer, he sought to solve the institution's political crisis by closing the school for six weeks and expelling politically active students. Naturally, this only increased political activity, and there were soon physically divided meetings in the canteen with Communists on one side, Nazis on the other. The Communists argued that you could only be a true *Bauhäusler* if you were a Marxist, as Marxism alone stood for freedom and progress. This led to factionalism on the left and increased power for the rightwing students, who were early adopters of the swastika, painting it on the studio door of junior master Gunta Stölzl, who was married to the Jewish student, Arieh Sharon. When the school closed in 1933, Franz Ehrlich, a noted Communist, helped produce an anti-Nazi journal for which he was sent to the Buchenwald Concentration Camp. To survive, Ehrlich designed the motto that appeared above the camp's gates, *Jedem das Seine* – 'To Each His Own' – and in a chilling turn, utilised the sans serif font forged at the Bauhaus. In a few brief years, the political polarisation at the school had led to an afterlife where a Communist anti-Nazi had become a collaborator with the National Socialist State. The revelation that Nazis were operating among the student body strikes a powerful red line through the school's textbook image of liberal unity and is perhaps the book's most persuasive argument for rewriting its official history.

Much of the new material Otto has uncovered is significant in expanding our understanding of Germany's cultural and political contradictions in the interwar period, particularly in how they intersected at the Bauhaus. Its provocations regarding gender fluidity and the decentering of the school's major figures are likely to spur ongoing debate. However, it is the peculiar irony of much art historical writing that even when exploring the most aesthetically exuberant and revolutionary works of art, it often reads neutrally. The dictum of looking coldly at an object or performance in order to comprehend its cultural property becomes evermore frustrating when there is so much happening in the frame. The problem here is not Otto's alone, whose prose conforms to the broader strictures of academic writing. There will be no joining in of the orgy, the scholar says; one must decorously observe the revelry from afar.

While there is a resistance in *Haunted Bauhaus* to the austere monarchy of sex, there is an adherence to the austere monarchy of language, where objects are held at a distance and ideas hemmed into stony sentences, ready for inspection. There are nods and polite finger wags and the occasional shrug, but there is no place in the language of this book for the vomiting, defecating, dancing and fucking it so laboriously and repetitively describes. None of the artists appear to be at play, despite the fact we are told they are always playing. For all the school's liberating tendencies, the story of its liberation is one of rote description and note taking, not inhabitation or playfulness.

Nathan Dunne

Bernard Stiegler, 1952-2020

Gerald Moore

The death of Bernard Stiegler in August, aged 68, will surely be met by a glut of biographies documenting a far from conventional philosophical eccentric. It is undeniable that he could be difficult, and not just because of the density of his prose and tendency to write exclusively in neologisms; but he could also be extraordinarily hospitable and at ease with others from all walks of life, not least, perhaps, because he had walked so many lives himself. Both of his grandfathers were German immigrants. One raced cars. His father, Robert, was a self-taught television engineer, among the first of his kind. Stiegler's childhood was mostly spent in Sarcelles, at a time when the village quadrupled in size, transitioning from a sleepy rural backwater to a multicultural satellite of rapidly modernising Paris. He grew up, in other words, at the outset of what he would later theorise as a period of profound technological and social disruption – the 'age of acceleration' spanning from the ever-expanding world of the car, plane and rocket, to the shrinking, retreating, microspheres of the pocket screen.

The turbulence of postwar France left its mark on him. A hardline sixteen-year-old communist who dropped out of school around May '68, he would come to depict the protests as individualistic and lifestyle-oriented. The first great symptom of hyperindustrial decadence: consumerism dissolving the social super-ego that served as a precondition of the very desire that the protesters sought to unleash. His own post-'68 drifting matched his later diagnosis of an era slipping into nihilism, occasioned by the relentlessly disadjusting rapidity of change. Glimpses of this period are offered up in the unusually autobiographical *Age of Disruption* (2016), which recounts how he fantasised about becoming a saxophonist, novelist or poet, but stumbled over having nothing to say. At the age of nineteen he fathered a child – the philosopher Barbara Stiegler – and suffered a psychotic break after being sent to a psychiatric hospital, due to alcoholism, from which he hitchhiked an escape after meeting a patient so institutionalised that they could not leave. He was homeless and living in a car when a farmer took pity on him and gave him land. There Stiegler raised goats and a pet monkey, Zoë, who swung freely through the trees until she got jealous of his first wife and took to attacking her. When drought killed off the farm he transformed a brothel into a jazz club, one frequented by his first philosophical mentor Gérard Granel, until the police drove him out of business following his refusal to turn informer on local mobsters using his premises to sell heroin. Famously, Stiegler then turned to robbing banks, before getting caught on his fourth go. During a five-year stint in prison he went on hunger strike, turning his teeth black, until he was granted a single-occupancy cell where he became obsessed with the image of four-dimensional spirals and read Mallarmé and Husserl in silence, seeing confinement as a real-life version of the phenomenological *epokhē*. He had once been funny, he would later reflect, but prison put an end to that. Henceforth, although still capable of considerable humour, he bore the weight of the world and became a centre of gravity, a point around which others would rotate. His incarceration only became public in a 2003 talk, 'How I Became a Philosopher', published in *Acting Out* and given just as he rose to superstardom. There, Stiegler recalled that, amidst enforced solitude, he saw how, in stripping away the outside, prison also strips out interiority, forcing us to begin rebuilding a world, and by extension, a self, from scratch. He reiterated the message in interviews given during Covid-induced lockdown, and was a pliant prisoner now, as then – a model convert who, upon his release in 1983, declined involvement with Michel Foucault's reform movement, the *Groupe d'information sur les prisons*.

Granel saw in Stielger incipient genius, not to mention the significance of the spiral – 'voilà c'est ça, ta philosophie!' – distance-supervising a first thesis on Plato and Marx as thinkers of technology, before steering Stiegler towards Derrida and the École des hautes études en sciences sociales for a PhD. *The Fault of Epimetheus* was submitted in 1993 and published a year later as Volume One of the *Technics and Time* series. It was here that Stiegler laid out his philosophical stall, combining Greek mythology and Husserlian phenomenology with Heidegger, Derrida, biology, the history of technology, the paleoanthropology of André Leroi-Gourhan and the transductive relations of Gilbert Simondon, to argue that humans – whom he would later claim are only ever 'intermittently *not* inhuman' – only exist, or rather 'consist', through technics. By this time, he had married Derrida's other *protégée*, Catherine Malabou, whom he continued to describe as the 'most *brilliant* philosopher' long after their divorce, and passed through the Collège international de philosophie, on his way to the Université de technologie de Compiègne, where he stayed, albeit minimally, alongside recurring professorial stints at Goldsmiths and later Nanjing, until his retirement in 2018. He had mooted the plan of continuing to work in the United States, using the salaries on offer to subsidise his many other projects. The robberies, however, returned to haunt him in the Trump era: despite his criminal record having been expunged, he was blocked from a spell at Brown planned for the same year.

Derrida's philosophy of the trace described how earlier terms in a series are retroactively constituted and thereby also transformed by their subsequent and future iterations. Stiegler thought his friend and mentor equivocated on whether traces operated within nature, and not just in the structures of writing that deconstruction analysed. Derrida was similarly unpersuaded that a driver might 'read' and 'write' a car, or a musician an instrument, in the way that an author would a book. In addition to the random, mutating, iterations of Darwinian evolution, which change the way we read the history of a given organism, Stiegler proposed that we should also recognise how technical objects transform the bodies of their users. The *Fault of Epimetheus* refers to the Titan who forgot to give people qualities, thereby necessitating our constitution through technics, understood as a supplement that both conditions and makes impossible the very subjects it brings into existence. The book goes on to recast Derridean *différance* as a theory of the reciprocal reinvention, or 'co-individuation', of the 'what' and the 'who', the tool and the tool-user. The *who* invents the *what*, which in turn reinvents the who, transforming the interiority of the subject – the experience of time as memory and anticipation, attention, desire and knowledge – whose increased mastery of the tool means that it, too, can be reinvented, and so on. This is Stiegler's image of the spiral, oscillating between tool and user as it projects forward in time, anticipating the future in a *potentially* never-ending process of mutual refinement. Nowadays, however, that potential is largely unrealised, on account of what Stiegler theorised, reworking Marx, as 'proletarianisation': the externalisation of know-how and life skills (*savoir-faire* and *savoir-vivre*) into machines without there being any corresponding re-internalisation of knowledge on the part of users, who find themselves henceforth reduced to the vitiating passivity of consumption without production. It is not just labour that is nowadays proletarianised, but also desire and thought, which are increasingly automated by marketing and the algorithms that make decisions for us, he argued, most notably in *The Automatic Society, 1: The Future of Work* (2015).

Stiegler's politics started to come to the fore in the second and third volumes of *Technics and Time: Disorientation* (1996) and *The Time of Cinema and the Question of Ill-Being* (2001). The latter has been described by his friend and fellow-traveller Jean-Hugues Barthélémy as Stiegler's *magnum opus*, marking the transition from the 'philosophical anthropo(techno)logy' of his earlier work to what was, *per* the title of a book from 2009, a 'new critique of a political economy'. The two later volumes are marked by an emerging activism, signaling the birth of a project rooted in what Barthélémy calls the methodology of '*prolongement-dépassement*', or extension that also goes beyond.

Stiegler went beyond deconstruction by extending Derrida into technics, psychoanalysis and 'libidinal economy', but also because, over and above just breaking down our relationship with technology, he sought to 'recompose' it. The future is not just already out there, waiting to come, but must actively be created if we are to avoid the entropy of mere 'becoming'. Stiegler's way of doing this was to campaign for an inversion of the economic model that allows market-produced technologies to determine who we get to be, in favour of developing tools of 'de-proletarianisation' that would allow us to contribute to constructing the world and people we would like to see. Creating 'an industrial policy of technologies of the spirit', and later an 'economy of contribution', were the stated manifesto goals of Ars Industrialis, the think-tank-cum-lobby-group-cum-charity Stiegler co-founded in 2005 with others including his third wife Caroline Stiegler (née Fayat), then a legal advisor to his literary agent, now a judge. The birth of Ars Industrialis went hand in hand with Stiegler's founding (with Vincent Puig) of the *Institut de recherche et d'innovation* (IRI), following his directorship of several other centres designed to bridge industrial and academic research: Institut national de l'audiovisuel (INA), Pierre Boulez's Institut de recherche et coordination acoustique/musique (IRCAM) and the Department of Cultural Development at the Centre Pompidou. Also based at the Pompidou, IRI ultimately became independent and remained the principal hub of Stiegler's activities up until his death.

These institutional inventions came in the middle of an astonishingly prolific period of writing during which Stiegler wrote or lead-authored over twenty books, including multiple series, in the seven years between 2003 and 2010. Among the most important works of these years are the triple-volumed *Disbelief and Discredit* (2004-6) and double-volumed *Symbolic Misery* (2004, 2005), both of which drew heavily on Freud to revisit the fate of desire under consumerism. The problem, Stiegler now argued, is that consumerist technologies, surrounded by marketing, the user lock-in of warranties and guarantees, and built-in obsolescence, make us (the *who*) without enabling us to make them (the *what*) in return. The average iPhone addict cannot pull off its back and tamper with the black box of smartphone technology to come up with alternative modes of use. We no longer get the feeling of self-worth ('primordial narcissism') that comes from using technics to shape the world, and by extension ourselves. The result is a prevailing feeling of nothingness and despair that is common also to terrorists – desperate to perform the sublime they cannot feel – and those seduced by the return of the extreme right.

In his middle (libidinal economic or 'general organological') period of work, *différance* became the '*différance* of pleasure', with desire 'sublimated' into existence through the deferral of satisfaction, which is itself regulated by the social organisations that govern our adoption of technology. When society tells us to consume without limits, that process of deferral and anticipation never happens, giving way to 'drive-based', compulsive behaviours. We are automated by prescribed habits to crave the next dopamine buzz. Here is where Stiegler differs from Deleuze and Guattari: desire is not just out there, 'natural', and revolutionary, kept castrated by its reduction, by capitalism, to impotent fantasy. It has to be nurtured and created. It is fragile and can collapse.

'General organology' names what Stiegler saw as the new discipline of thinking biology ('physiological', or, later, 'endosomatic' organs) and technics ('artifactual', later 'exosomatic', organs) alongside social organisation, which regulates our interactions with technologies, by prescribing limits on when we use them, and for what. Understood as 'digital studies' – also the name of the international research network Stiegler founded in 2012 – cultural history becomes the study of the transformations of thought and experience opened up when bodies are 'grammatised', or 'de- and re-functionalised', by revolutions in the technical systems that organise society – from knapped flints and cave paintings to writing, printing and, ultimately, the digital. By the time of *What Makes Life Worth Living* (2010), the Platonic-Derridean concept of the *pharmakon*, a simultaneous remedy and poison, had taken centre stage in the presentation of this argument. Just as the smartphone frees up time and eliminates space while also weakening memory and detaching us from our immediate surroundings, Stiegler argued, all technologies are both curative and toxic, opening up and closing down possibility. Regimes of politics and libidinal economy are differentiated by whether they reign in the toxic side, or whether, like late capitalism, they cultivate it by eliminating constraints and failing to develop new educational norms.

The question of education preoccupied Stiegler between *Taking Care of Youth and the Generations* (2008) and *States of Shock: Stupidity and Knowledge in the 21st Century* (2012), which picked up on the relationship between screen exposure and attention deficit disorders. To some this confirmed the impression of Stiegler as a bit of a panic-merchant, yet accusations of Luddism routinely fail to account for his work on creating alternatives: to experiment, for example, with the possibilities of digital education. He hated the attritional consumerism

110

of MOOCS, but was among the first to pioneer smaller-scale digital teaching. IRI developed digital distance participation tools for annotating and categorising film and text, which Stiegler put to use in his own doctoral seminars from 2010. When plans to turn Caroline's family home in Épineuil-le-Fleuriel into a school proved too ambitious, he settled for a summer school, launched in 2011 via his website, Pharmakon.fr. For several years as many as eighty-odd visitors would camp and eat for free (or rather, pay voluntary contributions) around his beloved medieval millpond, while up to two thousand followed from afar. Participants would sit with minimal breaks through gruelling ten-hour days of philosophical discussion capped by evening sessions on experimental art, all in Stiegler's disused concrete barn. The debates were often explosive. In 2016, for instance, Stiegler bawled out visitors from the popular student-led movement *Nuit debout*, then busy protesting reforms to French employment law. He accused them of 'lacking gravity', standing around doing nothing, because they were not actively involved in the creation of new knowledge.

For all its toxicity, he insisted, neoliberalism had succeeded because the knowledge it created had been therapeutic – at least to some, if only for a while. In so arguing, he alienated his guests but hinted at the central concept of his final monographic series, *Qu'appelle-t-on panser?*, a pun on Heidegger's *What Is Called Thinking?*, where *penser* (thinking) is inseparable from salving (*panser*). The problem with contemporary knowledge-production is not just that academics are proletarianised and unable to understand the import of the technologies on which they rely to make their claims, but that knowledge, subject to profit motives and hyper-specialisation, has become divorced from its original, 'negentropic', 'antientropic', function of enabling us to live better. The references to thermodynamics had been there, lurking, from the start, but now pointed to Stiegler's main focus, thanks to the major late influences of the economist Nicholas Georgescu-Roegen and the biologist Alfred Lotka. After Stiegler's first, foundational, discovery of the technical constitution of 'noetic', 'exosomatic' (intermittently not inhuman) life, he held that his second great contribution to philosophy was to grasp how we employ technics to defer entropic collapse. That collapse is now staring us in the face in the form of the 'Entropocene'. If fake news and climate-change-disavowal have gained traction, it is only because they do more to salve than the academic abstractions that currently pass for truth.

Stiegler's summer school was discontinued in 2017, partly because of his annoyance at the rise of 'philosophical tourists' but mostly so he could focus instead on his next project, the 'experimental learning territory of Plaine commune', set up in Seine-Saint-Denis in conjunction with national and local government and a range of corporate investors. The aim of Plaine Commune was to take one of the most deprived and multicultural areas of France, considered to be particularly susceptible to the disruptive automation of employment, and engage its citizens in using digital tools for urban regeneration and the creation of 'negentropic localities'. For all Stiegler's relentlessness and in spite of subsequent success, the project was initially beset by funding issues, court cases, political opportunism and the half-hearted participation of municipalities the project sought to serve.

The fire in an increasingly exhausted Stiegler was starting to flicker. He considered *The Automatic Society, 1* to be his most important work – aside from that which would appear just before his death, *Bifurquer: Il n'y a pas d'alternative* (2020) – and laboured on a sequel that just would not come. As his output slowed, so the number of promised titles increased. Substantial drafts of *Technics and Time 4, Symbols and Diabols*, were in private circulation by 2004, but it was never released because it grew into volume 5, *Le Défaut qu'il faut*, which needed a prequel to fill in gaps in the argument. By 2018, *Le Défaut qu'il faut* had been pushed back to volume 7 – one of ten or so books, or fragments of books, which might make up his archive, including volume 2 of *The Automatic Society*, volume 4 of *Disbelief and Discredit*, two volumes on aesthetics, *De la mystagogie*, originally scheduled for publication around 2011, and a third volume of *Qu'appelle-t-on panser?*

Back in 2016, it took the unexpected *Age of Disruption*, subtitled 'How not to go mad?' in the original French, to break the writing deadlock. The book saw the philosopher open up about his experience of depression and the fundamental role he accorded to writing as a form of self-therapy – a clue, perhaps, as to why he can read to others as though writing primarily for himself. He also waded in on the epidemic of suicides afflicting all ends of society, from the abandonment of the *banlieues* to the hopeless youth and jaded disruptors of wealthy Palo Alto. He would ultimately return to this thought via Arnold Toynbee: a society 'always dies from suicide or murder – and nearly always from the former'.

The final flurry of Stiegler's work combined negentropic locality with the need to avert this suicide, both individual and civilisational. In December 2019, Ars Industrialis was relaunched as the Association of Friends of the Thunberg Generation, in coalition with the French wings of Youth for Climate and Extinction Rebellion, to fight for the dream of a 'Neganthropocene'. And, this summer, the work he oversaw and co-authored with the Internation Collective was published – *Bifurquer (Bifuricate: There is No Alternative)*. The former had long been in the offing. Ars Industrialis was well down on its peak membership of over 40,000 and relied on Stiegler's royalties for revenue. The insuperable rise of big tech meant that its mission, and the free software movement to which it had hitched itself, had failed in Stiegler's eyes, and his energies were now more focused on the planet. *Bifurquer* had begun life in September 2018 at the Serpentine Gallery's 'Work Marathon', and was intended as a follow-up to the 'Scientists' Final Warning' on climate change of earlier that year, bringing together over fifty researchers from across the disciplines to lay out the theoretical groundwork for how contributive economic neganthropy might take off. A draft was presented to the United Nations on the hundredth anniversary of its foundation in January 2020, with publication following in July, after monumental editorial efforts that included a near-fatal bout of sepsis. He wound down in hospital with a bit of light work, drafting multiple proposals for a global 'Network of Ecologically Smart Territories' (NEST), including the Galapagos, which he planned to launch on return from what proved to be his last family holiday in Corsica. Of *Bifurquer*, Stiegler euphorically insisted, 'It's the best book I have ever read!' By his own definition it was a 'miracle', a hitherto impossible bifurcation able to provide hope in the face of 'absolute nihilism'.

The man whose list of institutions pointed to a longing for collectivity ever since the disappointments of May '68 had finally, he hoped, made a group to succeed him.

Gerald Moore is Associate Professor at Durham University and chair of the Collège scientifique *at the IRI.*

Neil Davidson, 1957-2020

Steve Edwards

Neil Davidson – the most significant Scottish intellectual of the radical left – died at the beginning of May 2020 from a brain tumour. He was 62.

Davidson was a prolific writer of historical sociology and a critical analyst of contemporary politics, particularly the Scottish scene. His learning was immense, his reading power prodigious and his intellect both generous and daring. His book collection installed in a garage at his home, Cauther Ha', West Lothian, actually required library stacks. Davidson was author of three monographs: *The Origins of Scottish Nationhood* (2000); *Discovering the Scottish Revolution 1692-1746* (2003), which was awarded both the Isaac & Tamara Deutscher Memorial Prize and the Saltire Society's Andrew Fletcher of Saltoun award; and the monumental *How Revolutionary were the Bourgeois Revolutions?* (2012). He published three collections of essays and, always committed to collaborative work, co-edited significant works: *Alasdair MacIntyre's Engagement with Marxism* (2008); *Neoliberal Scotland* (2010); *The Longue Durée of the Far-Right* (2014); and *No Problem Here: Understanding Racism in Scotland* (2018).[1] This bibliography gives only a limited sense of his work, because he published on a wide range of topics in Marxist theory, history and politics in academic journals, the press and the publications of the far left. He was also a frequent speaker on campaign platforms and at socialist gatherings. In an appreciation of Davidson and his work, George Kerevan, journalist and one-time MP (SNP) for East Lothian, observed that he accomplished enough to fill three academic lifetimes.[2]

This record was all the more noteworthy because it was only in 2008 that Davidson was appointed to his first university position at Strathclyde, moving in 2013 to the Sociology Department at Glasgow and he never occupied a position above the basic lecturer grade. Davidson was born in Aberdeen, into a working-class family, with some relatives still working the land.[3] One grandfather was a farm servant who moved to the city in the 1920s and an aunt worked as a shepherdess (the Scottish peasantry survived in the area much longer than the rest of mainland Britain and Davidson's family history finds its echo in the greatest work of British Marxist modernism: Lewis Grassic Gibbon's *Sunset Song* of 1932). Throughout his life he was acutely aware of his class origins; his only academic qualification came much later with an Open University degree (he studied modern art and popular culture). He began his working life as a clerk in the health service and then took the civil service exam. After living for a short period in London, Davidson moved to Edinburgh to work in the Scottish Office, whose functions were transferred to the Scottish Executive in 1999, rising to provide advice on policy implementation to the Permanent Secretary to the Scottish First Minister, Alex Salmond. Yet while he occupied a position as a state manager, he was also a leading socialist activist, having joined the Socialist Workers Party in 1978. An active member for thirty-five years, he would later break with that group, but its particular theoretical contribution and militant ethos remained enduring influences.[4]

While working as a civil servant Davidson would read and write before dawn. It was during this period that he published his two major studies of the development of capitalism in Scotland.[5] Scotland was a very uneven social formation: the lowland area centred on Edinburgh was an advanced commercial centre, producing major Enlightenment thinkers such as Adam Smith, Adam Ferguson, David Hume, James Steuart and the stadial historians who influenced Marx, but the highlands remained dominated by peasant agriculture under control of feudal warrior chiefs organised in Clans. The consolidation of capitalism in Britain involved the destruction of clan society and the brutal 'highland clearances'.[6] Employing categories that would become central to his subsequent work, he viewed the emergence of modern Scotland as an outcome of 'uneven and combined development' (Trotsky) and 'passive revolution' from above (Gramsci). Scotland was, he said, the very first example of a capitalist modernisation carried out from above. Importantly, for understanding modern Scottish politics, he demonstrated that a national structure of feeling was not based on some enduring *'Braveheart* effect', rather it was a decidedly modern construction. It was only with the Act of Union that the British state eradicated the contradiction of distinct highland and lowland social formations. The British state, he argues, was ultimately only cemented with the defeat of the Jacobite Lords at Cullodon in 1746.

Neil at Ian Hamilton Finlay's *Little Sparta*.

What might seem like a local matter turned out to be an occurrence of epochal significance in establishing the international predominance of British capitalism.

The rout of the Jacobites eradicated the remaining power base for an Absolutist alternative to the rule of capital. Scotland supplied the British regime, at home and in its colonial forms, with important resources – a key port and industrial commodities in the form of fish, jute, tobacco, and later engineering - but also many of its military and administrative cadre. The Scots played a central role in Imperial project and they conceived of themselves as Britons. As Keravan observes, Davidson may not have been aware of it at this time, but these studies allow for an understanding of current Scottish national consciousness as a distinctly modern development with anti-systemic dimensions that would break the hegemony of Labour and pose a serious challenge to the integrity of the British state. Davidson's work thus involves a challenge to both defenders of the Union and cherished mythemes of Scottish nationalism. It is said that on being advised that to understand Scottish history he needed to read these works, Alex Salmond was astonished to find that a member of his staff was a Marxist!

In 2012 Davidson published his major work: *How Revolutionary were the Bourgeois Revolutions?*[7] In *New Left Review*, Dylan Riley summarised the ambitions of the book:

> Epic in scale, *How Revolutionary?* is by any standards a significant achievement. Its intellectual scope is commendably wide-ranging; no one else has put together such a broad field of references on this subject, or conjoined such widely dispersed historical and theoretical arguments. In addition, Davidson discusses virtually every key issue in Marxist political sociology, sweeping from the tributary mode to the nation-state, the differentiation of the peasantry to the revolution *en permanence*.[8]

This assessment is all the more telling, because of Riley's very substantial disagreements with key aspects of Davidson's argument. Across 700 pages, Davidson explored the genealogy of the concept of bourgeois revolution along with conditions for the rise of capitalism, arguing that by 1749 capitalism existed as a world system and there could be no retreat to pre-capitalist social relations, only a path beyond to socialism. The book is an outstanding work of history and sociology, commanding a huge literature, but rooted in the idea of uneven and combined development and the distinction between revolution from below and from above (Gramsci's 'passive revolution'). He also insisted on demarcating genuine social revolutions that inaugurated a new mode of production from merely political revolutions, which changed the staff, but left the prevailing property relations in place. The major turning points in the consolidation of capitalism involve both revolutions from below: England in the seventeenth century, France in 1789; and a series of passive revolutions: Bismarck's defeat of Denmark in 1864 and the unification of the German states, the Meiji Restoration and the Risorgimento. One central point of the book is to confront Stalinist mystification that described as 'socialist' or 'on the socialist path' states created without popular upheavals. It was a misconception that gave rise to a devastating catalogue of defeats. As Jamie Allinson noted, 'Even the national liberation states of the latter twentieth century, garlanded with red flags and portraits of Lenin', followed the same pattern.[9] It is noteworthy that critics of *How Revolutionary?* have largely avoided the challenge of thinking about how these states morphed, without break, into forms of capitalism.[10] Davidson was remorseless in pointing out the contradictions of those who held illusions in these societies and grasped better than anyone that any robust account of bourgeois revolution would have to test the concept against the post-Stalinist societies.

Setting aside World Systems Theory, on the Marxist Left there are currently three schools of thought on the development of capitalism (it goes without saying that they all have implications for current political understanding). One position associated with the 'Political Marxism' of Robert Brenner and his followers, sees capitalism developing uniquely in Southern England (possibly in Holland and Catalonia as well – they disagree over this) as a result of the historic weakness of English feudal property relations that enabled the development of market-dependent free-wage labour to develop. Some Political Marxists argue there was no capitalism in France until after 1871, and, in one extreme case, until the 1950s. International capitalism from this perspective is an effect of British predominance. Although, in his own *Merchants and Revolution* Bob Brenner does speak to the seventh-century revolution in Britain, his followers have little use for the idea of 'bourgeois revolution', particularly as it applies to 1789. In *The Origins of Capitalism* Ellen Wood presents the concept as a hopeless mess. Davidson was particularly opposed to purism of the Brenner School, which he felt did not grasp the uneven and combined

character of *particular* capitalist formations. In his final intellectual appearance Davidson organised a large conference on UCD in Glasgow where he debated Brenner. (Part way through that conference, disoriented, he went to hospital and received his diagnosis.)

A second globalist approach emphasises 'trajectories of accumulation' developing within existing non-capitalist societies, which leverage internal transformations, creating centres of capitalism. Here we could cite: Banaji, Beckert, Liu and Van der Linden. For this trend, bourgeois revolution is not essential to the development of capitalism and Maurice Dobb and the British Marxist historians may have done a mis-service in making the category the focus of socialist attention. Davidson's book is the main modern defence of the third approach: the idea that revolutionary upheavals instigated major transformations in modes of production. Rather than a misconceived importation of liberal historiography into Marxism as some suggest, for Davidson bourgeois revolution was a necessary idea for Marx and Engels that allowed them to break with evolutionist schemas. Responding to revisionists on all sides, he argued for a 'consequentialist' position, acknowledging that the revolutions from below were not led by a conscious capitalist class. Consequentialists suggest that revolutions can aid capitalist transformation by removing legal and other state impediments to accumulation and these need not involve consciously capitalist actors. The mass involvement of plebeians in these events have often pushed the gentlemen at the top much further than they would have gone if left to themselves. Right or wrong on any of these points, Davidson's critics all acknowledge that he energised the discussion to the point where Bridget Fowler could describe the exchanges that ensued as 'the Davidson debate'.

An activist to his bones, throughout his life Neil was a committed trade unionist; he was a founder of the anti-war movement in Scotland and, when allegations of predatory sexual behaviour against a leading member tore the SWP apart, he resigned with the opposition and helped to create the breakaway organisation *rs21* (revolutionary socialism in the twenty-first century).[11] He was also an anti-nationalist advocate of Scottish independence, expressing disdain for 'left Unionists' who, in the name of abstract internationalism, accepted the continued existence of Scotland within the British state, 'a more pernicious nationalism', as he wrote in this journal.[12] Davidson was a leading intellectual figure in the Radical Independence Campaign (RIC), the left-wing alliance RISE (*Respect, Independence, Socialism and Environmentalism*) and the Scottish anti-capitalist platform *Conter*.[13] Several commentators have noted that Davidson and RIC played a central role in the referendum of 2014, taking the independence campaign to the housing estates and turning the referendum into a debate on neoliberal austerity. As he explains in his diagnosis of the campaign, the highest votes for independence came in exactly these working-class conurbations.[14] The Scottish radical left, at least partly inspired by his perspective, came close to fracturing the British state.

Neil was a fine polemical speaker, excelling in irony, though international audiences – and also many English ones – found his Doric inflection challenging. Despite this, he found appreciative audiences from Chicago to São Paulo. Most of all, Neil Davidson was a passionate socialist intellectual, both erudite and militant. Yet he was also one of the least pompous, or self-satisfied, men one could hope to meet, always encouraging to others. His energy was immense, forever writing, speaking and organising; he was continually involved in the next project to revive socialism from below, convinced of immediate possibilities. Deeply committed to working-class politics, Davidson maintained an attachment to intellectual continuity – to the work of Marx, Lenin, Trotsky, Luxemburg, Gramsci and Benjamin – yet he was also a theoretical innovator. At first sight, it might be difficult to grasp, but the spectrum of his concerns – bourgeois revolution, the emergence of the Scottish nation, racism, neoliberalism, radical independence, art and literature, and much more – was animated by an approach to uneven and combined development as a strategic perspective for current politics.

Steve Edwards is Professor of History and Theory of Photography at Birkbeck, University of London.

Notes

1. Neil Davidson, *Holding Fast to an Image of the Past: Explorations in the Marxist Tradition* (Chicago: Haymarket Books, 2014); *We Cannot Escape History: States and Revolutions* (Chicago: Haymarket Books, 2015); *Nation-states: Consciousness and Competition* (Chicago: Haymarket, 2016). He also co-edited four books: *Alasdair MacIntyre's Engagement with Marxism: Selected Writings, 1953-1974*, with Paul Blackledge (Leiden: Brill, 2008); *Neoliberal Scotland: Class and Society in a Stateless Nation*, with Patricia McCafferty and David Miller (Newcastle: Cambridge Scholars Publishing, 2010); *The Longue Duree of the Far-Right: An International Historical Sociology*, with Alexander Anievas, Adam Fabry and Richard Saul (Abingdon: Routledge, 2014); and *No Problem Here: Understanding Racism in Scotland*, with Minna Liinpaa, Maureen McBride and Satnam Virdee (Edinburgh: Luath Press, 2018). At least five further books are in the offing: *Marxism and Conservatism* and *The Meaning of Revolution Today*, both with Haymarket; a reply to critics of *How Revolutionary?* and the major study of *Uneven and Combined Development* in the Historical Materialism series; and a collection of essays on Scotland compiled by Jamie Allinson.

2. George Kerevan, 'Neil Davidson an Appreciation 1957-2020', Bella Caledonia, 2020, https://bellacaledonia.org.uk/2020/05/07/an-appreciation-of-neil-davidson-1957-2020/

3. Scotland was an independent Kingdom, which joined with England in The Acts of Union 1706 and 1707 to create the state of Great Britain.

4. Much of this information comes from conversations over a long period. The best source for Davidson's biography is George Souvlis, 'The National Question, Class and the European Union: an Interview with Neil Davidson', *Salvage* (2017), https://salvage.zone/online-exclusive/the-national-question-class-and-the-european-union-neil-davidson/

5. *The Origins of Scottish Nationhood* (London: Pluto Press, 2000); *Discovering the Scottish Revolution, 1692-1746* (London: Pluto Press, 2003).

6. Neil Davidson, 'Marx and Engels on the Scottish Highlands', *Science & Society* 65: 3 (2001), 286–326.

7. Neil Davidson, *How Revolutionary Were the Bourgeois Revolutions?* (Chicago: Haymarket, 2012). Reviewed by John Kraniauskas in *Radical Philosophy* 184 (March-April 2014).

8. Dylan Riley, 'Property Leading the People', *New Left Review* 95 (2015), 117. *How Revolutionary?* begins with an account of Delacroix's painting *Liberty Leading the People* of 1830.

9. Jamie Allinson, 'In memoriam: Neil Davidson, 9 October 1957 – 3 May 2020', https://www.versobooks.com/blogs/4697-in-memoriam-neil-davidson-9-october-1957-3-may-2020

10. Davidson presses home this weak spot in the arguments of his critics – both orthodox Trotskyists and sublimated Stalinists – in his forthcoming *Why Marxism needs the Concept of Bourgeois Revolution* (Leiden: Brill, 2021). See also Linda Matar, 'Twilight of "State Capitalism" in Formerly "Socialist" Arab States', *The Journal of North African Studies* 18:3 (2013), 416–430.

11. Articles on uneven and combined development that form the basis of this book appeared on the rs21 website, https://www.rs21.org.uk/.

12. Neil Davidson, '"Yes": a Non-nationalist Argument for Scottish Independence', *Radical Philosophy* 185 (May-June 2014), 2–7.

13. Conter is organised around a website: https://www.conter.co.u

14. Neil Davidson, 'A Scottish Watershed', *New Left Review* 89 (2014), 5–26.